CONTENTS

PRODUCTION *BOGART*

DIRECTOR *D. Norman.*   **CAMERAMAN** *MM n.*

SCENE MAN AND MYTH   **TAKE** 1

DATE *n.v.n.*

Every generation has its idols, but thanks to advanced communications modern society frequently finds itself faced with an ever widening and often confusing choice. The satelite that brings into our living rooms the battle zone, the earthquake and the world title fight as they occur makes it difficult for us to believe in the studio product. But idols we must have, and if the astronaut and the athlete have replaced the war lover and the hoodlum that is probably no bad thing.

At the movies, as in most other places, an idol is something exclusive to one particular generation, and only rarely is one star's pulling power sufficient to sustain him beyond that. Time has a habit of showing up the cracks and our fashion-conscious, idol-hungry minds, tire easily of the imperfect.

The American cinema has never been short of idols, nor has it spared us perfection of one kind or another. Recalling the heart-shaped lips of Clara Bow, the inspired bickering of Ollie and Stan, Gable's horse laugh, Monroe, Garfield, Brando. . .who can accuse the dream peddlars of yesterday of not doing their jobs well? Nostalgia is fine, but would we dig into our pockets and face a hard night's drizzle to see them all over again? Clearly, we would not, for those who organize such screenings, exist on financial support from official sources and not on ticket sales.

When Humphrey Bogart burst onto the screen as the tough ravaged killer Duke Mantee in *The Petrified Forest* in 1935, nobody could have foreseen that those wolverine features and raspy voice would break every rule about fan-worship.

During his lifetime, and following his ascendancy to the upper echelons of stardom, his career followed the conventional route, for instance, memorable moments with a lot of ordinariness in between, followed by the inevitable years of decline – in Bogart's case not as many as some, for he died of cancer in 1957, less than six years after deservedly winning an Academy Award for his work in *The African Queen*.

With most other actors it would have ended there, and apart from the occasional flurry of nostalgia when TV screenings nudged our memories, nothing more would be heard of them. But with Bogart the clock never stopped. Nearly twenty-five years after his death he has more fans, and his movies are in greater demand than at any time during his life, with the bulk of his new following being youngsters who weren't born when his movies went the rounds first time.

When the Classic Cinema in London's Baker Street put on a festival of Bogart movies during the '70's, the opening night of *Casablanca* (1942) could have been mistaken for a world premiere with lines fifty yards long either side an hour before the theater opened. In the nearby West End, movies with stars of the day were playing to half-empty houses.

At a recent all-night marathon of Bogart movies it was the same again. All seats were sold within hours of the program being announced, but that did not deter hundreds of young hopefuls who turned up without a ticket and waited in line for nearly six hours until the midnight commencement on the off-chance of a few tickets being returned.

The story is similar wherever Bogart movies are shown. A few years ago the London Sunday Times asked its readers which movies they would most like to see again. Over 1,500 letters shot back and the movie most hotly demanded was *The African Queen* (1951). In second place, and a mere one vote behind the winner came *Casablanca* (1942), *The Maltese Falcon* (1941) came sixth and *Treasure of the Sierra Madre* (1948) eleventh. Four Bogart movies had been placed in the top twelve movies of all time, a record that no other actor past or present came anywhere near to equalling.

In all this, Britain – and latterly, France – were merely reflecting the mood of young America where during the mid-sixties (and indeed, to this day) on college campuses and in off-track movie houses Bogart Festivals had become the 'in' culture. Interest all over the world has never been higher and no one can say when it will all stop.

Definitions of what constitutes individual appeal must, by their very nature, be suspect since those who attempt the definition and those on the receiving end can never see it through the same viewpoints. In this area Bogart presents an interesting challenge, for one is faced with a personality so popular and so hugely known, what for a lesser actor might seem an in-depth appraisal must, for Bogart, remain frustratingly superficial however deep one strikes. The comparison is between moons and meteorites.

It is important, firstly, to separate the popular screen image from the man himself. Inevitably these were areas of overlap which deepened with the years, but the Bogart of popular myth was a projection, a manufactured product that bore only a passing resemblance, as we shall see, to Bogart the man.

The screen Bogart had one foot planted squarely in life and the other in inspired fantasy. His favorite habitat was the city jungle after dark, alive with real and imagined perils, but for Bogart, survivor of a million past encounters with the sleek dangerous beasts who prowled and took possession of the urban night, they were presented not so much danger but excitement. Bogart lived close to the edge, rising like some unshaven phoenix from the solitary squalor of a downtown rooming-house to play violent games with the underworld and the law.

In his earlier roles, whatever side he chose to be on, automatically put moral right on the opposing side and he died dozens of defiant, bullet-ridden deaths to satisfy Hays Code. Later, when world events had mellowed the wry brute and moral right had crossed over to where he stood, we loved him all the more because he still didn't give a damn, and the snarl and the evil leer were ever more than an inch or two behind his lips.

Bogart was living proof of what too many cheap rented rooms with only cheap liquor for company can do to someone. There was nothing noble about his isolation, but he met it with a raddled insolence that made him both king and outcast in his chosen jungle. His existence was relevant only to himself and then only relevant to him while he could go on being his own man, owing allegiance to nothing but the occasional tarnished cause he picked up along the way.

Once hooked he was intractable, held beyond the reach of those who would scare him or buy him off by his knowledge of the deadly game and more than a share of mule cussedness.

The backbone of Bogart's appeal lies in his dour refusal to accept anyone except on his own terms or to auction his integrity. Cynical idealists had been adrift in an alien world before Bogart came by, but his style, representing the ultimate absence of style, closed the book on that particular characterization. Nobody coming after him could hope to survive comparison, even from this safe distance, because it was not the qualities that the character presented which were unique so much as the manner of the delivery. And that, it is fairly safe to say, will not be improved upon.

Interesting though the popular image was, and is, the man behind it is even more so, and to the intrigued observer a vintage blend of complexity and paradox he presents.

According to Bosley Crowther, distinguishing one from the other is not easy, because the dividing line has been purposely fudged 'by writers and directors of his films who created roles for Bogey that conformed to the shape his image took. The total myth is far from a reflection of the man that Bogart was, yet Bogart himself was not really the man he appeared to be. . .'

Kenneth Tynan was another reviewer intrigued by the paradox presented by Bogart and his screen persona, and has made no secret of the fact that admiring the latter put him under no obligation to like the former. He once witnessed Bogey behaving ungallantly in a nightclub and that was about as close as he got – or, indeed, wanted to get – to Bogey. But of the screen character, he wrote:

'He was "inner-directed", steering by a private compass that paid no attention to storm signals from outside. Moreover, if the needle led him (as it usually did) into a hail of bullets he would die with a shrug, no complaints, no apologies, no hard feelings. Indeed he rarely displayed strong feelings of any kind and this in an age when stars were supposed to emote and be vibrant was something else we admired.

'It reflected, in part, the emotional tact of a man who seemed repelled by sentimentality; and

Sam Spade or Philip Marlowe – The classic movie pose

in part the professional assurance of an actor who knew damned well that he could get along without it!'

The complexity in his nature was probably inherited, from an unremarkable but tension-filled childhood spent in a fashionable part of New York City where he was born, the eldest of three children, just before the turn of the last century.

Humphrey's mother was a headstrong, talented magazine illustrator and his father was a doctor. As the eldest of the children, Humphrey bore the brunt of his parents' frequent quarrelling, a role he was emotionally not quite up to.

He flunked college and to escape their combined wrath joined the US Navy and took part in some dangerous Atlantic crossings during World War I. Not a courageous man but better prepared to face the German U-boats than his parents, this shows how bad it must have been at home.

In 1920 Humphrey returned to a New York he scarcely recognized. While his back had been turned it had transformed itself into the most fun-conscious, wide awake city in the world. A war had come and gone and a new generation – his generation – had taken over.

Coney Island. Harlem jazz. The speakeasies of mid-town Manhattan. Wild bohemian nights in Greenwich Village. Cars. Gramophone records. Radio broadcasting. Even tabloid newspapers. And more fun-seeking girls to the square mile than Humphrey could have imagined existed. During the early twenties his home town presented to his unaccustomed eyes a labyrinth of mouth-watering delights. Back home, the tensions persisted, but with so many excitements to catch up on outside, he scarcely noticed them.

Humphrey blundered into a theatrical career, initially as a trainee house manager, after numerous attempts by his father had failed to place him in more respectable employment. It was a theatrical-producer friend of Dr Bogart who took him under his wing and started him off on the road to eventual success, but it was to be a long, heartbreaking road that would almost break him, mentally and physically.

By the time he won the part in *The Petrified Forest* in 1935, the production which transformed everything for him, Bogart had spent an unbelievably static fourteen years around Broadway and the movie studios playing slick young men and second leads that mostly came to nothing.

Louise Brooks, an actress-contemporary of Bogart's, recalled vividly in Sight & Sound (Winter 1966) how it was for him before he got the part in the film version of *The Petrified Forest*. He had played in the New York stage production opposite Leslie Howard, but when Warner Brothers acquired the film rights along with Howard to star, they intended Bogart's role for Edward G. Robinson, their established gangster star. With one wrecked marriage behind him and another going on the rocks and nothing to look forward to after fourteen years of hard slog but obscure summer stock at Skowhegan, Maine, Bogart had gone to Tony's Restaurant in New York to drink away the blues with an actor friend, Thomas Mitchell.

Miss Brooks recalls that after Mitchell paid his bill and left, Bogart settled down alone 'drinking with weary determination. His head drooped lower and lower. When I left he had fallen into an exhausted sleep with his head sunk in his arms on the table. Poor Humphrey. . .he's finally licked.'

Leslie Howard helped him break the jinx, and the story of how the British star, vacationing in Scotland prior to returning to America for the film, cabled Warners with the ultimatum that if Bogart wasn't signed he wouldn't be back either, is part of movie history.

Warners consented, and Bogart made such an impact as a gangster-on-the-run that for several years he played little else, mostly overshadowed by James Cagney and Edward G. Robinson and frequently ending up as a foil for them.

But the experience was not, as he once pointed out, wholly unrewarding: 'When the "heavy", full of crime and bitterness grabs his wounds and talks about death in a husky voice, the audience is his and his alone!'

By a curious mischance – Edward G. and George Raft having both declined the part – Bogart was signed for *High Sierra* (1941) in a role not dissimilar to, but softer edged than, his *Petrified Forest* gangster. *High Sierra* was to the gangster what *The Wild Bunch*, almost thirty years later, was to the Western – pinpointing the close of the era, when time and modern civilization catches up with the outlaw turning him into an anachronism and luring him into a suicidal trail of strength – in Bogart's case, on the side of a mountain.

The box office success of *High Sierra*, and the providential meeting with John Huston on the set – Huston was the co-screenwriter – led to

The Maltese Falcon and five other collaborations, most notably *The Treasure of the Sierra Madre* and *The African Queen*. It is through Huston's movies plus two directed by Howard Hawks, *To Have and Have Not* (1944) and *The Big Sleep* (1946) and the stylish *Casablanca* (1942), directed by Michael Curtiz, that the Bogart legend lives.

In the days before advanced communications, before satellites, before television, it was as indicated earlier much easier to believe in the make-believe. Fan magazines, with the blessings of the big studios, pandered to our illusions, fuzzing the edges between the real and the imagined. The Doris Day that emerged from the fanmag profile differed only marginally from the daffy girl-next-door type she invariably portrayed. When he spoke to journalists at all, which was not very often, Brando sounded like a cross between Stanley Kowalski and Terry Malloy, two of his popular early characterizations – but well removed, as we have since learned, from the studious, articulate extrovert he really is.

Errol Flynn and Alan Ladd were tough heroes on the screen, but were driven in the end to despise the glossy caricatures they had allowed themselves to become. Both died from an excess of alcohol at the age of fifty.

Bogart was into his forties when star status overtook him finally. That itself was a blessing in disguise, for he had had long enough to come to terms with himself, and having learned to live with disappointment for half a lifetime it was moderately easy to adjust to success. Unlike the overnight 'discovery' who arrives dazzled and friendless in the big city, Bogart had long before staked out his patch of dust in Beverly Hills and acquired a circle of colorful pals who viewed his success with little more than benign indifference.

Adjustments were comparatively minor and at no time was he in any danger of losing his head. On the contrary, he tended to view the level of acclaim given to him as simply events catching up with what he had known all along. Edward G. Robinson once admitted: 'I loved

Bogey. I knew his eccentricities and could handle them. He was frustrated he'd had to wait so long for recognition. In his last pictures he was getting so good as an actor – and so good as a man, too.'

Bogart took a keen interest in his publicity and cooperated good-naturedly with every request, not because he believed it would do him any good but because it appealed to his gallows humor.

Publicists were dark schemers weaving their plots behind locked doors and Bogart admired schemers of any color. Later on, when he was a star in his own right he needed neither help nor prompting to dream up outrageous stunts of his own.

His love of a good stunt, plus the gaggle of newspaper columnists that he kept strategically in tow, served two purposes. He could play-act shamelessly in real life, a sport he enjoyed almost as much as filming, and at the same time the play-acting created a handy smokescreen behind which the more serious-minded Bogart could safely retreat, to the solitude of his boat, his den of books and his small circle of close friends.

For this reason many of the antics that were faithfully chronicled by his columnist-biographers, while authentic, tell us little about the man himself.

On one occasion, Bogart was reported as having stuffed the remains of a broken cocktail glass into his mouth and chewed it, apparently to prove his toughness to a Frenchman who ate glass. Confronted with the story, he smiled ruefully, 'I may be a little nuts, but I don't think I'm that nuts!'

Many people were puzzled at the way he and Clifton Webb had to be physically pulled apart when they met at Hollywood parties because of the insults and threats that passed between them. What they did not know was that Bogart and Webb were great chums from the Broadway stage during the twenties, and the insults routine was a running gag intended to liven up dull social get-togethers. Bogart had a similar long-standing arrangement with Broderick Crawford.

Webb, who remembered Bogart as a 'charming, charming, warm friendly fellow' told a reporter: 'He's never done any of the things he's supposed to do in public places when I'm around. I've never seen him in a brawl.   . .In this particular business people think you are like what you play on the screen. This is sometimes completely erroneous but if that's what they want to think let them go ahead.'

Robert Morley, who starred with Bogart in his two British made productions, *The African Queen* and *Beat the Devil* (1954), told me, 'perhaps the most endearing thing about him was the fact that he was not in the least what one would expect from his public image. Deep down, he was a kindly, gentle man. And enormously modest.'

But kindly or otherwise, he could be a difficult taskmaster on the movie set. Long years in the theater had taught him exceptional concentration. 'I may drink but I do my work,' he would say, and those who watched could only nod appreciatively. It irritated him to have to go through numerous re-takes for the benefit of lesser experienced performers, and he did little to conceal his impatience.

In *Sabrina Fair* (1954) he played opposite Audrey Hepburn, a former ballet student who had rocketed to fame one year previously in *Roman Holiday* and with next to no film experience, she needed expert and patient handling. Bogart was exasperated and not very helpful. When Clifton Webb asked him shortly after the movie's completion, 'How do you like that dream girl?' Bogart replied morosely, 'Okay, if you like to do thirty-six takes.'

Sabrina Fair was his least happy film and he quarrelled bitterly with director Billy Wilder and his other co-star William Holden, whom he had worked with in Holden's early picture, *Invisible Stripes* (1939).

Wilder and Holden had won the Oscar that year for *Stalag 17*, and Bogart felt that Wilder was trying to make it Holden's picture. He got his revenge by needling and being difficult, and mockingly calling Holden 'Smiling Jim' behind his back – a reference to all the useless, juvenile parts Holden had played in the past. Holden, who had coined the name himself and joked about it among his friends, was incensed when he learned that Bogart, whom he disliked acutely, was using the name derisively around the set. To this day, all any reporter needs to do to make Holden's bland mask drop away and have him cursing like a trouper is to mention Bogart and *Sabrina Fair*.

Warner's bosses were frequently targets for Bogart's wrath – mostly over the allocation of roles. But in that, it was situation normal – all Warners stars rebelled from time to time for the same reason. While the others favored legal redress, Bogart would adopt more colorful forms of protest, and once surprised studio chief Jack L. Warner by riding around the studio on a bicycle clad in a pair of crumpled pyjamas.

Bogart's sudden loss of hair in his mid-forties, due to massive hormone injections caused Warner a few worries. Would his top star's popularity vanish along with the thatch? – that was the nagging question. Warner called Bogart to his office and demanded that a toupée should be worn in public at all times. There was, of course, no way that Warner could insist on his wishes being carried out, and Bogart knew this. So whenever he felt like putting Warner in his place – and he needed little encouragement for that – he would make a point of turning up where he knew Warner would be, with his head bare and the baldness showing. As Bosley Crowther pointed out: 'Though comparatively trivial, this.   . .was characteristic of his fractious and anti-authoritarian attitude.'

Bogart made no secret of the fact that his shenanagins with Warner had their amusing side. After finally leaving the studio, he said: 'I kinda miss the arguments.   . .it's like when you've fought with your wife and gotten a divorce. You kind of miss the fighting!'

On the subject of marriage and divorce, by the time he left Warners, Bogart ought to have been something of an authority. But the chances were that he wasn't – in some areas, he was slower to learn than others.

Bogart married four times, on each occasion to an actress he had worked with and mostly within days of the previous divorce. His first wife was Helen Menken, a former child actress he met during a touring production of *Drifting*, produced by William A. Brady, in 1921. Bogart was infatuated with her from the start, but the fact that she was an established star and he a mere bit player didn't make for a cosy romance.

Helen was frail and intelligent, the epitome of coolness and sophistication, groomed for stardom from early childhood and effortlessly charming. She talked endlessly and knowledgeably about the theater and mingled with the famous in and around Broadway. Bogart, at twenty-one, had survived a jagged chronology of censure and mishap and was not especially knowledgeable about anything, and he felt the strain acutely.

Although this hurdle had been satisfactorily overcome by the time they married, in 1926, much greater ones stood in the way of their happiness. At twenty-five, after a lengthy career, Helen was ready for the comforts and security of marriage, but to Bogart acclaim was a new toy. It seemed to fill the vacuum left by a childhood of

basic loneliness and unacceptance, as if winning applause could cancel out every disappointment he had ever had.

Disillusioned, Helen threw herself back into her career. The moment of crisis occurred when she received an invitation to star at the Strand Theatre in London in Austin Strong's *Seventh Heaven*, opening in September 1927. The marriage failed to survive the separation and a divorce quickly followed Helen's return to New York, where she had another hit play, *The Captive*, waiting for her. They had been married for less than eighteen months.

In April 1928 he married Mary Phillips who had earlier appeared with him in another William A. Brady production *Nerves* at the Comedy Theatre. The marriage endured ten years, through the bleakest periods of Bogart's career. Not a great deal is known about Mary, for she remained tolerantly in the background and in later years Bogart would say nothing about her. She was certainly a clear-headed stabilizing influence on him and, as Louise Brooks observed, 'Mary was exactly right for him during the time he required comfort more than inspiration'.

While they were both based in New York, and working there, the marriage held together, but after Bogart went to California for *The Petrified Forest*, success held him there and Mary was soon faced with the choice of either staying in Hollywood and not working – movie stardom for actresses would be extremely unlikely if they are past thirty, which Mary was, unless they are either exceptional actresses or well established in the theater, which Mary was not – or returning to Broadway where she could get a job, and risk the long separations.

The offer of a substantial part in *The Postman Always Rings Twice* on Broadway – later filmed as a starring vehicle for Lana Turner in 1946 – brought Mary back to New York, and their marriage, effectively, to an end.

Five days after his divorce from Mary, in August 1938, he married Mayo Methot, a cut-price Mae West whom he had met on the set of *Marked Woman* (1937) at Warners. Mayo was different from his previous wives in that she had more stamina for a fight and while she achieved little in the way of an acting career for herself, her spectacular public brawls with Bogart were glossy productions in their own right and often looked as if they had been choreographed beforehand.

Mayo was a firecracker, glamorous and

Bogart and Mayo Methot (center) with (l-r) Rosemary Lane, Jane Wyman, John Payne and Priscilla Lane at the Premiere of Errol Flynn's [Dodge City] (1939)

impulsive, with no intention of fading into the background. Despite their knockabout physical relationship – Jaik Rosenstein recalled for me an occasion when he came out of a fashionable restaurant on Sunset Strip and encountered Mayo astride Bogart determinedly banging his head on the sidewalk – it was a love match of sorts. But with the onset of his huge personal triumphs in *The Maltese Falcon* and *Casablanca* and the beginning of the war, Bogart and his audiences – and indeed the world – had quickly rounded the point where the supposed drunken antics of a middle-aged roustabout, even a famous one, deserved anyone's attention.

By 1942 Bogart had achieved what he had desperately wanted for over twenty years – to be taken seriously as an actor – and Mayo, who had abandoned her own career when they married and thus had no career to return to, openly resented it. Bogart had enjoyed himself in the temporary role of after-hours desperado, but he was anxious not to push it on his fans to the point of boredom. Long training in the theater had shown him that the time to leave your audience is when they are calling for more, and by 1942 they had probably had enough.

Their relationship soured when Mayo – the least intelligent of his wives – couldn't adapt to a change of pace. She clung on grimly, drank too much, and became a general nuisance both at home and at the studios where she frequently followed him screaming about infidelity or some other imagined grievance. Knowing his weakness for leading ladies (he had become infatuated with Mary while married to Helen, and with Mayo herself while married to Mary) her jealousy of Ingrid Bergman during the shooting of *Casablanca* was not entirely unfounded, but the pattern was not repeated until he met Lauren Bacall in Howard Hawks' office before filming began of *To Have and Have Not* . Cool, shrewd, ambitious Betty Bacall – she loathed her studio name Lauren and to this day refuses to answer to it – was only twenty when Bogart, then in his

Bogart and Betty Bacall with their son Stephen

mid-forties, met her, but she had maturity and a remarkable degree of self-assurance which, as the movie shows, compensated for her obvious lack of acting experience. A former New York model, she had appeared on the cover of Harpers Bazaar in March 1943 and been spotted by the wife of Howard Hawks, who invited her to Hollywood and tested her immediately for *To Have and Have Not* which he was by then setting up.

When Jack Warner saw the test he was delighted with Hawks' discovery and authorized the film's commencement.

The day after his divorce from Mayo in May 1945 Bogart married Betty Bacall in a quiet, private ceremony at the Ohio home of novelist Louis Bromfield, one of his closest friends. After three unsuccessful attempts, cynics thought it would be just a matter of time before Bogart would be making another enormous settlement – Mayo had been awarded $75,000 by the divorce judge – but Bacall knew how to handle him.

He wanted a stable home life, but he still wanted acclaim, so she gave him both, as an acting partner during the late forties she shared in several of his screen successes, until the birth of their son, Stephen Humphrey, in 1949.

At the christening, Bogart said: 'She (Betty) is everything that I ever wanted and now Stephen, my son, completes the picture.' The picture, and the family, was not complete, however, until the birth in 1952, of his daughter, whom he named Leslie Howard Bogart in memory of the British star who had made so much of his success and happiness possible by insisting he and no-one else would be the movie Mantee, and whose life had been so tragically cut short in a wartime plane disaster.

Ordinarily a stout defender of liberalism, Bogart had his fingers burnt when he stepped in, as he so frequently did when the cause was right, and chartered a plane to fly many notable movie people to Washington to protest about the Communist witch-hunts in the film industry during the McCarthy investigations of 1947.

Movie people, including actors, writers, directors and indeed anyone connected with movies, were being selectively called to testify before the powerful House of Un-American Activities and declare their political affiliations. When several prominent writers and directors refused to cooperate or rat on their fellow artists, Bogart organized a planeload of supporters, including Bacall, Danny Kaye, Richard Conte and others, and flew to Washington to deliver their protest personally.

When ten of the obdurate witnesses later confessed to having been Communists, Bogart, who must have known it and who of all the protesters unquestionably wielded the most influence, shocked his fellow liberals by publicly and unreservedly recanting, describing the trip to Washington in a statement as 'ill-advised, foolish and impetuous'.

It was an ugly time for the industry with many prominent people being blacklisted and driven out of Hollywood and clearly it would have taken a strong nerve to speak out against what was going on. Many were appalled at what was happening and had looked to Bogart, a sturdy liberal, for support and, under pressure, they felt he had stabbed them in the back. It was an act of dubious intent which a lot of film people could not forgive easily and could account, no doubt, for some of the sour relationships he subsequently had with members of his own profession.

After winning the Oscar in 1951 for his superb performance in *The African Queen*, Bogart's career began to decline steadily. All the old fire was gone, and apart from one redeeming portrayal as the demented Captain Queeg in *The Caine Mutiny* (1955) it never revived. One reason was that, in common with Gable, Flynn, Cooper, Tracy and all his great contemporaries, he took on parts that would have better suited younger actors.

He was a stern critic of the Method style of acting, and bitterly resented the influx of Strasberg-trained actors from New York, and the prominence they quickly attained, particularly Marlon Brando whom he misguidedly accused of being 'the same in every part he plays'.

Predictably there were arguments on the set of *The Harder They Fall* (1956), Bogart's last film in which he was co-starred with Rod Steiger, a fellow student and declared admirer of Brando. Steiger took it in his powerful stride, sensing that something more serious was wrong. And he had guessed correctly, for shortly after the movie's completion, in March 1956, Bogart was transferred to hospital for an eight hour operation for cancer of the oesophagus.

Optimistic at first about his chances of recovery and reassured by his doctors that the cancer in his throat had been caught in time – Bogart had insisted in being told the grim medical details of his illness from the time it was

Bogart's moment of triumph as Claire Trevor presents him with the oscar for his role in [The African Queen] (1951)

first diagnosed – as the year wore on he continued to lose weight and grow weaker until by Christmas, despite contradictions which he authorized to appear in the press, it was pathetically obvious that he was not going to beat it.

The central fact of his last months was his exemplary display of physical courage and endurance, witnessed by a small knot of his closest friends.

The New York Herald Tribune's comment summed up the widespread admiration which his bold fight against the illness drew from every quarter of American life: '(Bogart) seemed to be defying fate to do its worst and when it did it found him calm and courageous'.

John Huston was one of those who saw him often during those final months. Huston recalled: 'He demonstrated a unique, purely animal courage. After the first visit, nothing more was needed to reinforce the first shock caused by his devastating appearance. One quickly became aware of the greatness it hid.'

Another close friend, writer-director Joseph L. Mankiewicz, who directed Bogart in *The Barefoot Contessa* (1954) felt that his tremendous courage at the end was based on the fact that Bogart wasn't too unhappy about dying.

Apart from the obvious benefits of living longer, such as seeing his children grow and sinking a few more crates of scotch, there were no new worlds for him to conquer, no new statements for him to make that could have any effect on what movie historians, and the rest of us, would make of him. He had been part of the movies roadshow from shortly after the development of sound until its eclipse by television and he had tasted more success and more disappointments, at both artistic and personal levels, than is good for any one human being. Mankiewicz believed that Bogart, like the weary, cynical character he portrayed in *The Barefoot Contessa*, had had his fill of the phonies and the fatcats, and that he genuinely enjoyed the sad little drama being played out because it gave him a respectable reason for wanting to see his friends and he didn't much mind what was waiting for him at the end.

He died in his sleep during the early hours of

BOGART

January 14, 1957.

The real Bogart, I suspect, can be found somewhere between the myth that has grown up around him, and the quiet determination of a man who, in Tynan's words, was 'not perhaps very lovable but, at least, was unbought.'

His appeal is undiminished a quarter of a century after his death because the qualities he represented are, in fact, ageless. Bosley Crowther observed: 'Today's young man, cynical and anxious about the way things are going in the world, sees in the character of Bogey a cheering model of firm contempt and cool aplomb.' The ladies, too, see depths of self-assurance and more than just a hint of mockery in those sad, thoughtful eyes.

Florence Marly, Bogart's co-star in one of his own productions *Tokyo Joe* (1949), recalled: 'There was a nobility in that man, and I could feel it. . .' From a greater distance, British film writer Allan Eyles reflected: 'Bogart deserves to be remembered for the uncommonly fine and sensitive actor he was. It is not necessary to embrace the simple-minded adulation of the camp crowd and the cult-makers to respond warmly to his particular qualities as a performer and to find a topical relevance in his style. Of course, luck played its part. Though stardom came late to Bogart it gave him a good number of great films in which to develop and display his persona to great effect.'

Respected movie historian David Shipman, in his excellent compilation *The Great Movie Stars*, wrote:

'He was much acclaimed while he was alive but his intrinsic appeal seems even stronger now. Interest centers not on his ability, or even on the overall Bogart, but on the screen character he played in his middle years. Still, even after he had remarkably extended his range he was always Bogart.'

'He took on all sorts of characteristics and varying situations and made them fit the Bogart persona. That persona gave him a head start as an actor because it was a compound of opposing qualities, mixed sometimes ambiguously.'

Kenneth Tynan came closest, in my view, to articulating the popular viewpoint when he declared: 'I don't think we can say he was a great actor but he remained, to the end, a great behaver. Without effort and with classic economy he could transfer the essence of himself to a camera and be sure that it would be eloquent on a screen.'

Two days after Bogart died, Alistair Cooke summed up what the actor had meant to him, both as a personality and as a man. Bogart was, according to Cooke, 'a vastly more intelligent man than the trade he practised, a touchy man who found the world more corrupt than he had hoped for, a man with a tough shell and a fine core. He invented the Bogart character, and it fitted his deceptive purpose like a glove. By showily neglecting his outward forms of grace he kept inferior men at a distance, for he lived in a town crowded with malign poseurs, fake ascetics, studio panders, the pimps of the press. From all of them he was determined to keep his secret – the rather shameful secret, in the realistic world we inhabit, of being a gallant man, and an idealist.'

Biographical details about Bogart's early years differ according to the viewpoint of the writer. On one point however, there is little argument. Bogart's childhood was fairly uneventful. Born the eldest of three children to an indifferent Manhattan surgeon and his formidable, headstrong artist-wife, he quickly discovered that the benefits of being upper-class could be starkly counterpointed by his parents' cold reserve. All too frequently the buffer between them, Bogart took early refuge behind a mask of daydreams and moody introspection, nurtured a profound dislike of all things authoritarian, and, in a crisis, learned to pull down a curtain of wafer-thin defiance. He never abandoned these characteristics.

At each school he attended, the behavioral pattern was consistent – initial enthusiasm being slowly overlapped by a systematic withdrawal. It was a total lack of personal horizon more than gross misconduct which got him the boot from

Bogart aged two years

Phillips Academy in Massachusetts, an experience from which the harassed rector Dr Alfred Stearns felt Bogart might 'profit greatly.'

Two years service with the U.S. Navy showed him to be the same shallow prig he had been in college. It was during this period he suffered a permanent injury to his lip which was responsible for that unique lisp. The actual explanation advanced by Warner Brothers was that a splinter had hit him in the face during an encounter with the German Navy, but Bogart's brother-in-law, Stuart Rose discounts this, relating the injury to a scuffle with a prisoner when Bogart was on escort duty.

Indoctrination in the theater, through his boyhood friendship with the son of Broadway producer William A. Brady, came in the form of stage management with the Brady office.

But being blessed with vaguely Valentinoesque features and the sudden onrush of vanity that seems to have affected all American youth in 1920, Bogart badgered his employer to let him perform in a touring play.

He won his chance on January 22, 1922, at Brady's Playhouse Theatre, in *Drifting*, directed by John Cromwell, who 25 years later would direct Bogart in *Dead Reckoning* for Columbia. A member of the cast was Robert Warwick, later to appear with Bogart in the Fox 1931 production *A Holy Terror*, and, more memorably, in that cryptical film *In A Lonely Place*, cameoing an aging, redundant Shakespearian actor.

Bogart flopped in his second play with Brady, the 3-act comedy *Swiftly* by John Peter Toohey and W. C. Percival, but by now, the light of battle was in his eyes. The American theater was coming alive in a strident way. A new school of playwrights had surfaced and new ideas abounded.

The 1920-21 season had seen a total of 157 Broadway productions, topped the following year by thirty more, and the 1922-23 season reached a heady 200. The trend was to continue, until the all-time pinnacle of 280 was reached during the 1927-28 season – the last before the financial crisis hit Wall Street.

Producer Rosalie Stewart picked Bogart to play in Lynn Starling's 3-act comedy *Meet the Wife*, with Mary Boland and Clifton Webb. The production kept the Klaw Theatre busy for 232 performances, despite energetic opposition from Eugene O'Neill's *Desire Under the Elms*, Kaufmann and Connelly's *Beggar on Horseback*,

John Barrymore's record-breaking *Hamlet* and Sidney Howard's *They Knew What They Wanted*. Moviegoers were seeing Lon Chaney as Quasimodo, Nazimova as Salome, Valentino as the Sheik and the flamboyant Fairbanks Sr as Robin Hood.

Brady's son Bill, Bogart's boyhood friend, produced the actor's next – and last – assignment for Brady, John Farrar and Stephen Benet's war play *Nerves*, Somerset Maugham's *Rain*, with Jeanne Eagels as Sadie Thompson, opened the same night, and stole the spotlight. A few weeks later, the Maxwell Anderson-Laurence Stalling's play *What Price Glory*, a war drama as raw and bitingly lifelike as *Nerves* was hollow and contrived, erupted on Broadway and *Nerves* folded, joining the string of elegant flops which Brady had managed since the war. A basically inflexible man with neither the formal education nor the intuitive talents of his rivals, Brady clung resolutely to the style of pre-Twenties drama he had always been associated with, refusing to concede an inch.

His inflexibility decided Bogart it was time to strike out for himself. Brady was slowly becoming a backwater, whereas Bogart's heart lay with the big fish, among the strong currents of the expanding commercial theater.

In January 1925, he co-starred with Shirley Booth in the Barry Connors comedy *Hells Bells* at Wallacks Theatre. The production weathered 120 performances, qualifying as one of the many minor hits of an excellent Broadway season that had leavened serious modern drama – Eden Phillpots' *Farmer's Wife*, Laszlo Fodor's *The Stork*, – with plenty of music and chocolate-box romance – *The Student Prince* and *The Desert Song*.

Director Hassard Short reunited Bogart next with Mary Bland in *Cradle Snatchers*, a 3-act comedy by Russel Medcraft and Norma Mitchell. It proved to be the hit of the season, with an unrivaled 332 performances, and more than any other previous work, established his name on Broadway.

Many of the lesser-knowns around Broadway in 1925 would cross pathways with Bogart, before a decade was out.

At the Palace Theatre, James Cagney hoofed his way through the *Out of Town Capers* revue. Theatre Guild players Spencer Tracy and Edward G. Robinson, were warmly received in Molnar's *R.U.R.* and *Juarez and Maximilian* respectively. Tracy's room-mate Pat O'Brien was appearing in *Gertie* at the Nora Bayes Theatre on 44th Street with the fresh-faced Elisha Cook Jr (Wilmer in *The Maltese Falcon*).

Paul Muni earned rave notices for his first English-speaking part in *We Americans* while former ballroom gigolo George Raft was partnered by Elsie Pincer in the musical *Gay Paree* . But not everyone was having successes. At the Eva La Gallienne Civic Repertory Theatre the hopeful Bette Davis had just been dismissed for lack of promise.

Baby Mine , Margaret Mayo's 3-act comedy brought Bogart and Lee Patrick (Spade's secretary in *The Maltese Falcon*) together for the first time.

Star of *Baby Mine* was Roscoe 'Fatty' Arbuckle, one-time slapstick comedian hounded from the screens by scandal. It soon became apparent that his enforced layoff since the three

Bogart, Paul Kelly and 2nd wife Mary Phillips in the stage play [Nerves] *(1923)*

legendary trials five years before which had acquitted him of the rape and manslaughter of actress Virginia Rappe – had not enhanced his sense of comedy. After the twelfth performance, the show folded. Arbuckle was thereafter reduced to writing comedy material under a pseudonym.

The 1928 season was the last big bonanza year before the New York stock market crashed. When *The Jazz Singer* hit Broadway in October 1927, bringing the era of silent movies to an abrupt halt, Bogart was out of work, but a big hit was not far away, replacing Roger Pryor in Maxwell Anderson's Broadway success *Saturday's Children*. He joined the cast towards the end of its 310 performances, after it had transferred from the Forrest Theatre – where it opened – to the Actors Theatre. On January 11, 1929, Bogart transferred to the Lyceum for his second-in-a-row assignment for director Guthrie McClintic, *Skyrocket* by Mark Reed in a cast that included his second wife Mary Phillips.

In August 1929, Bogart starred in the Laurence Johnson comedy *It's A Wise Child* staged by David Belasco, which clocked up 378 performances, apparently unaffected by the collapse of Wall Street ten weeks after the play opened, and the plethora of personal and commercial tragedies that followed.

Bogart made his first trip to Hollywood, at the invitation of the Fox Studios, in 1930, shortly after the closure of *Saturday's Children*. He made six films during the year's try out, after which his contract lapsed, and forced his return to New York.

The first to be released, *Up the River* directed by John Ford from a subject by thriller-writer Maurine Watkins, featured another Broadway refugee named Spencer Tracy in his first Hollywood assignment. Originally devised by Watkins as a serious treatise on prison rioting – and based on contemporary headlines about the troubled Auburn Prison – Metro Studios had beaten Fox to the prison yard with *The Big House*, starring Chester Morris and Robert Montgomery, also based on the explosive Auburn situation.

Fearful of being labeled a plagiarist, Fox production chief Winfield Sheehan insisted on severe modifications and Ford obliged with a largely improvized comedy treatment which soothed Sheehan and satisfied the critics.

New York Times writer Mordaunt Hall described the film as 'violently funny' and said that Tracy had acted 'particularly well'. British film magazine Bioscope further praised Tracy's 'excellent' performance but added 'the story is told in a jerky manner and is destitute of dramatic tension. However there is adequate compensation in the abundant humor. . .'

Richard Watts, in the London Herald-Tribune, complimented Tracy on his 'usual excellent performance,' overlooking, in his enthusiasm, that *Up the River* was, in fact, Tracy's debut film.

Bogart's second assignment was alongside Victor McLaglen in *A Devil With Women*, a rewrite of the Clements Ripley novel *Dust and Sun*. Bioscope called the film 'a typical McLaglen offering,' indicating that he was 'the only one who really matters, and his performance far outshines any other member of the cast.' The New York Times noted McLaglen's preference for playing the same rough diamond character in every film, but added 'judging by the merriment he arouses, there seems no need for him to change.

The New York Times also mentioned McLaglen's 'irritating friend. . .Humphrey Bogart, who makes his debut in talking pictures and gives an ingratiating performance. Mr Bogart is both good-looking and intelligent. . .'

His intelligence was barely scratched in *Body and Soul*, a Jules Furthman adaption of A. E. Thomas's play *Squadrons*, co-starring with Charles Farrell. Alfred Santell directed with scarcely a sidelong glance.

Due partly to the slow emergence of scripts – itself a reflection of the studios playing safe policy – written exclusively for sound cameras, many films of the early thirties were remakes in sound of popular silent productions. Such was *Bad Sister*, a novelettish rehash by Hobart Henley of Booth Tarkington's *The Flirt*, Universal's big success of 1924. The film starred Conrad Nagel and Universal discovery Sidney Fox, with Bette Davis and Bogart in support.

The New York Times called it 'a woodenly and insecurely presented story. . .lost in the general shuffle of adaptors, dialogue writers and modernizers.'

Bioscope saw it as 'the type of entertainment which appeals strongly to the average fan, and excellent direction makes the most of it.' All critics were wowed by Sidney Fox who died tragically ten years later. 'Effectively vivacious,' crooned Bioscope, 'certainly a hit in her first starring role.'

"Steve" and Claire Luce – [Up the River] (1930)

BOGART

A small part in Fox's *Women of All Nations* reunited Bogart with the boisterous McLaglen, and introduced him to Raoul Walsh, who would later direct him for Warners. Last of a cycle based on the *What Price Glory* twosome Flagg and Quirt, the film had McLaglen and Edmund Lowe as the racy Army sergeants, with Bogart playing a cautious friend. With their impertinent leers and outrageous bonhomie, Flagg and Quirt were figures outside their natural habitat, the war game, and consequently, interest had cooled. What had been box-office magic in 1925 proved unsuccessful for the thirties. The New York Times called the film 'a fractious tale which might pass for Rabelaisian humor.'

Bogart's last film for Fox was *A Holy Terror*, starring George O'Brien and Sally Eilers. The critics hated it. ' *A Holy Terror* is here to take its meagre bow,' said the New York Times.

Bogart's only recorded stage appearance during 1931 was in John Van Druten's comedy *After All* staged by Dwight Deere Wiman at the Booth Theatre, on the corner of Sixth Avenue and 23rd Street. Notices were bad and the production collapsed after twenty performances.

Back in Hollywood, Columbia cast him as a flying instructor in Thornton Freeland's gals-and-gadgets epic *Love Affair* with ex-Ziegfeld dancer Dorothy Mackaill. Jo Swerling's dialogue proved no more inspired than had Ursula Parrot's original story, but the film was saved from total catastrophe by some incisive camerawork by Teddy Tetzlaff.

During 1932 Bogart made two films for Warner Brothers, the studio which would control his destiny for thirteen years. *Big City Blues*, adapted by Ward Morehouse and Lillian Hayward from Morehouse's stage play *New York Town* and directed by Mervyn LeRoy was a grim crosshatch of razzamatazz melodrama and solemn eulogy. Bogart was listed tenth in order of importance. During the thirties LeRoy directed over three dozen major features, and with such a prodigious output, some variation in quality was inevitable. The New York Times summed up everyone's feelings with the comment

"Tom Standish" and Mona Maris – [A Devil with Women] (1930)

'quite painful to observe.'

Kubec Glasmon and John Bright – former crime reporters turned scenarists who had written *Public Enemy* for Cagney – devised *Three on a Match*, Bogart's next for Warners. Set against the familiar Warner backdrop of big-city low-life, the story explored the differing fortunes and ambitions of three girls ten years after their college graduation. Directed by Mervyn LeRoy, Bogart suckled his first gangster role, with obvious relish. The New York Times called it 'tedious and distasteful.' But Hollywood Filmograph disagreed. 'Hardhitting, fast melodrama, handled with real motion picture intelligence. . .' ran its banner.

In New York, Bogart surfaced on October 11, 1932 in *I Loved You Wednesday* a romantic comedy by William du Bois and Molly Ricardel, presented at the Harris Theatre by Crosby Gaige. The play sank after sixty-three performances, by which time Bogart was rehearsing *Chrysalis*, the Rose Albert Porter melodrama, for Martin Beck.

The fate of *Chrysalis* – it died after 23 performances – was symptomatic of the kind of season Broadway was having. The effects of the Wall Street crash had burrowed deep. Bankruptcies and foreclosures were commonplace. The success ratio had plunged from one in three productions staged to less than one in five. Not even Broadway giants like the Schubert and the Erlanger organizations could cope – both collapsed within weeks of each other.

March 1933 saw Bogart in *Our Wife*, a 3-act romantic comedy by Lyon Mearson and Lillian Day, staged by Thomas Brotherton and Abe Halle at the Booth. Ten patrons turned up for opening night.

At the Guild Theatre, he managed to shake off the jinx in Somerset Maugham's translation of the Luigi Chiarelli comedy *La Maschera e il Volte* ('The Mask and the Face'). First performed in Rome in 1916, the play had been initially adapted for English-speaking audiences by C. B. Fernauld in 1924. Maugham's translation nine years later, scored a minor hit with forty performances and a cast that included Shirley Booth, Judith Anderson and Leo G. Carroll.

To ease the overstretched production facilities in Hollywood, several major studios had production units operating in and around New York. Among Universal's program of east coast productions in December 1933 was *Midnight*, a thriller by husband and wife writing team Paul and Claire Sigton, which director Chester Erskine had adapted for actress Sidney Fox. The film also featured Australian actor O. P. Heggie and Henry Hull, who was one of Hollywood's most versatile characters in a career that began in 1916 in *The Little Rebel*.

When one of the supporting players fell ill at the last minute, Lynne Overman, also in the film, got Bogart the part. Overman had been drinking with Bogart the previous evening at the El Morocco, and knew how desperate he was for work.

The New York Times called it 'a story of unusual interest. . .a nervous and somewhat hysterical tale, blurred occasionally in the telling, but consistently compelling.' Apart from panning O. P. Heggie for repeatedly 'suffering at the top of his lungs. . .' the Times complimented the 'admirable' players in a film that was destined for 'certain success.'

In April 1934, playwright Robert Emmet Sherwood was living in Reno, Nevada, for the statutory six weeks to fly the cage from a troubled and unrewarding marriage.

During his stay in Reno, Sherwood wrote *The Petrified Forest*, and it was from Reno's checkerboard of humanity that he drew his inspiration.

Aboard the Cunard liner "Majestic," en route to England where with Arthur Wimperis he was to co-script the Alexander Korda film *The Scarlet Pimpernel*, Sherwood encountered the star of the film, Leslie Howard, voyaging home with actor William Gargan, who had just finished filming with Howard in *Secret Agent*, and their wives.

Howard was intrigued by Sherwood's outline of the plot of *The Petrified Forest* and in particular, with the scope and fiber of the play's central character, the panhandling intellectual Alan Squier.

Later the same night, Ruth Howard awoke rather suddenly, and caught sight of her husband, enveloped in pipesmoke, scribbling furiously on the ship's crested notepaper. He had read the play several times, and was making preliminary notes on how he would interpret the Alan Squier part.

Sherwood returned to New York ahead of Howard, and in association with Howard's partner Gilbert Miller and producer Arthur Hopkins tackled the preliminaries. The assembled cast included Peggy Conkin, Charles Dow Clarke

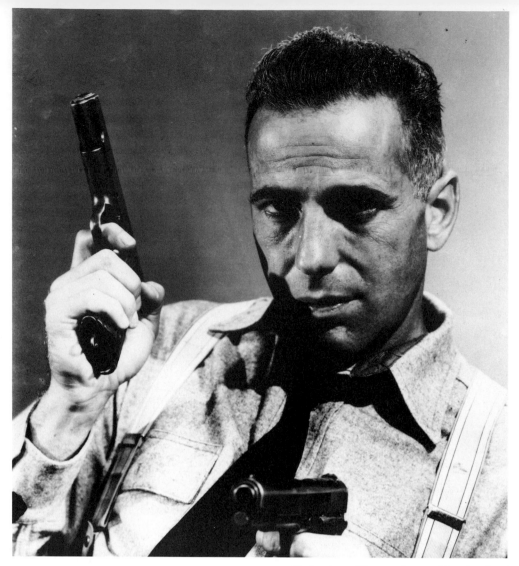

Studio pose as "Duke Mantee", setting a trend for screen gangsters – [The Petrified Forest] (1936)

and Blanche Sweet. For one of the remaining unfilled parts, the heroine's handsome but mouthy footballer boyfriend, Sherwood suggested Humphrey Bogart, whom he knew through Bill Brady Jr. – Humphrey's best pal – who had produced the playwright's very first work, *The Road to Rome* at the Playhouse in 1927.

Bogart was tracked down by Arthur Hopkins at the Masque Theatre, in Rufus King's melodrama *Invitation to a Murder* with Gale Sonnegaard, Walter Abel and Jane Seymour. Hopkins, architect of a full score of Broadway smashes ranging in style and pace from the legendary Barrymore Hamlet to *What Price Glory*, told an unbelieving Sherwood that Humphrey would make a more impactive Duke Mantee – the second male lead, yet to be filled.

Knowing Hopkins' immaculate track record, Sherwood concealed his initial scepticism, confident that either Howard or Miller, or both, would share his view that Bogart was no Mantee.

But when Howard saw him in *Invitation to a Murder*, growling commands in that pained, gravelly monotone, peering out into the auditorium like a cornered wolf, there was never any doubt in his mind. He endorsed Hopkins choice, and the search for Duke Mantee ended.

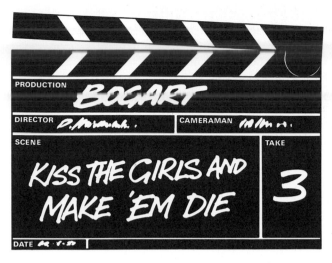

The Wall Street crash, bookended by savage gang warfare and grim unemployment, brought the curtain down with resonant finality on the madcap twenties. The resultant hardening of attitudes coincided with the rise in popularity of the gangster film. Suddenly disillusioned with traditional hero figures, the youth of America saw in the spread of organized gangsterdom a vicious parody on the ethics of big business. This was the direction the world was taking – legitimate commerce scrabbling around on its knees while organized crime flourished.

Gangster films had appeared before the advent of the soundtrack. Von Sternberg's *Underworld* (1927) and Milestone's *The Racket* (1928) both had impact, but sound permitted moviemakers to step inside the harsh metallic world of the gangster.

Of the many actors catapulted to fame through their gangster portrayals during the thirties, three occupy an indisputable supremacy – Humphrey Bogart, James Cagney and Edward G. Robinson.

All three were weathered Broadway performers wooed by the Hollywood machine after sound had discarded dozens of mime artistes with thick, foreign accents. Each brought to the screen a distinctive trademark – Robinson's cobra eyes and mean slit of a mouth, Cagney's lithe stride and leprechaun smile, Bogart's famished wolf face. All three of these actors flourished at Warner Brothers studios. The true-life rags to riches story of the Warner brothers possessed all the elements of high drama and low comedy that was their staple product for four generations. Having gambled their limited resources on a chain of nickelodeons, the four immigrant Warners barely survived the twenties, but with the coming of sound – which they more than any other studio pioneered – they quickly became the hottest working unit in Hollywood. Even after attaining solvency, however, the rigid internal economies persisted, resulting in a studio system whose footage, like everything else, was pruned to the bone.

In visual terms, this translated crisply into pace and vigor, the hallmark of the gangster movie. Although the League of Decency backlash in 1933 successfully dampened the swell of crime films, the style was established and survived, with a subtle revision of emphasis, till the outbreak of World War II.

The Cagney-Robinson characters were hard and megalomaniacal, evidence of a social rather than personal maladjustment. Cagney's wise-cracking slum kid driven to the rackets through lack of opportunity for his legitimate talents was only a shave from the truth. In *The Roaring Twenties*, he returns from the trenches to find his job taken, his status nil. Gangland beckons, but only after society has slammed the door in his face.

Bogart differed fundamentally by portraying psychological rather than social maladjustment. Unlike the other two, he was pragmatically American. In *The Petrified Forest* he is exonerated by a fellow trueblood: 'Gangsters are foreigners. He's an American. . .' In *Black Legion* he captures the disillusion of working-class America during the thirties, susceptible to political exploitation.

But it was through his wartime, and immediate post-war characterizations that he reflected so strongly the national character. In *Casablanca* he is isolationist America plotting a cautious neutral course. A year later, in *Action in the North Atlantic*, he is off the fence and even ready to love the Russians. *Sahara* finds him marshalling a United Nations of stragglers under a Free World banner, and in *Passage to Marseille*, he blisters the French collaborators. In *To Have and Have Not* he abandons cosy neutrality to assist the underground Free French to hit back at the Vichy authorities. No sequence of films by any one actor capture so expressly

*"James Frazier" and Jimmy Cagney – [Angels
with Dirty Faces](1938)*

the American attitude between 1941-1945.

The memorable CagBog confrontations
spanned three films in under two years – *Angels
With Dirty Faces*, *The Roaring Twenties* and
The Oklahoma Kid.

Several interesting parallels occur in the first
two. Both times, Cagney's downfall/redemption –
one being indivisable from the other – springs
from an inner morality, his refusal to stand aloof
when chums are menaced. Comradeship is
everything, even though his pivotal violence in
their defense carries more hint of a poignant
appeal for their affection than of an instinctive
violent personality in full charge.

In *Angels With Dirty Faces*, rhetoric street
urchin Rocky Sullivan (Cagney) lands up in the
reformatory more through bravado than criminal
intent – his first haul is a worthless cache of pens.
From there, the system takes over, and Rocky is
propelled in and out of prison, like someone
caught in a revolving door.

Rocky is anxious to recoup some hot money
from his shifty lawyer Frazier (Bogart) who had

sieved the bankroll into a thriving nightclub
business in partnership with a grasping politician
Keefer (George Bancroft).

Stung by the dissipation of his flock that
Rocky's presence creates, Father Connally (Pat
O'Brien) hot gospels about the evil in their midst,
and gets his name on a Frazier bullet, but before
it can be arranged, Rocky's latent choirboy
morality runs amok, and he wraps up Frazier in
grand style. Making his escape, he is forced to
kill a policeman. Abrasive and buoyant, even in
the death cell, he finally consents to putting on a
convincing weasel act to the gas chamber, to
alienate himself from the army of slumkids who
would otherwise ape him all the way to the
penitentiary.

The film is full of good things, like the early
montage of Cagney's regression into criminal
grey, and his wryly aggressive refereeing of an
ill-matched basketball game (Cagney
demonstrating his authority by gouging the
gougers). Scene after scene mirrors the vicious
world of the bluff, ill-fated Sullivan. He is
alternately sadistic and cherubic. 'Nice day for a
murder,' he chirps at a gaggle of policemen. His
gently-needling catchphrase, 'Whaddya know,

whaddya say!' mixes cocky self-assuredness with an appealing naivety.

From the opening panshot of tenement squalor – reminiscent of the rooftops opening to *Dead End* – to the chilling climax of death mile as Cagney pleads for his life, his trousers ripped to the knee to receive the electrodes, Curtiz keeps the narrative in high gear, sensitively nibbling at rather than indicating the causative sociological factors.

Only in the pious bromides of the priest, and in the mock-redemption of the gangster does he let the softening light of sentimentality pervade.

The Motion Picture Herald described Cagney as 'functioning with throttle wide open, and mainly as a lone wolf. He's never done this kind of thing better, if as well.' Bogart, it went on, 'plays the second-string criminal. . .softening his touch considerably for the job.' Critic William Weaver concluded that the movie was 'a strong, swift, pungent melodrama, crammed with excellent performances.'

The Monthly Film Bulletin, while commending everyone, pointed out 'that the tendency of this film is to glorify the gangster.' The Daily Film Renter said that Cagney 'garnished the role with character strokes that make for terrific conviction' but thought that Pat O'Brien 'even in his customary robustness, seems a trifle dissipated in his clerical trapping. . .' Bogart displayed 'every competence'.

The London Sunday Times put that film in the same tradition of *Quick Millions* and *Scarface*. 'So lively and natural is the writing, so spontaneous and engaging the acting of James Cagney, that I am not sure *Angels With Dirty Faces* is not the best gangster melodrama ever made. . .fresh, witty and continuously entertaining, and the emotional impact is terrific.'

In *The Roaring Twenties*, Cagney is again the catalyst between good and evil. Three rookies strike up a wary camaraderie in the trenches of World War I. Back home, former jobs are filled by surly dodgers, prospects are grim. Eddie Bartlett (Cagney) begins running errands for mobsters, where his distinctive flair and resourcefulness promptly earns him the attention of the bigger fish.

Lloyd Hart (Jeffrey Lynn), resuming his law practise is persuaded against his better judgment to become Bartlett's attorney, and soon, with the merest encouragement, Bartlett's long-suffering songstress girlfriend Jean (Priscilla Lane) is gobbling him up in her torch-songs.

An audacious off-shore hyjack of bootleg liquor reunites Bartlett with George Hally (Bogart) who is riding shotgun for mobster Nicky Brown (Paul Kelly). They decide to pool their resources and split the shipment. The methodical slaying of Brown characterizes their abrasive alliance.

Preoccupied with his business affairs, Bartlett fails to notice Jean's attachment for the lawyer, who, by this time, had had more than enough of gangsters, and wants only to settle down with Jean.

The years pass. Lloyd becomes a blazing meteorite in the D.A.'s office, and duty insists he indict Hally on criminal proceedings, despite the threat that his infant son will be harmed – a prospect which naturally panics Jean. Bartlett turns up, tough as usual but penniless, and decides to tackle his former partner personally.

His run-in with Hally is superb Cagney. 'Goodbye and Happy New Year' sneers Hally, despatching him for the obligatory car-ride, but a moment later he is cornered and groveling. Hally's mob, waiting downstairs, nail him as he sprints away. 'He used to be a big-shot,' explains nightclub queen Gladys George to a curious patrolman as Bartlett dies in the snow.

Mark Hellinger's frothy story – based on a real life New York character Larry Fay – initially entrusted to director Anatole Litvak, became the high-spot of Walsh's erratic thirties. Its recreation of the corrosive effects of war, and the hazardous readjustment is bitingly accurate. Everything is harsh and volatile and grubby. Deserted wharves and dark streets bristle with hidden menace. The texture of the period is so authentic that we are drawn into it, we become almost part of the events.

Again, brilliant montages set the pace. Bartlett's progress up the racketeering ladder is encapsulated in short, savage machinegun bursts of action. No unnecessary fat is left hanging on the bones. Moods and relationships are established with a cold economy. One profound little scene near the beginning rationalizes the contrast – social v. psychological malformation – between Bogart and Cagney.

Pinned down by enemy fire their rifle sights collide on the same advancing German. 'He can't be more than fifteen,' observes Cagney, instinctively lowering his weapon. 'He'll never be sixteen,' growls Bogart, squeezing the trigger.

The CagBog confrontations – there are more here than in *Angels With Dirty Faces* – delight

RT-2

with their usual wry venom. At no time is the toughness feigned, the dialogue forced. It is bright steel versus salt water, with Cagney doing most of the stabbing and splashing and Bogart needling away with the quiet corrosiveness of his, but the film sags disappointingly from the point where Cagney becomes the victim of events instead of their architect.

His spectacular slump is poorly advocated, and the suggestion that his moll's defection causes it is illogical in view of what has gone on before. Lloyd's character makes no concession to a lifetime of thunderous violence – the trenches, then gangsters – and his lame-duck affair with Jean is all too plausible, if only for the mutual dullness they exhibit.

But Gladys George's faded rose, who genuinely loved her clip-joint suckers, especially Cagney, deserves the Oscar which Claire Trevor won for an identical characterization in *Key Largo* eight years later.

Spectator critic Basil Wright describes Cagney as 'the only actor who can personify the evil of the world in its proper guise of amiability. . . In gesture and in timing, he is one of the most accomplished and convincing of actors; there are indeed few whom one can watch with greater pleasure.' The film was 'a brilliantly-made thriller'.

Film Weekly thought it 'vivid as a newsreel'.

The Oklahoma Kid , conceptually and visually less interesting than the two previous films, nevertheless remains an intriguing museum piece. Neither actor was ever totally at ease in a western and the routine theatrics of the story offered little by way of extra comfort. Made before the western movie had learnt to pace itself, everything happens with unnerving speed, the galloping horses in the famous land-rush carbon of *Cimarron* recall the dizzy days of Mack Sennett, and the tight editing, normally so effective in urban melodrama, ill-suited the great sepia outdoors.

The plot is strictly one dimensional. Outlaw Jim Kincaid, alias the Oklahoma Kid (Cagney) emerges from hiding to extricate his father from the wrath of powerful gambler McCord (Bogart). For openly opposing McCord's presence in the small frontier community of Cherokee Strip, Kincaid Snr is about to be hanged – on a trumped-up murder charge.

"George Hally" in the trenches – [*The Roaring Twenties*] *(1939)*

Aside from the grinning and wincing that passes between Cagney, in fringed buckskin, and Bogart, in symbolic black, there is precious little to hold the attention. The final shoot-out is nicely frenzied and Cagney's redemption is achieved without the usual pious overtones.

Graham Greene wrote in the Spectator that Cagney 'takes perhaps a little less kindly to the big hat and the tight breeches and the intense sexual purity than Mr Bogart as the badman in black. But Mr Cagney can do nothing which is not worth watching. On his light hoofer's feet, with his quick nervous hands and his magnificent unconsciousness of the camera, he can pluck distinction out of the least promising part, and this part has plenty of meat.' Greene concluded it was 'a direct and competent picture.'

Peter Galway, in the New Statesman, thought of it as, simply, a 'horse opera. . .but immensely enjoyable.' The Monthly Film Bulletin described Bogart as Cagney's 'effective opposite number, as sinister a villain as could be wished for,' while Kine Weekly condensed it further by referring to him as a 'powerful adversary'.

Paul Mooney, in the Motion Picture Herald, commented on the upsurge of westerns, and put *The Oklahoma Kid* 'pretty close to the top of the list' for 1939, adding: 'The real force of the production is Cagney. . .he completely dominates the picture as he has many others. Humphrey Bogart is seen in one of his typical villain roles, a role, incidentally, which Bogart seems to revel in, for he plays it to the hilt. . .'

Four of Bogart's five films with Edward G. Robinson were made before *High Sierra* (1941) – a fact which excludes objective comparisons. *Key Largo* (1948) represents the only clash of these two consummate styles, and on sheer forcefulness alone, Robinson dominated from that first cold-bath shot of him sweltering on the end of a giant cigar.

Megalomaniac gangboss Rocco (Robinson) instals himself, plus his entourage of jaded uglies, in a ramshackle hotel on the south-westerly tip of Florida. All nervously await the arrival from Cuba of a fellow-gangleader, the flamboyant Ziggy (Marc Lawrence). The fierce hurricane which delays Ziggy traps inside the hotel, its crippled proprietor Temple (Lionel Barrymore in a muted growl), his daughter-in-law Nora (Lauren Bacall) and Major Frank McCloud (Bogart) a morose, disillusioned war hero newly arrived in Florida to explain personally the heroic circumstances of Nora's husband's death.

"Frank McCloud", Claire Trevor and Bacall –
[Key Largo] (1948)

As the hurricane lashes the hotel, uprooting palm trees and nudging glasses off the shelves, Rocco begins to crack. Stung by taunts from the wheel-chaired Temple, and goaded along by Nora's stony contempt, he murders an over-zealous police-deputy, who has snatched an empty revolver intended for McCloud's use.

McCloud alone pays lip service to the monster. 'One Rocco more or less isn't worth dying for,' he reasons – not entirely with Nora's approval. But with the deal with Ziggy successfully concluded, and McCloud pressured into ferrying to Cuba the Rocco gang – minus blowsy torch-singer Gaye (a jarring portrayal by Claire Trevor) – the screen is cleared for the long-awaited showdown. Twelve miles out to sea, McCloud seizes the initiative and in a frenzy of methodical blood-letting, he cooly reserves Rocco till last.

As usual, Huston uses a moderately bizarre situation to probe the effects of conflicting characters and hostile environments on each other. Karl Freund's expressionistic cameras dissect the long night with a cold clinical authority, flashing stridently from single to group shot, from long shot to close-up, from shouts to whispers.

He purposely hangs on to Rocco's boorishness, zooming into the foaming venom as it spills from the trench-slit mouth, eavesdropping on the treacherous gaiety of his reunions with Ziggy, taunting him with his own terror when the hurricane stretches to its peak.

Bogart's embittered army major is shrouded in mystery. He is simply a man who has stopped thinking, a man of principle soured by the impotence of mere ideas. He functions on a personal level only – intervening when Rocco humiliates his faded moll ('You had to help her,' Nora tells him. 'Your head said one thing but your whole life said another. . .') but declaring cold neutrality on a patriotic level. ('What do I care if Johnny Rocco comes back to America? Let him be President if he wants. . .').

Huston uses the familiar Bogart persona – wary isolationism giving way to flip sentimentality – to flesh out his timid post-war allegory. For gangsters read politicians (Rocco and Ziggy dividing the spoils of a duped electorate) while old-world decency and patriotic fervor (the Temples) watch stifled and defenseless against the muscle and corruption.

Bogart's negativeness reflects the quiet unease of the post-war America, weary of cant and platitude, unsettled by the threats from within.

The Largo Hotel is a microcosm of American betrayal and vengeance. Rocco's bland refusal to allocate Gaye the drink she has humiliated herself for and Gaye's subsequent arming of McCloud is a subtle, though eloquent warning of where the ultimate power lies.

Opinions on *Key Largo* differed widely. The Monthly Film Bulletin saw it as 'a series of outstanding, forceful moments rather than a dramatic whole,' and whilst being critical of Bogart, Barrymore and Robinson – 'their performances are full of their own tricks and gestures' notes that 'the best performance comes from Claire Trevor – she gives real feeling to what is too often dangerously artificial.' Claire Trevor subsequently won an Academy Award for her performance.

The Sunday Times felt that Huston 'has failed to create the fluency and movement which belongs properly in the cinema, and the end of the story jerks with a broken spine.' Ewart Hodgson called it 'a thunderous film of its kind, filled with imaginative direction, true writing and a battle for acting honors that I have seldom seen.'

'A well-known vehicle from the old assembly line dressed up with a dollar's worth of shiny new fittings,' was the London Daily Telegraph's verdict, chiding director Huston for having 'done very skillfully something that a man of talent might well have left undone.'

The Daily Herald ended its criticism – 'a second class Hollywood gangster thriller with guns going off and bodies everywhere' – with the advice to 'see this film right up to the moment when Bogart says 'You can't shoot the wind.' Then grab your hat and your girl and go. . .before it is too late.'

The Daily Mail was saddened by the film's apparent failure to offer 'anything new' on the subject of the Little Caesar figure, 'The picture, therefore, has the air of being terribly profound about nothing,' it went on, while conceding that 'as an exercise in tension, the film is pretty good.'

The Sunday Chronicle summed it up thus: 'Despite a hurricane which bends a number of artificial trees double and whips the seawater in the studio tank to a stiff froth, the pace is largo

and the key is minor.'

Kid Galahad offers Bogart and Robinson as rival fight promoters in Michael Curtiz' florid skit on big-time boxing. Donati (Robinson) hosts a giant bender to ease the humiliation of having his top prospect hammered by the vicious McGraw, a protegee of Turkey Morgan (Bogart). Not content with merely winning, Morgan gatecrashes the party to flaunt his unbruised fighter, whose boorish incivility in front of Donati's girlfriend (Bette Davis) gets him floored by the moonstruck bellhop, Ward (Wayne Morris). Donati senses immediately the fighter-potential in the brawny bellhop, and a deal spontaneously hatches between them. Renamed Kid Galahad by the lady he defended, and under Donati's seasoned eye, the fledgling fighter reveals an explosive natural ability.

Unknown to Galahad, Donati is incestuously jealous of his younger sister Marie (Jane Bryan) whose declaration of fondness for the fighter triggers off his morbid rage. Hoping to dispose of Galahad, he matches him with the vastly improved McGraw, but Galahad weathers the onslaught to finally drop his opponent after a grand slam finale.

Convinced that he has been double-crossed by Donati – who prophesied Galahad's ruin so forcefully that Morgan backed his own fighter down to his last cent – Morgan corners him in the shower-room, and the guns blaze up. With that supreme clarity of vision which often attaches itself to bullet-riddled fight managers, Donati concedes he was a trifle underhand with Galahad and Marie and they, bless them, are equally reckless with their forgiveness.

Curtiz observes the corrosive, grubby world of the fight game with an affectionate detachment which occasionally spills over into plausible broad satire, witness Donati's spree early on in the film. A puzzled barber, scything through Donati's black hair amid awry furniture and pie-eyed guests, recalls a similar party in progress the last time he cut Donati's hair. 'Same party,' whispers Donati, with a racked smile.

Too frequently for the film's overall balance, Curtiz diverts us from his central theme, i.e. Galahad's rise to fame in the ring. Donati's irrational jealousy – like Muni's in *Scarface* – is never adequately explained, and in view of his dying observations, remains the one irritating hang-up in a film that is otherwise lucid and direct.

Christopher Shawe, in the Spectator, wrote:

'Although the impetus of this film is largely due to Robinson's energy, I am a little tired of the whole paraphernalia of toughness. . . the film is noted for good dialogue and the point with which it is spoken by the charming Bette Davis and for the discovery of Wayne Morris. . .

'Before the radiance of this dumbhohegrin, Robinsons and Cagneys and Mae Wests look like so many Teremunds and Ortruds. And the manner of their passing may be foreseen in the last moments of the film which show Robinson muttering his dying words to the sound of soaring violins, reinforced by the distant peal of tubular bells as the heavy eyelids close. Goodnight sweet thug, And flights of Wurlitzers sing thee to thy rest!'

The Film Daily called it 'easily one of the best fight pictures ever screened. It has authenticity, suspense and romance.' Film Weekly complimented Bogart for bringing 'his distinctive

'Nick 'Bugs' Fenner' with Edward G. Robinson – [Bullets or Ballots] (1936)

brand of menace most powerfully to the role of the crooked promoter,' and called the film 'outstanding, vigorous entertainment'.

In William Keighley's *Bullets or Ballots*, the umbilical relationship between politics and crime comes under harsh scrutiny.

Johnny Blake (Robinson), former head of New York's crime squad, is drummed from the force for punching the Commissioner. Gangboss Kruger (Barton MacLane), lone middleman to the faceless syndicate who controls the city's underworld activities, promptly puts Blake's knowledge – and hatred – of the law to work for the syndicate.

Kruger's triggerman Fenner (Bogart), however, refuses to accept Blake as an ally, but his dependence on Kruger's protection temporarily sobers him.

Blake's fast words and unstoppable nature ingratiates him so successfully with his new employers that when Kruger is killed (by Fenner, after a quarrel) he gains access to their identities, and promptly sinks the entire brigade – he was an undercover cop all along – but vindictive girlfriend (Joan Blondell), purposefully excluded from the truth, sets Fenner onto him. The

inevitable exchange of shots kill them both, although once again Robinson indulges his favorite pastime of outliving Bogey by two clear minutes.

'American studios excel at this sort of picture,' observed the London Sunday Times. 'They practically monopolize the market. . . completely satisfying.'

'Hollywood is never happier than when it is playing cops-and-robbers, and in *Bullets or Ballots* it comes back to this exciting recreation with all the gusto of rediscovery – the thrill of remembering a favorite game after a long while,' wrote the Observer. 'Mr Bogart is a. . . most successful tough guy, and I should say the chances are entirely remote that he will ever be allowed to play a law-abiding citizen again.'

'Considered simply as a gangster melodrama, it is a satisfying piece of work,' said Film Weekly, 'with as much vigorous story-telling, deftly managed thrills and fights and cunningly built-up suspense as anyone could wish for.'

Kine Weekly praised its 'punch and slickness,' noting that Bogart and Barton MacLane scored off each other 'with fine dramatic effect' – the first of eight such encounters (*Maltese Falcon* , *Treasure of the Sierra Madre* et al).

'William Keighley's direction maintains suspense and keeps the story moving at an exciting pace,' recorded Film Weekly. 'Humphrey Bogart is once more strikingly sinister as a killer.' The Monthly Film Bulletin called it 'first rate' with a story 'well constructed, full of exciting moments and with a good seasoning of comedy.'

'Those who like vivid and vigorous melodrama will not be disappointed,' wrote the London Evening News, 'even if one cannot award it superlative praise.'

Film Pictorial added 'There's action practically all the way. . . this is not a film to which to take the children, but for adults it is an unusual thriller.'

In *The Amazing Doctor Clitterhouse* , Robinson plays the title role psychiatrist whose researches into criminal psychology submerge him totally in their twilight world. Chief object of his scrutiny is Rocks Valentine (Bogart) jewel thief extraordinary, whose killer instincts are markedly heightened by his girlfriend's defection to the more articulate Clitterhouse.

With his studies completed the doctor's return to a life of respectability is blocked by the persuasive Rocks, now co-guardian of his secret.

Clitterhouse blithely poisons him, to little purpose, since bodyguard Maxie Rosenbloom, languishing in police custody, has already unwittingly fingered the doctor as the brains behind the organization.

At his trial, Clitterhouse's threadbare defense – an insanity plea – is badly holed by his balanced testimony. But the jury have serious doubts about the sanity of any defendant who could so determinedly blow his own defense and the verdict is Not Guilty.

As a straight treatise on the corrosive effects of criminology on all who come into contact with it, *The Amazing Doctor Clitterhouse* could, with more definition and purpose, have turned into a worthwhile social drama.

Regrettably, the screenplay – by John Huston and John Wexley –broke no new ground, and the rather blasé, satirical note struck by Barré Lyndon's original stage play was allowed too much free rein. The result was a patchy, though fundamentally satisfactory, crime story, held together – as so many of these rugged little dramas were – by the sheer force of Robinson's personality.

Claire Trevor's Jo was predictably tart-with-a-heart although not one of the more exciting profiles from the actress's wide range of brassy, butch heroines.

Brother Orchid , Lloyd Bacon's ornate satire about a gangster-monk's search for class was again Robinson's film, but Bogart's Jack Buck, though still the one-dimensional neanderthal of a dozen earlier films, managed to transmit occasional flashes of brutish candor. When Little John Sarto (Robinson) deputizes Buck to manage the gang's affairs while he takes a vacation in Europe to 'absorb a little class', he miscalculates Buck's smouldering ambitions. Chastened and weary after an unrewarding trip, he returns to a frosty welcome, not only from his former accomplices but also from daffy girlfriend Flo (Ann Sothern, imitating to perfection a mynah bird), whose fortunes have taken a distinctive upturn since Sarto last saw her, thanks to a rich, fawning hick named Clarence (Ralph Bellamy).

Sarto's loyal sidekick Willie (Allen Jenkins), refuging from Buck in a mental sanitorium ('He's got a nerve – going crazy just when I need him!') is despatched to recruit some new heavies. Sensing a showdown, Buck dupes the simple-minded Flo into isolating Sarto from his gang in a neutral upstate café, but the subsequent assassination attempt misfires, and Sarto, badly

"Jack Buck" and Edward G. Robinson –
[Brother Orchid] (1940)

wounded, flees until he drops, exhausted, in the
courtyard of a secluded monastery.

The brothers are pleased to welcome the
resourceful Sarto to their ranks as he –
rechristened *Brother Orchid* – is to lie low for a
while ('I'm okay and in a swell hideout run by the
biggest chumps in the world. . .' he cables
Willie).

Flo's publicized marriage plans (to Clarence)
flushes a scornful Sarto from hiding, but in the
end he grudgingly concedes that his rival is the
only logical choice. ('All the real love I have for
Flo you could stick in your eye'). Monastery life,
he concludes, wryly tossing aside what's left of
his worldly goods, is the 'real class.'

Brother Orchid showed Robinson with his
spikes off, and a surprising amount of its original
luster is preserved in his deliciously tongue-in-
cheek performance. His subtle conversion from
vulgar slob to responsive human being contains
moments of real sensitivity. Many scenes – like
Sarto mistaking the inquisitive monks grouped
around his sickbed for St Peter's welcoming

committee – are hugely amusing. Ann Sothern's
precocious gump ('If the cops nail him he'll get a
hundred years, maybe life!') is a refreshing
about-face on Robinson's customary hard-boiled
ladies of pleasure, and her feigned drunkenness
to lure the over-protective Sarti to Fat Duchy's,
and Buck's hired assassins, conveys a neat,
persuasive, eroticism. The monks are suitably
clockwork, although Cecil Kellaway's expressive
moonface, forever helplessly it seems on the
point of irrepressible laughter, makes up for all
that overt piety.

Heinz Roemheld's atmospheric music score –
the monastery scenes' limpid strings
counterpointing the brassy discordance of the
outside world – upholds Tony (*High Sierra*)
Gaudio's mobile camerawork (Sarto's near-
murder and escape is a masterpiece of light and
movement) and Don Siegel's evocative montages
of Sarto being skinned in Europe preface the
same craftsman's touch responsible for Bogart's
Parisian dalliance in *Casablanca* .

'A monastery garden is hardly a suitable
background for the exploits of a gangster,' ran
the Times comment, 'and even when the gangster
reforms, the film does not cease to embarrass
and jar. And Edward G. Robinson. . .cannot

disguise either the general weakness of the film's construction or its unfortunate confusion of moods.

'Mr Humphrey Bogart gives another of his smooth, cold exercises in villainy. . .'

The London Daily Sketch commended both Robinson for almost making the characterization credible, 'which proves what an excellent actor Edward G. Robinson is,' and the production for its 'several nice ironic moments.'

'Robinson keeps the different moods of the film together,' wrote William Whitebait. 'Here, more than ever, he sets out to be lovable though tough, and succeeds.'

The Daily Film Renter suggested there was 'plenty of originality and resource and inventiveness at the core of this brisk and competently made offering. . . With its well-turned dialogue, slick production and dominant theme, its box-office response is assured.'

'So cleverly does the story steer a middle course between the serious and the comic that it is able to make a monkey, and an entertaining one at that, out of morality without offending the tenderest susceptibilities,' noted Kine Weekly. '. . . Humphrey Bogart contributes another convincing gangster cameo. . . Its secret is realistic detail, clever pungent characterization and smart dialogue.'

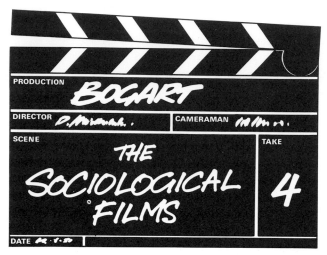

PRODUCTION BOGART

DIRECTOR D. Niven.

CAMERAMAN M Mi.

SCENE THE SOCIOLOGICAL FILMS

TAKE 4

DATE

During the first hectic years of sound, movie genres pursued each other frenziedly. In 1931 alone, fifty gangster movies emerged in the wake of *Little Caesar*. Prison yard dramas tumbled out in quick succession after *The Big House*, and *The Front Page* theme resurfaced countless times.

Although the quality of these movies were uneven, film-makers of distinction were at work, dispensing on average five feature films every year. Against this prodigious output, variations in quality are inevitable.

One of the most durable cycles was the sociological drama, remarkable for the force and tenacity with which it probed conventional areas of public unrest. Sermons on private and civic responsibility, delivered with everything from the fur glove to the mailed fist, indicated that every other director in Hollywood was having crusading seizures. But there was a more basic explanation for it – public demand. As it had done with sound, Warner Brothers, more than any other studio, gave birth to the restless idealism that swept through the cinema of the thirties.

The three surviving Warners had seen enough social injustice to pack out a hundred movies since their impoverished disembarkation from Warsaw. To their proven flair for converting headline issues into solid box-office was added a crisp sense of patriotic responsibility. The result was a pageant of violent

little morality plays, retrospectively stylized by their harsh static photography and gloomy interiors, from which no contract player was exempt and no excessively punitive system safe – except their own.

Bogart's most persuasive sermon-on-the-slums was *Dead End*, Sidney Kingsley's grim, claustrophobic drama of the New York waterfront, made with Bogart on loan to Sam Goldwyn. Lillian Hellman's faithful adaptation moved like a biologist's probe, feeling out the ugly truths, repelled but morbidly fascinated by what registers.

The opening and closing sequences of the movie convey exactly this feeling. After the credits, rolled onto a smoky, shuttered skyline, Gregg Toland's camera plunges downwards, ominously, until it picks out a huddle of teenagers splashing about in a polluted backwash of New York's East River. Trapped like helpless wharf-rats between the slimy water and the high walls of the nearby residential quarter, locked away from sunshine, and any hope of legitimate prosperity, these no-hopers group into marauding packs-by-night, aping and envying the more established mobsters already spawned from their own ranks.

The final sequence floats us back to the rooftops again, and we can gratefully breathe clean air. Kingsley's bitter odyssey is driven home by William Wyler's insistent direction. Wyler neither moralizes nor condemns. He gives Toland the freedom to make lucid observations, to mingle unnoticed with the waterfront low-life, and absorb rather than comment on its sad predicament.

Accompanied by fellow mobster Hunk (Allen Jenkins), Babyface Martin (Bogart) takes temporary refuge in the waterfront of his childhood, where his killer reputation has made him the local tearaways' idol. Like his relationships, Martin's reunions are less than satisfactory.

Rebuffed by his destitute mother, he learns that girlfriend Francey (Claire Trevor) has taken to the streets. ('Why didn't you starve first?') Still, the kids admire him, and he re-establishes their approval in the now-famous scene when he flicks a knife into a tree above their heads.

Martin badly needs money so, with Hunk and Tommy (Billy Halop), leader of the tearaways, he plans to kidnap a rich man's son, but his troubles compound when Dave (Joel McCrea) an unemployed architect, recognizes him and plans to trade him in for the reward money.

Though he eventually kills Martin, Dave never gets to fly the cage – for the reward money is swallowed up helping Dave's future brother-in-law Tommy beat the complicity rap.

'Savage realism and the magnificent work of Humphrey Bogart and a team of boys make it arresting entertainment,' said Film Weekly. 'In Bogart's brilliant characterization there is plain crime and the odd psychology of the killer. . . One brief and deeply moving scene (between Bogart and Claire Trevor) is tragic poetry.'

London's New Statesman noted that 'Wyler's direction, Toland's photography and Lillian Hellman's dialogue are alike, swift, cunning and aware of beauty. . . There are no dead patches; you hardly care to light a cigarette for fear of missing something. And at the end when the camera, retracing its initial steps, lifts you back among the pinnacles of Manhattan, you feel

"Baby Face Martin", Joel McCrea and Allan Jenkin on the set of [Dead End] (1937) – Director William Wyler in shirt sleeves sits behind the camera

murderous towards the idiots who fumble for their coats and cannot wait.'

'Stark sociological plot illustrating the genesis of the gangster,' proclaimed Kine Weekly, adding how effectively the Dead End Kids 'steal the picture. . . They demonstrate graphically the power of environment in the molding of character for good or ill, and at the same time, blend the many by-plots into an arresting whole.'

Basil Wright complimented 'the acting of the slum boys. . . unerringly and absolutely the real thing. While they are before us, which fortunately is most of the time, the staginess and melodrama vanish, and the film becomes documentary in the highest sense of that burdened and unattractive word.' Motion Picture Herald singled out for special mention Marjorie Main's 'two minute cameo of a broken mother, without parallel in screen history.'

Crime School was the next logical step in the checkered regression of the Dead End Kids. Delivered into the hands of a brutish reformatory superintendent, the alienation process begun so effectively in the slums continues.

Mark Braden (Bogart), an attorney-at-law

"Mark Braden" with Leo Gorcey, Bernard Punsley and Bobby Jordan of 'The Dead End Kids' – [Crime School] (1938)

with specific responsibility for juvenile offenders, witnesses the committal proceedings of a gang of unrulies (Dead End Kids). Once behind bars, their open defiance of Superintendent Morgan (Cy Kendall) earns their leader Frankie Warren (Billy Halop) a savage flogging. Through Warren's elder sister Sue (Gale Page), Braden's interest in the case is kept alive, and with his appointment as New York's Commissioner of Corrections, Braden decides to study more closely the plight of juvenile offenders.

Finding the institution a hotbed of graft and brutality, Braden suspends the sadistic superintendent, but mistakenly retains his head warden Cooper, who has managed to conceal his allegiance to Morgan.

The warden poisons Frankie's mind against Braden with veiled allegations about his relationship with Sue.

With the gang's hatred of Braden stirred to murder pitch, he skillfully engineers their escape, making certain beforehand that Braden's humane methods will be blamed for the breakout. But before they can add further indiscretions to their lengthy list, the Commissioner manages to prove his concern for them is genuine, and unmask the real menace.

Crime School's strength lies in the cool, arbitrary way it presents its case. There are no obvious tricks to make you sit up and take notice. No complications in the form of embittered mothers or fallen-angels. Adroit use of wisecracks portray more effectively than overt sermonizing the pathetic superficiality of the Kids' toughness.

Their exuberant adaptation to reform school routine is one of many highspots of the movie. Dialogue is, as expected, rock-hard, laced with some adept flashes of sardonic humor. On a tour of inspection, inmate Bobby Jordan's outsize trousers plunge to the floor. 'Take this boy away and make the punishment fit the crime!' thunders the outraged superintendent. Bogart flashes a thin smile. 'Wouldn't it be better,' he suggests, 'if you made the pants fit the boy.'

Monthly Film Bulletin complimented the director for 'handling a difficult subject in the main skillfully and sympathetically,' but remained unconvinced by the 'sudden and complete reformation of the boys at the end. . . Bogart has a difficult part. He acts with sincerity and is convincing and impressive.'

Film Weekly called Bogart's performance 'efficient, restrained and completely effective as always.' Kine Weekly marked his report card 'very good' and praised the production as 'a searching indictment of the American reform system. Neither axe-grinding nor occasional concessions to the gallery can impair its honest, sturdy equilibrium.'

If the sermon-on-the-slums was obliquely delivered in *Dead End* and *Crime School*, nobody could accuse *Knock on Any Door* of excessive subtlety. Regrettably, its high-toned moral indignation, its insistence on taking sides, ruined what might have been a worthwhile debate, begun in the courtroom when irascible big time lawyer Andrew Morton (Bogart) agrees to defend debonair slumboy Romano (John Derek in an attention-catching debut) on a murder charge.

Despite Romano's tragic-violent history (father dying in prison, pregnant suicidal teenage wife) – Morton believes in his innocence – a belief which is dramatically shredded by Romano's subsequent admission of guilt under D.A. George Macready's gentle needling. Romano goes to the chair, belatedly reformed, but not before Bogart dusts off some blustery clich'es at the rest of us for putting him there.

As a weapon of social enlightenment, i.e. the equation of crime with the environment, *Knock on Any Door* was inherently weaker than the earlier Bogart vehicles on the same subject. Admittedly, the talented Dead End Kids were no longer there to underline in visual terms – which they achieved so comically yet so movingly – the crux of his message, though agreeably cast, John Derek was never quite the same apostle of skid row as Billy Halop.

The movie failed to arouse compassion, either for Romano or those who wrangled over his fate. Bogart seemed to be merely toying with the part, playing the melancholy lawyer from outside as if he, too, felt a porosity of substance within. Making the lawyer a graduate of skid row, the guy who had made good against the current, so that his evocative closing speech in the courtroom – around which the entire plot appears to have been threaded – will ring more true was one more contrivance its already tottering legs had to try to support.

Monthly Film Bulletin thought Bogart 'more impressive than in his usual badman roles' and the film 'fast-moving except for a few lengthy courtroom speeches.'

'Mr Bogart stirs himself out of his impassivity to make the barrister's pleading earnest and eloquent,' wrote the Times, noting also the production's 'earnestness of purpose not always to be found in film stories of crime. . .although its message inclines to the sentimental and the superficial.'

Tribune called it 'an odd blend of social document and intellectual nothingness.' William Whitebait thought 'the moral-society's guilt towards the criminal monotonously overstressed. . . the movie fails to break loose of the conventions of its message and settings.'

The London Observer said it was 'a long and hideously depressing account of a juvenile delinquent's downward progress. . . the value might be increased if the film did not try so hard to find something noble about the criminal lapses of its highly undisciplined hero. Mr Bogart keeps on. . .blaming us and excusing his client, rather tiresomely.'

'We have rarely, if ever, looked upon so sustained an exposition of legal venom as in the taut courtroom sequence which occupies so much of the footage here,' said The Cinema. 'This compelling drama has been brilliantly portrayed by Humphrey Bogart as the defending counsel. The artist probably does better work here than in his more familiar badman characterizations.'

The Spectator wrote: 'We have known many courtrooms, but the heat in this one is so palpable that one can feel one's nerves twanging with exhaustion.'

Paul Holt struck a discordant note in The Film. 'A great big bore,' was his verdict. 'It is not so much a film as a tract. It combines the qualities of *Seven Nights in a Barroom* with *Broken Orphans*. It is becoming increasingly clear that Mr Bogart is rapidly becoming a social reformer. . .therefore we must not be too hard on him.'

The London Daily Mail concluded that the film was held together by 'the passionate sincerity of Mr Bogart's acting.'

To Western societies, the existence of a free press has long been a cherished bulwark. 'A free press is like a free life – always in danger,' growls Bogart in the first of two newspaper movies he made in the fifties, both gritty melodramas; the kind to which either Curtiz or Walsh might conceivably have laid claim fifteen years before.

The better of the two, *The Harder They Fall* was less a defense of a free press than an indictment of the moral catastrophes that could allow the existence of a bent one. *Deadline USA*, the earlier – and debatably less evocative – of the two, since the conflict was communal not personal, was scarcely front-page stuff, but made up into a commendable little filler.

Willis, the editorial dropout of *The Harder They Fall* might easily have been Ed Hutcheson, the campaigning editor of *Deadline USA* a few years on.

Willis is ravaged and, even to himself, over the hill. Hutcheson has fire in his belly and a hardnosed wryness to drape over his disillusionment, but that heavy symptomatic weariness is already there. True, at the end of *Deadline*, he is still printing the news, and has fumblingly hit it off again with his ex-wife Nora (Kim Hunter), but success for Hutcheson is always a transient, inconclusive thing. His finest moments are reprieves, never triumphs.

He inhabits a vista-less Hawksian world, devoid of the absolute, a dominion denied real winners and losers, where life is a timeless succession of bright notes and black ones. Tomorrow he could lose both the paper and Nora, but we know he would scrape himself together again. Even engulfed by black notes, it is only the bright ones that reach his ears.

Willis, on the other hand, lacks Hutcheson's raw boned optimism. Mere survival is the best he can hope for, and it is not enough. At the end of *The Harder They Fall*, he anticipates writing his campaigning articles from a hospital bed. Hutcheson would never have tolerated such folly. He would have pulled the rug from under Benko long before it ever got to that.

In *Deadline*, Hutcheson has three simultaneous running battles – against the newspaper's autocratic owners who are intent on merging the paper with its main rival. against a Capone-style ganglord, Rienzi (Martin Gable), and against time: his ex-wife Nora is planning to marry again.

The movie has several neat, if not bizarre, touches, like portly bespectacled Ed Begley grappling with the office pessimist, Joe de Santis being pushed to his death into a huge printing press, Bogart drunkenly returning to his ex-home and, forgetting he is divorced, tumbling into bed, and of course, the oily Rienzi, credibly manipulating an entire city. When Hutcheson's newshawk Burrows (Warren Stevens) is

half-clubbed to death by Rienzi thugs, the editor turns every available man onto the trail, and piece by piece Rienzi is implicated in the senseless murder of a camp-follower.

At the end, Rienzi has only the threat of death to offer Hutcheson if he prints the story – a threat majestically cut off in midsentence by the roar of Hutcheson's impatient presses.

Vincent Canby, in the Motion Picture Herald named it 'one of the most authentic and exciting newspaper dramas to come along in many a month. . .packed with touches which give it life.' Bogart's performance was 'assured throughout.'

'Somewhere along the way the film loses itself; the melodrama gets out of hand, as does the repeated insistence on the virtues of a free press,' complained the Monthly Film Bulletin. 'Technical assurance keeps the film moving, but the process becomes increasingly mechanical.'

Kine Weekly applauded the movie's 'integrity and punch,' and Bogart's 'ideal casting in the leading role. . . the importance of a free press is established in breathtaking circumstances. The timing of the intriguing and spectacular highlights is perfect, and the dialogue crackles.'

'More forcefully than any other recent film,' said Today's Cinema, 'this film gives a clear and dramatic account of the workings of a big newspaper and of the assorted types who work for it, and its amazing resource in digging up the often unsavory truth. Sharp, hard-hitting dialogue, and completely convincing characterization never allow the excitement to flag. . .'

'Richard Brooks' scripting and direction have bite and precision. . .Humphrey Bogart gives a characteristically tense and interesting performance as the editor, and makes his lines hit home. . .an intelligent true-to-life theme handled with snap and authority.'

The Daily Film Renter wrote: 'Photographically, it's as hard as a deep etched block. Directorially, it's reasonably fast on the street but not front pagely overdone. Actingly, it's terrific from new faces and characters. . . The talk is good, fast newspaper talk with few false notes. . .'

In *The Harder They Fall*, based on a bestselling Budd Schulberg exposé, Eddie Willis (Bogart) is engaged by a slippery boxing promoter Nick Benko (Rod Steiger) to further the contender prospects of a lame giant from

*"Eddie Willis" and Mike Lane – [The Harder
They Fall] (1956)*

South America. Accordingly, Willis creates via
the press, whose ranks he recently left, a
Frankenstein without substance, a brawler-cum-
sacrificial lamb whose route to a title fight is
sweetened with fixes and payola.

Destruction awaits the gentle giant at the
gloves of reigning champ Brannen, (Max Baer in
guying form) incensed at the imposter's
assertions of invinsibility, particularly in
connexion with the death of an ailing opponent.
Brannen's vengeful demolition of the giant is
among one of the bloodiest boxing sequences
ever shot – the sight of the giant pawing his way
sightlessly round the canvas, gumshield dangling
like a baby's teething ring from his mashed lips,
reminds one of what bear-baiting must have been
like.

His investment now worthless, Benko
recoups what he can by thinning down the
fighter's prize-money to 49 dollars – a move
which drives the final wedge between Benko and
Willis, who hustles the broken fighter on a plane
back to his native pampas before taking up his
own personal fight with Benko 'for every bum

whoever got his brains knocked loose in a ring.'
Faced with such indefatigable logic, Benko can
only utter a Steigerish wail from the heart and
retreat through a cloud of sweat.

Motion Picture Herald described *The
Harder They Fall* as 'realistic bitter and
pointed. . . Its scenes, be they tender, tragic or
tingling, are always fascinating.'

Jaik Rosenstein, in the Hollywood Reporter,
called the movie 'a hunk of red, raw meat, it has
the most intense acting duel in many years, that
between Bogart and Steiger, in which the latter
has an initial advantage as the script's aggressor
and uses it, and his brilliant talent, like a whip.
But Bogey rides the tiger, gives better than he
gets, and turns in his most outstanding
performance since *The Petrified Forest*.'

'Bogart brings his best laconic manner to a
piece of special leading called *The Harder They
Fall*,' wrote Isabel Quigly in Spectator 'and saves
it from seeming, as it nearly does, hysterical.'
Alan Brien noted 'too many flaws in the
argument to make a true indictment. But bad
logic still does not destroy exciting film-making.
The battle between Bogart and Steiger is screen
acting at its best.'

'A funny, cynical, hardhitting picture with more pace and drive than any picture since *Waterfront*' was Film Daily's verdict. 'What gives this one special distinction is a brilliant utilization of comic style. . .there's always an angry emotion lurking beneath the satire.'

Film Culture thought *The Harder They Fall* 'often recalls the finest achievements of the crusading American cinema of the late thirties.' But Monthly Film Bulletin remained characteristically unconvinced: '. . .the atmosphere of shabbily corrupt double-dealing, of hotel room conferences and ringside intrigue, is synthetic in its calculated toughness. . .Bogart plays with rather jaded competence. Steiger. . .gives a highly mannered impression of cold brutality, its force blunted by a too apparent reliance on a somewhat limited battery of vocal tricks.'

The London Sunday Times' Ken Pearson noted 'Mr Steiger is surrounded by many lesser lights each in his small way quite effective, an actor who in repose still manages to threaten one's peace of mind. And all of them overshadowed by Humphrey Bogart, whose cynical columnist remains the one anchor of humanity.'

'In the acting, and in Mark Robson's direction of this tough film, there is no fault at all,' was the Guardian's comment. 'Bogart has never done better in his harsh, leathery yet likeable way.'

The Financial Times called it 'well-made and rather meretricious with detailed observation. . .cleverly to the point.' Bogart played with 'nice, dry, smoke-cured cynicism,' a comment which differed little from his 'granite imperturbability' of the Cinema's report. The Daily Telegraph summed up the Bogart-Steiger acting battle as a victory for Steiger, who 'walks away with the picture'. By comparison, Bogart 'roars like a sucking dove'.

Black Legion , based on a story by Robert Lord (who produced all four movies for Bogart's Santana Company), hit out at that sinister element of American society, the secret society. During the twenties, organizations like the Ku Klux Klan preyed on foreigners and negroes, purging alien minorities with ritualistic savagery.

"Frank Taylor" surrounded by press and police – [Black Legion] (1937)

Bogart plays Frank Taylor, an automobile assembler stung into joining the legion by the appointment, over his head, of an affable foreigner. The Legion, ostensibly a patriotic brotherhood sworn to defend national interests, but in reality a cover for a lucrative swindle, presents Frank with the opportunity to burn his rival's home and thereby flush him from the community.

Though clearly no hothead, Frank allows himself to be manipulated, and his rejection, and subsequent murder, of his best friend personalizes the kind of nightmare Americans have had to learn to live with – the smouldering violence that threatens an easy surface calm.

It is not until the Legion discredits itself sufficiently in Frank's eyes – as the public indiscretions of the real Klan's leaders did in 1928 – by clearly undermining the same personal freedoms it espouses to protect, that Frank finds his voice and sacrifices his own skin to smash the evil network.

The New York Times voted *Black Legion* 'editorial cinema at its best'; the Herald Tribune called it 'outstanding and memorable', And the Daily News 'as up-to-the-minute as today's newspapers'.

These were symptomatic of the general response to *Black Legion* .

'Starkly naturalistic acting and narration give the story complete reality,' wrote Film Weekly. 'Some of the most vital incidents have the reality of a good newsreel. . . Bogart gives a magnificent performance. He wins sympathy for the character but never whitewashes it, or even deliberately plays on one's feelings.'

C. A. Lejeune, in the London Observer, declared the movie gave Bogart – 'a far from robust Bogart' – 'the chance to act his best work since *The Petrified Forest* . The film itself is obviously one of Warner Brothers movies with a mission. . .so seriously played And so hotly argued that nobody can miss the point, but not everybody, I'm afraid, will share the passion.'

Daily Film Renter called the acting 'particularly brilliant – Humphrey Bogart fully sensing the surly resentment of one of the artisan class. . .a strong taut story which left most of the audience with something to talk about.'

With three Bogart films simultaneously on show in London, the Spectator's Christopher Shawe looked forward enthusiastically to a Bogart boom. 'For he brings to the screen directness and ease and the ability to seem an ordinary guy without ever becoming commonplace.'

Film Daily ventured it might 'be just a little too stark, just a little too grim, and therefore 'refrained from recommending it wholeheartedly, but conceded 'it is a brilliantly acted film. Bogart leaps into the Muni class, a great study.'

The flourishing years of murder-by-contract occurred, paradoxically, in the States between the wars. Denied a target abroad, Americans turned on themselves, energetically and bloodily, using highly paid professionals to eliminate commercial and political competition. It was the gutter tactics of the gangster overspilling into legitimate business and the silk-smooth efficiency demonstrated by these 'hit' men insured that hundreds of statistical accidents were never even suspected.

In *The Enforcer* , assistant district attorney Ferguson (Bogart), a punctual, pragmatic man by nature, takes on the task of smashing a murder ring, the formidable brains of which he has singled out for personal attention.

One by one, the State's witnesses are either eliminated or compromised, until a surprising discovery about an earlier contract victim yields Ferguson the one vital witness he needs to send Mendoza, the killer-gang leader (Everett Sloane), to the electric chair.

Ferguson's chief problem is keeping the lady alive until a grand jury can hear her deposition – a tactical victory which in the end takes every ounce of his spaniel cunning and determination.

The Times thought that Bogart's earlier work as a gangster 'had more heart in it' than he displayed in *The Enforcer* , a view obviously shared by Time & Tide who chose the word 'subdued' to describe his performance.

'A bloodbath for the boys,' was the London Daily Mirror's verdict. The London Evening Star began with the prediction, 'at fifty-one, Bogart has attained that agelessness that time bestows on all the best personality actors; and his trademarks – the lazy sewage snarl, the gnarled lisp of a voice, the face that looks like a triumph of plastic surgery – should see him safely through another ten years at the top.' It described the film as 'a clean and classic thriller, melodrama bared to the bone.'

Monthly Film Bulletin complimented director Bretaigne Windust for 'prising from Bogart a more natural and plausible performance than he has given in some of his recent films.'

'Except for a few policemen, all the faces are

evil, weak or mad,' complained the Spectator, 'and one can but cower back in one's seat, hating and yet fascinated by the poison they exude from every eyelash, hating yet gripped by every move in the sordid game. . .a very good film indeed.'

The Sunday Chronicle called it 'a mere X certificate which brilliantly deserves to be x-squared,' while New Statesman, noting that it 'very nearly but not quite' captured the grim authenticity required, went no further than naming it 'a good thriller.'

'Enough horror for the strongest stomach,' proclaimed the London Evening News, 'Not for a moment is its intention of being ugly softened by comedy or love-making.' The Daily Express considered that it salted 'its brutish facts with some artificial thrills,' and applauded Windust for directing 'a first-rate film.'

C. A. Lejeune, in the Observer, most tellingly summed up British feelings on the film: '. . .my objection still stands to scenes showing people undergoing mental and physical suffering, in a work not on the highest plane, in a place of entertainment. But it must be said at once that the director does not stop to gloat over them, and that a great deal of the film, as a piece of craftsmanship, is singularly intelligent and sure. The first fifteen minutes of the movie is about as powerful and rapid a sketch of tension as I can recall for seasons. The last fifteen minutes might make Hitchcock weep with envy.'

More polished – though certainly less rivetting – social comment is available in The Barefoot Contessa, Joseph Mankiewicz's word-weary souffl'e of disappointment and tragedy among the tiaras. Harry Dawes (Bogart), a dog-eared movie director salvaged from the scrapheap (where he instinctively belongs) by a fish-eyed fledgling Mike Todd named Edwards, (Warren Stevens), stumbles into an Italian nightclub with Edwards and a flashy sycophantic press agent, Muldoon (Edmond O'Brien impersonating Jack Carson from A Star Is Born – Carson did not get the Oscar. O'Brien, surprisingly, did).

Edwards is intrigued by beautiful cabaret star Maria Vargas (Ava Gardner) whom he has visions of transforming overnight into a movie queen/international socialite, but his borish attempts to secure her services only succeed in stirring her hot Latin blood to angry recrimination. But with a combination of wry honesty and fatherly concern, Dawes saves the day ('You want to hate Kirk Edwards?' he asks.

'Then you're on the end of a long, long line.'), and she consents to work for the mogul-in-the-making on condition Dawes is retained as her personal director.

After the resounding success of their first movie together Black Dawn, others follow. Dawes is amused at being a marketable commodity again, but for Maria, the transformation from peasant to movie star is too sudden, and even with Dawes' fatherly hand at her elbow, she succumbs to several punishing love affairs, the last of which, with a sexually-incapable Italian nobleman, ends in her murder.

The movie recounts, through repetitive flashbacks, Marie's rise and fall, seen through the eyes of her men, notably Dawes, a South American playboy and the impotent nobleman.

The Barefoot Contessa aspires to the grandeur of an eight-course banquet, without ever rising above the culinary standards of a pub lunch. Mankiewicz's usual acrid wit sustains in places the huge, static word drama, but long before the end, the dialogue, as if gushing simultaneously from half a dozen burst pipes, manages to swamp everyone. Bogart's Dawes is the only compassionate figure in sight; his lines have a nice, abandoned irony that a less weathered face would have had difficulty in realizing.

Ava Gardner brings a heady smoulder to her Cinderella-in-reverse, but fails to ignite our feelings, one way or another. It touches us on superficial levels only – the Riviera color shots, implied decadence, Saganesque sub-plots – arguably because Mankiewicz cannot suppress his own private disgust with everyone except Dawes, the anchorman, our reason for watching. All the characters are deservedly murderable, so that whoever killed whom is scarcely important. We watch only for Dawes' measured reactions, hardly reason enough for enduring its untidy self-satisfied 160 minutes.

'Brilliantly conceived and sensitively executed,' announced the Motion Picture Herald. 'A tribute to all concerned.'

Today's Cinema wrote: 'The inevitably slow development of a complicated examination of motives such as Mankiewicz has chosen to write and direct is finely offset by some brilliant satire and bold observation on the complex state of war between men and women. In one dramatic scene after another, he uses all his experience to intensify a basically entertaining story to the pitch of real sympathy for all concerned. Bogart

"Harry Dawes" and Ava Gardner – [The Barefoot Contessa] (1954)

is at his best as Harry Dawes.'

Hollywood Reporter: 'It was a brilliant stroke of box-office and character casting to put Ava Gardner and Humphrey Bogart together, for their drawing power is as powerful as their performances are stunning. The story is a pungent mixture of drama and laughter, cutting at times into the movie-making scene with sharp, satirical insights. Mankiewicz's dialogue sparkles and bursts like vintage Burgundy.'

Sight & Sound: 'Mankiewicz, whether to circumvent censorship or to show off a natural talent for obscurity, had buried this fundamentally novelettish story in an immense cocoon of verbiage. . . The film has a vulgarity that deprives its considerable pretensions of any approach to grandeur. And as the story gradually uncoils, its prodigious length, curiosity – for at least the opening sequences have a certain bizarre appeal – gives way to boredom, boredom to near stupefaction.

'Bogart plays with stalwart determination through an alcoholic haze, and Ava Gardner, called on to personify Cinderella, a symbol of desirability and all the rest of it, affects an elegant undaunted impassivity.'

Time Magazine: 'The film has a few startlingly good lines and situations, and several embarrassingly bad ones, but even the neat lines, Bogart's expert delivery and some effectively acid scenes fail to make *Contessa* much more than an international set soap opera.'

Campbell Dixon, in the London Daily Telegraph, described the movie 'a thinnish slice of the old baloney,' but warmed to Bogart's harsh voice and ravaged face which lifts the kindly director above facile sentimentality.' Fred Majdalanay settled for the movie's ability 'to arouse considerable differences of opinion,' for 'that alone is a distinction very few films are intelligent enough to achieve.'

Kinematograph Weekly's verdict was 'witty, moving and provocative, superbly acted, dialogued and dressed, this bitter-sweet draught, rich in bouquet, is bound to intrigue and thrill.' Bogart's performance it called 'impeccable.' Monthly Film Bulletin thought it shared, with *Johnny Guitar*, the distinction of being 'the silliest movie of the year,' while Derek Granger, in the Financial Times, was aghast at 'the phoney literary echoes of Scott Fitzgerald and D. H. Lawrence and so on which litter this vastly blown-up example of the higher tosh.'

Despite the mixed British reaction, Bogart was repeatedly singled out for praise. 'Seldom has his air of weary disillusion been seen to better advantage,' said the Times. Roy Nash, in the London Star wrote 'Bogart reminds us, once again, that 1954 is his year so far as acting is concerned.' Sunday Express called him the 'magnificent centrepiece of the film.' William Whitebait in New Statesman, sympathized when 'poor old Bogart stands hunched in the rain and worries his way through the loquacious fog.' 'His misery,' concluded Whitebait, 'is nothing compared to ours.'

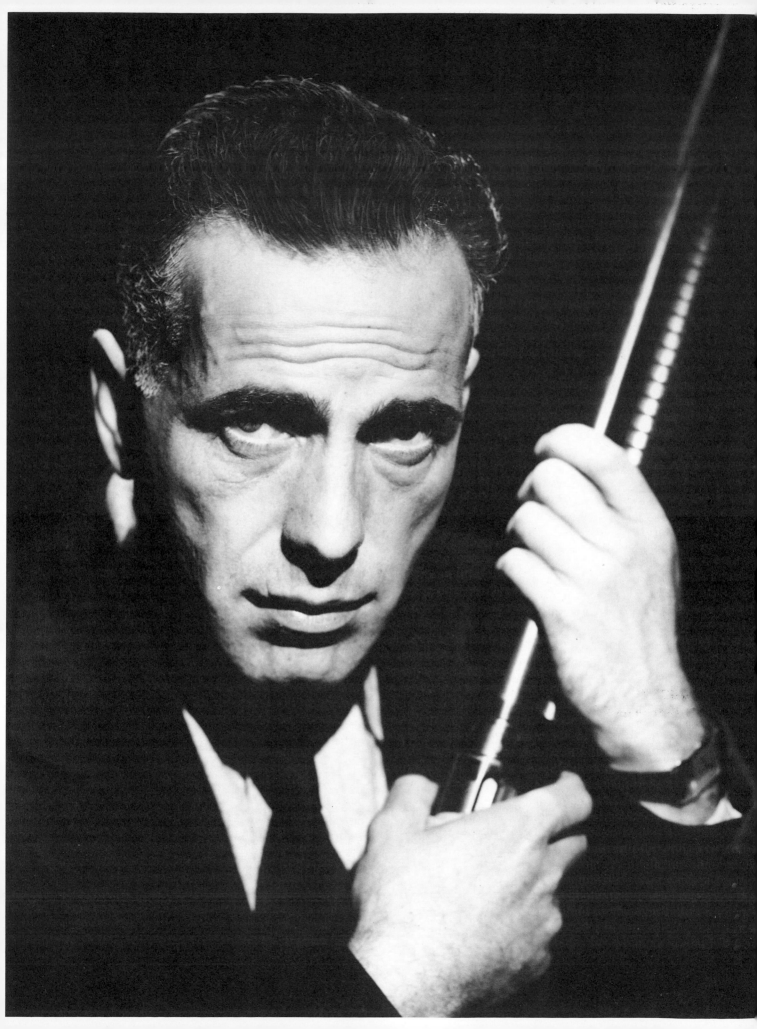

PRODUCTION *BOGART*

DIRECTOR *D. Newnah.*   CAMERAMAN

SCENE

AN ACTOR OF CONSIDERABLE MERIT

TAKE **5**

DATE

Bogart and John Huston met on the set of *High Sierra*. It was an historic sparking off of two compulsive talents – the gaunt, footloose writer/director and the dessicated screen heavy – each on the point of breakthrough. 'Mad Dog' Earle was Bogart's big chance, after George Raft had declined the part, and history shows that Raft would have been as wrong for it as Bogart was right.

Earle is a newly paroled, aging, Dillingeresque mobster – 'let me look at the trees to see if they're still growing!' he growls, emerging from prison grey.

En route to the mountain hideout where his last doomed robbery will be formulated, Earle encounters, and falls unexpectedly in love with, a young, Ohio cripple (Joan Leslie), but she rejects him, despite his generous funding of the medical treatment which restores her to health. Earle sheathes his disappointment in the planning of the robbery which already has a distinctly fated feel.

Earle's getaway from the scene of the crime, hampered by a dancehall hostess Marie (Ida Lupino) and a friendly mongrel dog – in whom Earle sees his own circumstances mirrored – is eventually blockaded on the ridge of a high mountain pass. Cornered among the huge rocks, Earle is smoked out by the dog who leads the

"Roy Earle" in a studio pose from [High Sierra] (1941)

trigger-happy lawmen to the spot. A final hail of bullets brings Earle crashing down the mountain side.

Bogart's sympathetic performance was the keynote of an otherwise routine melodrama. The mature gangster, stamped indelibly with the tincture of defeat, and denied even that modest Indiana farmhouse that might have salvaged him from the ravages of his profession, combined toughness with wary vulnerability, at times veering close to little-boys-lost sentimentality, all delivered with that abrupt economy of expression of which Bogart was the master.

Unfortunately, too many elements were crudely overstated. The establishment of Earle as one of society's lost causes could have been more adroitly handled than making him so obvious a champion of lost causes – Marie, the dog, the crippled girl, etc – and there were times when these relationships bogged down the movie to a slow walking pace but the overall statement came across with spirit and honesty.

New Statesman applauded Bogart's 'shell-shocked gestures and suddenly bared teeth' in 'a goodish gangster piece, the last swallow, perhaps, of the gangster's summer.' Dilys Powell was 'exasperated' by a 'so nearly good film,' but noted that Bogart was 'one of the very few actors who can communicate a sinister physical presence.'

Today's Cinema judged that 'Bogart dwarfed everyone else in the cast' of an 'excellent' film. Monthly Film Bulletin called him 'dominating' and Picturegoer 'easy, natural and wholly convincing.'

'Bogart has had no assignment to match this since *The Petrified Forest*, if then,' wrote Motion Picture Herald. 'By painting a character with streaks of white which do not, however, dilute the black, John Huston and W. R. Burnett, who adapted it from a Burnett novel, drive home their point with power and conviction.'

As Dixon Steel, the neurotic screenwriter in Nicholas Ray's *In a Lonely Place*, Bogart's harsh, corrosive facade wilts underneath the influence of love, but unlike *High Sierra*, where love seemed to temporarily answer his needs, *In a Lonely Place* merely compounds his angry dilemmas to the point of near-disaster.

Whereas Earle's Dillingeresque mentality imprisons him to the dead era of gangsterdom, Steele's waspish tongue is his main defense against the cruel spines that flash along his natural habitat, Hollywood. When a hatcheck girl, whom he invited to his luxury pad for the comparitively innocent chore of reading to him a boring script, is found murdered, suspicions fall on Steele.

Even when his seductive neighbor Laurel (Gloria Grahame) provides him with a vital alibi, the police, who include wartime buddy Nicholai (Frank Lovejoy) remain curtly unconvinced.

For a brief interlude, Steele's whirlwind romance with Laurel masks the violent undercurrents of his nature, but gradually, under the strain of constant police surveillance and Laurel's own deepening suspicions, the facade crumbles.

Steele bursts in on Laurel as she is preparing to leave him, and his enraged attempts to strangle her are interrupted by the telephone. It is Nicholai with the ironic news that the hatcheck girl's murderer, a jealous boyfriend, has been apprehended. Steele is cleared, but alas, too late to square matters with Laurel, the one person most likely to have guided him back to normality.

In a Lonely Place was a bold venture, skippered through difficult waters by Nicholas Ray. Particularly effective were the secondary characters – Art Smith, Carl Benton Reid and the splendid Robert Warwick (Bogart's staunch friend since his early theater days with William A. Brady) – each as in Ray's earlier Bogart movie *Knock on Any Door* contributing handsomely towards the movie's overall authority.

Bogart's performance dominates the picture and every twist and turn of his peculiar cobra logic rings true. 'He catches admirably the emotional ups and downs of a deeply disturbed individual, grasping at straws for a return to normalcy,' was Motion Picture Herald's summary. The Observer's C. A. Lejeune called it 'one for the connoisseur's notebook.'

Daily Express accredited Bogart's splendid performance to the influence of Gloria Grahame – their scenes together certainly possessed an additional ingredient. 'She is so stimulating. . . she even persuades Bogart to get down to some acting. And the result is a film. . .witty, edgy worldly, ripe with crusty observation.'

New Statesman thought that 'Bogart gives his best performance for many a year,' predicting the movie 'will excite any moviegoer with that orthodox play upon nerves and feelings which is the charm of the thriller.' Today's Cinema labeled it 'melodrama cleverly camouflaged within a framework of realism.'

The movie was applauded for its 'crisp crackling dialogue' and 'eloquence and fire.' Not all criticisms were praises sung, however. Monthly Film Bulletin decided, against the tide, that it 'lacks the penetration which would have made it really interesting,' and slammed Ray for appearing 'to accept the script on its own level and not give it much of his own creativity,' a disappointment more acutely felt since 'in *Knock on Any Door* he did raise the level of an uncertain script by powerful and sensitive handling'.

Margaret Hinxman commented: 'Though a deficiency in the script has been overcome up to a point, the deficiency in Bogart's acting is the near ruin of the picture. Bogart has long ago passed that period when he could give a completely original performance. Not since Alan Ladd's appearance as Gatsby has the casting of a central role seemed so disastrously off the mark.'

Most directors are tempted to play at least one joke on their audiences. Huston has managed more than most (*List of Adrian Messenger* , *Beat the Devil* , et al) and in *Treasure of the Sierra Madre* (1948) he brews an elaborate snigger with laudable skill.

Dobbs (Bogart), an unkempt bully and scrounger, finds himself prospectless in Tampico, Mexico, with fellow-vagrant Curtin (Tim Holt). They sign up with a construction firm, but after days of sweating in the hot sun, construction boss (Barton MacLane) absconds with their wages, although later they catch up with him, and beat it out of him.

Consigned to the local flophouse, they overhear a garrulous old prospector, Howard (Walter Huston) recalling gold quests in Alaska, Colorado and the British Honduras. With nothing to retain their interest in Tampico, Dobbs and Curtin decide to dig for gold in the remote Sierra Madres, taking along Howard for his technical expertise. The old man ('part goat, part camel') proves an embarrassment, forging a blistering trail up the steep mountainside while Dobbs and Curtin, decades younger, curse and complain far below.

They strike it lucky, and despite an onrush of mutual distrust between the two younger men, in one glow of the campfire, the brittle surface friendship they share softens to a guarded reverie. Howard reveals that his ultimate ambition is to own a general store. Curtin has an obsession for fruit trees, while Dobbs, predictably, has his body comforts in fixed focus.

Despite the unwanted appearance of a

Texan prospector – conveniently disposed of by Mexican bandits before Dobbs can do the job – the trio accumulate all the wealth they need, and in expressing their solemn goodwill ('Thanks, mountain'), break up camp.

Mistaking Howard for a medicine man, a knot of friendly Indians entice him to their village to restore to consciousness a partially drowned infant, where success brings him an instant offer of tribe 'legislature' – 'the highest honor the village can bestow', plus an assortment of dusky maidens to take his mind off gold-dust.

Without the old man's restraining influence on Dobbs, old hatreds erupt culminating in a clumsy attempt on Curtin's life. Taking off for Durango, with all the gold secreted inside packs disguised as animal skins, Dobbs is intercepted by remnants of the Mexican bandits, who murder him for the animal skins.

Alerted by a Mexican boy, the other two prospectors race to the scene, but all that remains is an empty tattered saddlebag. High winds have carried the gold back to the mountain. Howard roars delightedly at the magnificent irony of the situation. 'Worth ten months suffering and labor this joke is,' he tells Curtin.

"Dobbs" and Young Hombre – [*Treasure of the Sierra Madre*] *(1948)*

'A film that will raise Hollywood's prestige to Himalayan heights. . . an immense, dramatic, ironic masculine movie,' proclaimed Daily Graphic.

'Every line tells. Every situation carries this towering drama a step forward until towards the end you may find yourself a little exhausted, and that's because of the tremendous impact of John Huston's writing and direction,' said London's News of the World.

Sunday Graphic commented: '. . .the success of the movie depends on Bogart, his face concealed for most of the movie behind a facade of whiskers and grime. He plays it perfectly. Of course, the movie has flaws, but they are so outweighed by its realism, its humor and its humanity.' Sunday Pictorial applauded its 'crisp dialogue, hard-hitting dramatic situations, powerful action and well-drawn exciting characters. . .something extra special. Director John Huston – take a bow.'

Motion Picture Herald thought 126 minutes 'a long and tenuous stretch for the dramatic material to hand,' but nevertheless approved of the movie's 'guts and substance.'

Virginia Grahame thought there was 'nothing very startling about this tale. . .yet Huston has invested the movie with a cloak of such harsh realism, and has woven the thread of morality so cunningly into its pattern. . .that it all seems new and exciting.'

Huston's treatment, 'direct, forceful and free of sentimentality' won praise from Peter Ericson in Sequence. 'His observation is brilliant but detached, he demonstrates rather than interprets. All his characters are presented with the same impersonal irony.'

Fred Majdalanay described Bogart as 'an angry old piece of shoe leather with hurt eyes.' Monthly Film Bulletin, described the movie as 'this powerful story of life in the raw, superbly acted by Humphrey Bogart. . .'

'A sweeping canvas of banditry and gold-digging. . .depicted with wit, irony, insight and verve,' was the News Chronicle's comment, which acidly went on to harangue Huston for 'the

"Dobbs", Walter Houston and Tim Holt with Mexican villagers – [Treasure of the Sierra Madre] (1948)

musical intrusion of Max Steiner which shatters with distracting emphasis scene after scene needing only silence or the human voice.'

In *The African Queen*, Charlie Allnut (Bogart) in a collapsed old boat, rescues prim Congo missionary Rose Sayer (Katherine Hepburn) from a German raid on her missionary headquarters in Central Africa in 1914. They make their getaway in Charlie's chug-a-lug mailboat. The movie spans their quixotic voyage downstream, and their ripening relationship, through a sequence of natural and self-invited hazards.

Rose quickly recognizes that the ennoblement of her profane rescuer could be the pinnacle of her life's work. Naturally, Charlie, resists, but the narrow tramp steamer affords him no refuge from either her genteel reproach or her biting sarcasm.

Charlie fights back with the few weapons he has to hand, like getting drunk, but even that is a poor defense against a woman who calmly empties his entire gin supply over the side and then uses prolonged stony silences to achieve total emancipation.

She concludes their journey by inducing him,

"Charlie Allnut" and Katherine Hepburn – [The African Queen] (1951)

at considerable personal risk, to ram a German gunboat, a piece of monumental folly which almost gets them hanged by their captors. But rescue, never fear, is close at hand, and after the German captain has obligingly married them – a last request before facing the gallows – the enemy are soon threshing about in the water.

C. S. Forester's novel might have been handwritten for Huston's purposes; durability and resourcefulness and nobility of the human spirit under physical stress is familiar Huston territory instanced by the prospector's ordeals in *Treasure of the Sierra Madre*, Private's laborious return to his regiment in *The Red Badge of Courage*, Ahab's obsessive pursuit of the monster whale in *Moby Dick*, Garfield's revolutionary tunnelling in *We Were Strangers*.

The vistas of Africa – captured with impressionistic zeal by Jack Cardiff's color lenses – provide an exotic backdrop for one of the most off-beat romances ever filmed. The mellowing of Rose from starchy self-righteousness at the opening of the story to full, warm womanhood, under love's influence, is achieved without any obvious tricks.

Variety called it 'engrossing. . .a picture with unassuming warmth and naturalness.' Many reviewers baulked at the slightly melodramatic ending, noting its change of mood from the rest of the movie.

'Justifiable only on the grounds that a depressing climax would be out of key with the rest, so indomitably cheerful, simple and patriotic,' wrote London's Daily Telegraph. 'Bogart's Allnutt is something quite new. He has chosen to play so many solemn neurotics that you might not suppose him capable of such kindly, likable humanity.'

'An adventure story with a happy, intelligent smile on its face,' summed up Daily Mail. 'The first jungle movie above schoolboy level,' wrote Richard Winnington (Bogart's favorite British reviewer). 'Should collect every Oscar award Hollywood has got under the counter,' predicted Ewart Hodgson confidently.

The Sunday Times thought it 'vastly exciting. As for Bogart, he has shaken himself out of the routine performance he has been giving lately and gone back to being the actor he was years ago.'

'Bogart's followers might require a bit of

time before accepting him in the sort of role he has here,' wavered Motion Picture Herald. Time Magazine dubbed it 'not great art but great fun.'

Monthly Film Bulletin wrote: 'There are scenes in which the absurd is effectively twisted into something real and touching, but the balance of the whole is not maintained and somehow a style, or an approach, is never firmly established.'

Today's Cinema called the movie 'a box office winner all the way. Bogart is entirely credible. It is a performance of rare comic distinction.' John McCarten in New Yorker observed 'Hepburn and Bogart come up with a couple of remarkable performances, and it's fortunate that they do, for the movie concentrates on them so singlemindedly that any conspicuous uncertainty in their acting would have left the whole thing high and dry.'

Clarissa Bowen, in Sight and Sound wrote: 'Huston's film wavers disconcertingly and a little aimlessly between life and fairy-tale. Both Hepburn and Bogart give brilliant performances of such detail and subtlety that it comes as a shock halfway through to recognize how far they have escaped from reality. Nothing in the cinema is more charming than fantasy, more absorbing than character in action, or more exciting than the pursuit of adventure. *The African Queen* has something of each of these qualities, but the difficult problem of resolving them into a satisfactory whole has not altogether been surmounted.'

With the possible exception of Hemingway, Bogart functioned best in works by acclaimed writers. *The Maltese Falcon*, *The Big Sleep*, *Knock on Any Door*, and *The African Queen* were all big-selling novels by accomplished novelists. The theater provided him with *The Petrified Forest*, *Dead End*, *We're No Angels* and *The Desperate Hours*.

The Caine Mutiny, Herman Wouk's engrossing saga of neurosis in naval high command had the twin advantages of Pulitzer-prize novel and smash play before Bogart took over the screen Queeg following Lloyd Nolan's inspired work in the Broadway and London stage versions.

As in the book, Kramer's production observes Commander Queeg (Bogart) through the eyes of a young Princetonian, Ensign Keith (Robert Francis) who joins the U.S.N. mine-sweeper Caine during the closing stages of World War II in the Pacific. But Queeg's forceful opening address to his officers – 'Substandard

performance is not permitted to exist, that I warn you' – soon begins to look bluff alongside the inexplicable rationale he displays in tight circumstances,

During a routine exercise, Queeg is distracted by the glimpse of a rating's shirt-tail and he spends so long bawling the man out that the ship executes a 180 degree turn and slices through its own towline, a mishap which Queeg hastily blames on the equipment. 'We can hardly be held responsible if we're given faulty cables that break the minute the ship turns a few degrees.'

Assigned the task of leading in a fleet of Marine landing craft which are establishing a beachhead, with orders to accompany the boats to within a hundred yards of the beach, Queeg deserts the landing craft long before the assigned zone, leaving the Marines vulnerable to enemy land artillery.

Events come to a head during a blinding typhoon, when Queeg's mishandling of the situation almost beaches the vessel. To save the lives of the crew, Meryck, the Caine's first officer, with Keith's support invokes Navy Article 134 and relieves Queeg of command.

Meryck and Keith are charged with mutiny on the high seas, and the court-martial follows predictable lines. Matched against Queeg's long, distinguished naval career, their defense looks tattered, until their attorney Greenwald (Jose Ferrer) barracks Queeg in the witness box. To the surprise of the court, Queeg loses his composure and involuntarily spews out a bewildering chain of contradictions, hatred and self-pity. Too late, he realizes his mistake, and sags back in his chair, jaw hanging slack tired eyes glassily scanning the startled faces of the tribunal.

It is the crowning moment of a long-drawn-out, wholly uneven movie which suffers badly from under-editing. An intrusive, meddlesome love affair between Keith and May Wynn – introduced one suspects, to counterpoint the otherwise all-male no-romance plot – could have been excised to everyone's benefit (including Keith's).

Hollywood Reporter said that 'Dmytryk with great skill. . . unifies the many personal stories into a taut, fast-moving whole. . .a great picture.' Variety noted that Bogart's performance 'will long be discussed among the pros. . .almost certain to make an Oscar bid when Academy time next rolls around.'

'Bogart adds a quality of almost noble despair to the Captain's sufferings,' wrote Time Magazine. Leonard Mosely commented: 'In *Caine* you can see Bogart on his personal mountain-top, monarch of his professional world and of all the other players. In his long career as a Hollywood hero, hoodlum, bar-fly philosopher or broken-down beachcomber, he had never been so acutely and affectingly good.' Mosely concluded that *The Caine Mutiny* 'blows up in your face like a touched-off mine every time Bogart is on the screen.'

Today's Cinema agreed that Bogart was 'outstanding. . .the exact note of haggard weariness and touchiness is maintained, and the shipboard atmosphere suggested is as authentic as that of *The Cruel Sea* , with which this production will inevitably be compared.'

The Times thought it 'a respectable rather than memorable film.' News Of The World conversely called 'Bogart's performance. . .a memorable and majestic achievement.' The Evening Standard, like several other reviewers, pinpointed the disintegration of Queeg in the witness box as the moment of glory for both the movie and Bogart. 'The change that comes over him is not merely in the expression of his face, but in his whole body. He ages as we gaze at him,' wrote the Standard's guest reviewer Sir Beverly Baxter, M.P.

Martita Wilsher noted 'Bogart's crack-up is horrifyingly effective. The pity is this fine performance has not been matched by the presentation.'

"Captain Queeg" is quizzed by José Ferrer, Van Johnson looks on – [The Caine Mutiny] (1954)

'Bogart's flickering and writhing surpasses anything he has previously done,' said Time & Tide. John MacCarten, in New Yorker, suggested that his scene with 'the celebrated ballbearings had a finesse that would get him a medical discharge from any but the most tolerant of navies.'

'Bogart takes this by no means easy part and wrings every drop of sourness and sadness from it, proving once again that when given the opportunity he is a master at his craft. . .' enthused Virginia Grahame.

A few discordant comments appeared. Henrietta Lehman in Films In Review, called it 'a mediocre movie. Bogart is not convincing as Captain Queeg, for his forte is projecting conviction, not uncertainty. . .his acting range is a narrow one. The court-martial itself, which is exploited so dramatically on the stage, is thrown away in the film.' Monthly Film Bulletin noted: 'The standard of success is not uniform. The other elements do not match Bogart's performance or the possibilities inherent in the situation. The trial, though mainly successful, would have benefited from a performance less self-satisfied and shallow than that of José Ferrer as the defending officer.'

would have paid far more.) But on the immediate issues Rick sticks his 'neck out for nobody' and Renaud approves his 'wise foreign policy'.

Strasser believes Rick's neutrality is a cover for anti-Nazi activities, but his 'informal' interrogation sheds no light. (Strasser: What's your nationality? Rick: I'm a drunkard. Strasser: Can you imagine us in London? Rick: When you get there, ask me. Strasser: Who do you think will win the war? Rick: I haven't the slightest idea.)

Laszlo and Ilsa arrive, to be told by a Norwegian ally that the nominated source of exit visas, Ugarte, is already in police custody. Ilsa recognizes the Negro pianist, who nervously evades all references to Rick. (Sam: Leave him alone, Miss Ilsa. You're bad luck to him. . .)

A few bars of 'As Time Goes By' played at Ilsa's insistence, flushes a petulant looking Rick out into the open, but confronted wih Laszlo and Capt Renaud as well as Ilsa, he suppresses his feelings, treating her as a stranger. After closing time, however, he broods about their former happiness, ('Of all the gin-joints in all the towns in all the world, she walks into mine. . .') finally dozing off among the empties.

Ilsa skulks in, and attempts to explain why she deserted him in Paris (they had planned to flee to Marseilles together but Rick is morbidly self-piteous and unresponsive. (Rick: How long was it we had, honey? Ilsa: I didn't count the days. Rick: I did. . . Mostly I remember the last one. The wow finish. A guy standing on a station platform in the rain with a comical look on his face, because his insides had been kicked out. . .).

Hounded by Strasser, Laszlo is coldly contemptuous of the German's promise of freedom in exchange for turning traitor, but nevertheless he is worried. Understandably, since his one hope of escape, Rick, is bleakly unmoved by his advocacy. (Laszlo: I have to reach America and continue my work. Rick: I'm not interested in politics. The problems of the world are not in my department.) Pressed to explain his personal acrimony towards Laszlo, Rick tells him to 'ask your wife'.

With Laszlo submerged in parochial resistance matters, Ilsa attempts to wrest the documents from Rick, but fares no better. (Rick: I'm the only cause I'm interested in. . .Ilsa: If you don't help, Victor Laszlo will die in Casablanca. Rick (stonily): What of it, I'll die in Casablanca. It's a good spot for it. . .)

Eventually, she drops the pretense, reaffirms her love for him, and insists that she cares only for Laszlo's safety. With the cards now falling his way Rick agrees to provide Laszlo with one authorized exit visa. He dupes Renaud, (although not completely, for the police chief manages to alert Strasser) and all four(Renaud, Ilsa, Laszlo and Rick) hotfoot it to the airport, where Rick double-takes about having Ilsa stay. ('If you stayed here, nine chances out of ten we'd both wind up in a concentration camp.')

Strasser's breathless arrival at the departure point almost spoils the plans – his finger is on the telephone dial as Rick shoots him. Gendarmes swarm around the dead German, only to be shooed off by Renaud to 'round up the usual suspects'. As the plane banks off towards Lisbon with Laszlo and Ilsa aboard, Renaud offers Rick a set of documents to 'disappear from Casablanca' to the nearby free French garrison at Brazzaville, in exchange for a defunct wager. The film ends as they stroll off into the mist, Rick murmuring, 'Louis, this could be the beginning of a beautiful friendship. . .'

The allegorical content of *Casablanca* mars an otherwise strong melodrama. Rick is America 1940, sanctimoniously neutral yet taking up a center stage position. A comic Russian barman shares Rick's diffidence, is painfully in love with one of Rick's discarded bargirls. Nazi Germany/Strasser swaggers in, wooed by a sycophantic Italian official. Renaud is the Vichy mouse, deferential to the German war machine, yet happy to nibble other cheeses.

Laszlo represents the oppressed non-Aryans and refugees, slippery in defeat, converting the virtuous and the uncommitted to their cause – represented by the beautiful Ilsa, and latterly, through her, Rick. Ugarte, the saboteur, murdered while in custody, stands for North Africa about to be steamrollered by the German Panzers.

Rick's Cafe becomes the European theater of war, fought with vices instead of armaments, a rousing duel of anthems. At the end, when Rick shoots Strasser to seal Laszlo's escape, with Renaud's tacit approval, the allegory runs full circle – America's overdue blow is struck for the Free World, occasioning Renaud's 'beautiful friendship' – the North Atlantic Alliance.

Despite its dated politics, *Casablanca* is elegant fun. Curtiz' complex tapestry of colorful interlocking pieces, none exceptional by itself, achieves a surprising consistency of dramatic

"Rick", Claude Rains, Paul Heinreid and Ingrid Bergman – [Casablanca] (1942)

build-up. Questions are posed and deliberately avoided. Is Renaud, for example, a repressed homosexual? His dialogue is blandly double-sided. (If I were a woman, and I wasn't there, I should be in love with Rick. . .) The gadfly is never seen alone in the company of a woman. He could readily pass for a 'poor corrupt official' – his self-description – in more ways than the obvious.

What then about Rick? Veiled hints about his sexuality occupy much of the film. There are several specific references to Renaud and, less directly, to Sam. (Renaud: Rick is neutral about everything, and that takes in the field of women. . .) Sam is much the sadder case, nervously jealous every time Ilsa appears to be making headway with Rick.

He forever stands in her way, urging Rick to dismiss her. He propels Rick away from her in Paris – an exquisite scene dissolves her parting words on rain-drenched notepaper – and insists they 'drive all night' to avoid her in Casablanca.

If rumors fly, Rick offers us little reassurance.

He prefers male company, his affair with Ilsa is conspicuously platonic – in Paris, her mind was with Laszlo and in Casablanca following their reconciliation there simply isn't time – and she leaves him at his own insistence. The excuse that her presence could propel them both into a concentration camp is an unlikely one, in view of Renaud's established duplicity.

Rick's breathless 'We'll always have Paris' speech at the end squirms with unconscious humor. Nevertheless, the movie jogs along with complete confidence, an articulate exoneration of the studio system, for nowhere today could artists of the caliber of Greenstreet, Lorre, Veidt or Rains be assembled for coloring purposes only. Their mere presence establishes a sophistication quite apart from any lines they speak, characterization is completed with effortless economy, and settings become mere instruments of the action (which is how it should be, but regrettably, rarely is today; an exotic location is often the only watchable ingredient in the modern cinema).

Directorially, the style is predictable but has complete authority. Swiftly the mood is established. Bogart's delayed appearance works brilliantly, cameras freezing on his bold scrawl and manicured hands, climbing upwards over the immaculate tuxedo onto his sober face. Seconds later he deflates a pompous banker. Curtiz lets us glimpse the inner man before hurriedly veiling him up for the Ugarte arrest ('I stick my neck out for nobody') and the Strasser/Ilsa/Laszlo confrontations.

Later we see the real Rick rigging the roulette wheel to pay for a pretty refugee's escape. The croupier's lack of surprise confirms our suspicions that Rick has done this sort of thing before.

'Despite an exciting plot, the characters never walk out of their magazine covers,' wrote William Whitebait. 'The love story that takes us from time to time into the past is horribly wooden, and clich´es everywhere lower the tension.'

Motion Picture Herald noted: 'a treatment that is often both sentimental and trite does not seriously detract from the general distinction of the film and the excellence of the performances. . . a wealth of drama for all tastes.' The Cinema called it 'one of the most arresting instances of political melodrama seen

"Sam Spade" and (Femme Fatale) Mary Astor – [The Maltese Falcon] (1941)

for many a day. . . Bogart strides off with all the honors.'

'Bulging with acting talent and breathless with warm, dramatic momentum,' cheered the Guardian, while Kine Weekly, reflected: 'The story, a veritable library of espionage fiction, easily outstrips fact in its cultivation of thrills and the unexpected and what's more, the attractive and talented cosmopolitan cast brilliantly augment its many exciting, tender and spell-binding facets.'

Sunday Times wrote: 'Starry with talent, pictorially often lovely, and directed with considerable spirit, (though without John Huston's gift for the febrile and the sinister) by Michael Curtiz.' Daily Film Renter noted: 'Like all truly inspiring and gripping dramas. . . everything which happens does so because it springs from the play and interplay of human character, foible, cowardice and sacrifice. One

"Rick" and Ingrid Bergman at 'La Belle Aurore' in Paris – [Casablanca] (1942)

feels that its events happen, not at the whim of the scenarists but because they must. Brilliantly acted by Bogart and a handpicked – not to say extravagantly used – bunch of supporting players, it never wavers in interest and suspense.'

'A drama of realism and romance in which their two forces perfectly merge,' wrote Picture Show.

Few directors preserve the flavor of original works as proficiently as John Huston. Though erratic and flaccid at times, when he strikes form none is his master at translating words into images. *The Maltese Falcon* – the first and arguably best of five directorial assignments with Bogart – offers him plenty of raw meat to exploit his uncanny insight into the human condition.

The Maltese Falcon is essentially a spirited tug-of-wits between Sam Spade (Bogart) a hardneck San Francisco private dick, and Kaspar Gutman (Sydney Greenstreet) ringmaster of a trio of compulsive thieves trying to get their hands on a priceless jewel-encrusted falcon, once the tribute from the crusading Knights of Rhodes to Emperor Charles of Spain in gratitude for giving them possession of the island of Malta in 1539.

Spade and his partner Archer (Jerome Cowan) are hired by the nervy brunette Brigid (Mary Astor), one of the thieves, to shadow mysterious Floyd Thursby whom she alleges is menacing her sister.

While tailing Thursby, Archer is murdered, and the cops (Barton MacLane and Ward Bond), knowing that Spade and his partner's wife are having an affair, suspect a crime of passion – although a less passionate soul would be hard to imagine. Thursby's death, also sudden, destroys this theory, but they hurriedly advance another, that Spade murdered Thursby to avenge Archer.

Gutman's appearance is foreshadowed by telling glimpses of his two tame pansies, one of whom Joel Cairo (Peter Lorre) persists in searching Spade's office despite being roughed up. The other, Wilmer (Elisha Cook Jnr), a ferretty gunman whom Spade delights in needling ('The cheaper the crook, the gaudier the patter') eventually leads him to Gutman.

The two superheels, after some stylized verbal sparring (Gutman the clear winner on points; his syrupy banter is a constant delight) predictably get down to carving each other up. Spade convinces them that he is a sharp cookie – which is true – but conceals his real motive, which is to trap Archer's killer.

Drugged and ditched by the crooks, Spade awakens to a vital clue, and moves one step ahead when the falcon is delivered to his office (by a bullet-ridden Walter Huston, on-camera for mere seconds, a good-luck appearance in his son's directorial debut.)

From there on, Spade calls the tune. The crooks duly materialize at his apartment, where Gutman, shaved of his usual bluster, recalls how Brigid doublecrossed him in Istanbul, and later in Hong Kong, and how Thursby, her protector at the time, had become an expensive guard-dog. Spade's secretary Effie (Lee Patrick) delivers the statuette next morning, but the euphoria is short-lived, for under scrutiny, it proves to be a fake.

Cairo erupts into tearful rage at Gutman ('You bungled it, you imbecile! You bloated idiot. . .') but the latter departs on a buoyant note. He intends to add a further year to the eighteen already spent chasing the falcon across the world – 'an additional expenditure in time of only 5 15/17ths per cent!'

His attempts to procure Spade's assistance ('Frankly, sir, I'd like to have you along. You're a man of nice judgment and many resources') are unsuccessful. Alone with Brigid, he barracks her mercilessly until she confesses to the murder of Archer. (Spade: You thought Thursby would tackle Miles, and one or other of them would go down. If Thursby was caught and sent up for it. . .you found Thursby wasn't going to tackle him, you borrowed his gun and did it yourself. . .) At first, she thinks his threat to hand her over to the law is merely for effect ('You do such wild and unpredictable things') but he is deadly serious. ('You killed Miles and you're going over for it').

The parting close-up of Brigid's tearful face is one to remember. Flanked by two impassive policemen, she waits in the elevator for the gates to close. Next moment her frightened lonely face is framed in the bars of the gate for a split second before she drops from view, symbolically hanged.

Legend had it that Huston had merely dissected Dashiell Hammett's original story into setpieces when Jack Warner, mistaking it for a final shooting script, gave it his blessing. Whatever the true explanation, Huston's fidelity to the original is striking. The film retains large slices of the book's dialogue, and most of its nervous energy. Huston tampered with the narrative only to tighten its jaws, with an

"Sam Spade", Peter Lorre, Mary Astor, Sydney Greenstreet and 'A Black Bird' – [The Maltese Falcon] (1941)

occasional curtsey toward the censor.

Gutman's daughter Rhea, for example, is excised from the story completely. The homosexuality of Cairo and Wilmer is tactfully played down – Cairo's objections to having Wilmer made the fall-guy, occasioned by his infatuation with the gunsel (Hammett's word for Wilmer, easily confused with 'gunman' but in fact meaning the object of a homosexual liaison) disappears in the film.

Spade's explicit sexual relationship with Brigid is also muted, consequently the powerful dilemma at the end, when he sacrifices her for killing Archer, a man he inwardly despised, is only marginally realized.

When Gutman palms the $1,000 bill during the final confrontation and Brigid is suspected, Spade takes her aside and callously has her strip. Huston sidesteps this issue by having Gutman turn the episode into a mild lesson in gamesmanship.

With his usual clarity, Huston echoes Hammett's detachment. He resists the temptation to take sides, to impose his own viewpoint, instead he concentrates his energies on creating stylish visuals. Everything pieces together so skillfully that you tend to forget the complex plot being borne along. His eye for economy, like his eye for detail, recalls Warner productions of leaner years. The finely-balanced contrasts of mood and character blend together to create a symphonic style and movement – Archer's preening himself in front of Brigid, Spade's instinctive mockery of the heavy-footed cops, Gutman's magnanimity in defeat contrasted by Cairo's tearful reproach – rarely seen in a director's debut.

Edeson's cameras accentuate the already bizarre, toasting the abrupt physical contrasts with candid irreverence. Low level narrow angles of Gutman in the early shots transform him into a huge gloating reptile, appraising the comparatively diminutive Spade like he would a beefsteak in a butchershop. That is the nearest Huston gets to making a personal statement. But then he counters the impression with sideshots of a casual, roguish Spade. The impotence of size, too, is nearly conveyed by the two burly detectives who dwarf him during questioning, but are never a material threat.

Huston's night shots are tangibly menacing – Archer's murder, Wilmer staked out in a doorway, deserted rain-swept streets and fluttering neons. Archer's death and its immediate aftermath epitomize the director's impartiality of style.

Cameras track back from signpost, pick up Archer middle-distance, the half-smile of recognition freezing on his lips as his killer (unseen) shoots him at close range. Cut to indoor shot, close-up of telephone ringing urgently, alarm clock shows 2.05 background, curtains flutter.

A hand gropes for the receiver, hauls it out of camera range. Muffled grunts off-camera establish (a) it is Spade's apartment, and (b) someone is informing him about his partner's death. Only after the news has been absorbed and he is phoning his secretary do we see Spade's impassive face. Again, Huston imposes no viewpoint, he purposefully locks his cameras leaving us free to decide for ourselves the exact manner of Spade's reactions. His cameras interpret the action, and in no way attempt to shape it.

The crooks' apprehension at the end – Spade's part in this seems a trifle harsh in view of their gentlemanly treatment of him – is disposed of in the policemen's matter-of-fact account of what happened. Gutman is spared the full visual ignominy Huston reserves for Brigid.

The characters complement each other so brilliantly, that one refuses to accept that the casting was simply a matter of luck. Mary Astor's Brigid is the exception, lacking both the cobra-cunning and the eroticism the part seems to demand. At no time are we conscious of a personality that men would murder for. In group scenes she is totally upstaged, and the impression formed is much less the practised enchantress as the nutty, expendable broad. When Spade offloads her at the end, her timid, agonized protests destroy a keynote of Hammett's story – that she is a resourceful and dangerous woman.

Without resorting to Hedy Lamarr-style derringers in her garters, she should have taken some kind of initiative. We never imagined her losing her cool, blubbering like a cornered Joel

"Sam Spade" and Mary Astor – [The Maltese Falcon] (1941)

Cairo. By comparison Lee Patrick, intelligent, mildly predatory and uncomplicated, in the minor role of Spade's secretary Effie suggests the ideal *femme fatale*. Huston had the real Brigid under his nose all the time.

Greenstreet's Gutman creates the blueprint for all fat, cultured swine. Cairo's temperamental fairy is less of a ghoul than in Hammett's original, and the part is consequently the less substantial, yet Lorre's whispering voice and affected mannerisms, such as addressing Spade via his cane in the office-searching scene, convey a neat, pristine sadism.

'The most interesting and imaginative detective film to come out of America, or anywhere else, since the first *Thin Man*, another Hammett story,' wrote Dilys Powell. 'Bogart is as good as he can be. The defensive, admiring and calculating stare on his first encounter with the beauty, the physical self-confidence he puts into their later meetings, his resentful, implacable rejection of her appeal at the last – who could do these scenes better, or as well?'

' *The Maltese Falcon* has nearly everything a mystery film should have,' observed New Statesman. 'Enough mystery to keep us guessing. . .a wonderfully convincing set of characters. . . admirable photography. . .dialogue that has no time to settle in corners and ask questions of life. The technique is one of strip poker, with everyone more or less losing to everyone else. Not even the detective in this case ends up with much in the way of winnings or glamour. . .rich in sardonic revelation, it belongs to the vintage period of American gangsterdom.'

Today's Cinema could not 'readily recall a more brilliantly acted picture of its type,' while sister-journal Kine Weekly applauded its 'brilliant characterization, resourceful direction and imaginative camerawork. Bogart is brilliant as the unethical Spade.'

'Brilliantly directed, brilliantly acted and somewhat unusual film of its type,' commented Monthly Film Bulletin. Evelyn Russell in Sight and Sound called it 'the best thriller so far this year.'

In Films & Filming, Allen Eyles wrote: 'The picture is more compact and unified than the novel and Huston has made precise deletions. It is finally a study of people affected by the weakness of greed, realized with a force and a psychological aptness that gives it moral purpose. . .and more than just a private eye

picture, this is a compelling study in human frailty.'

Comparisons between *The Maltese Falcon* and *The Big Sleep* are inevitable. Marlowe is Spade a world war later, the old self-assurance yellowing round the edges, the loneliness beginning to settle heavily after dusk.

Chandler's creation is more sympathetic than Hammett's, his solitary, unshaven squalor mirroring to perfection the grey hostile jowls of the big city. Spade is the slick opportunist, changing color at a stroke, the buoyant superheel surrounded by clowns, whereas Marlowe is more human, more vulnerable, more interested in establishing the dignity of human values than blocking crime. 'Marlowe has as much social conscience as a horse,' Chandler wrote to Dale Warren in 1945. 'He has a personal conscience, which is an entirely different matter.'

Acclaimed by such writers as Elizabeth Bowen, Somerset Maugham and J.B. Priestley, Chandler's *The Big Sleep* was the first Marlowe story, written in 1939. Ten years later Chandler conceded that none of his Marlowe stories equalled *The Big Sleep* for pace. If the happy confusion that millions of filmgoers have gone home with after seeing Howard Hawks' full-blooded 1947 version is anything to go by, Chandler is probably right.

Laconic private eye Marlowe (Bogart) is hired by the dessicated General Sternwood (Charles Waldron) to flush out a pornographer who is blackmailing his capricious younger daughter Carmen (Martha Vickers). Carmen's weakness for bad company attracts a pageant of twilight characters hoping to sting the old man, who waits for death – the 'big sleep' of the title – in a temperature-controlled greenhouse, like a bottled spider surrounded by tropical vegetation.

Sternwood is also concerned about the sudden disappearance of his chauffeur/confidant Regan. Marlowe's chipped-glass repartee establishes him well with his employer, but not with ice-cool elder daughter Vivian (Lauren Bacall) incidentally no slouch in the dialogue department, either. (Vivian: My, you're a mess, aren't you! Marlowe: I'm not very tall, either. Next time I'll come on stilts, wear a white tie and carry a tennis racquet.)

Investigation of the pornographer's bookshop plunges Marlowe into numerous rapid

"Philip Marlowe" and Bacall, at Eddie Mars' Nightspot – [The Big Sleep] (1946) ⇨

intrigues. The pornographer is murdered by Sternwood's replacement chauffeur Taylor, who is in love with Carmen. Taylor retrieves the blackmail photographs, but is in turn murdered by an ambitious petty crook named Brody (Louis Jean Heydt), an associate of the pornographer.

Recovering the photographs from Brody, minutes before he, too, is murdered, Marlowe concludes his assignment, but Sternwood presses him to accept another, to exonerate Regan from the blackmail attempts. Sternwood fears that the checkered Regan ('He was like my son, almost') may have abused his position of trust.

Marlowe learns that Regan has apparently absconded with the alluring wife of hardnose racketeer Eddie Mars (John Ridgely), whose plush gaming club is frequented by Vivian. Both Mars and Vivian attempt, in contrasting ways, to dissuade Marlowe from completing his investigations, but for Marlowe it has become a personal matter from which not even Mars' hatchetmen can divert him.

The plot is a maze of sharp bends from start to finish. Marlowe succeeds in absolving Regan, who was murdered by Carmen, jealous of an imaginary relationship between he and Vivian, who has subsequently been covering for Carmen, including payouts to silence Mars.

Eventually cornered by Mars' gunmen inside the dead pornographer's deserted house, Marlowe turns the tables on the smooth gangster and forces him out the front door where his own gang, expecting Marlowe, cut him down. The credits roll to the urgent sirens of converging patrol cars.

Despite Hawks' major concession to the box-office by switching Vivian from killer to stringalong – Bogart delivering Bacall to the hangman a la Mary Astor would, in view of their real-life romance and marriage, have been unthinkable – and several impromptu sketches to which Chandler could never claim authorship, *The Big Sleep* was the most accurate of all the Marlowe translations.

Bogart's abrasive maturity helped the relationships to gel satisfactorily, and the casual inner humanity which girds Marlowe through his darkest hours has never been so succinctly described. From the opening encounter between Marlowe and Sternwood, a pall of somber decadence hangs over everyone. Sternwood's world, like his tropical conservatory, cries out for ventilation, perhaps a trifle too loudly, for by the time Hawks has cantered through, there are no dark corners, and with one notable exception, no irredeemable characters.

This is Hawks' trademark. He avoids the posturing and polarization of characters favored by Chandler. His killers and blackmailers border on self-parody, his women, as usual, are luscious and competent. Minor characters grapple for the remaining laugh-lines, and despite half a dozen odious murders, the movie retains an air of mocking indifference. Its callow disregard for human life is countered by a total lack of relish for the sadism depicted.

Although the plot follows closely Chandler's original, Hawks frees us from Marlowe's consciousness – events in the book are all stated from Marlowe's viewpoint – in much the same way Bogart frees us from his irritating glibness.

Chandler's lines work too hard at establishing a smart-aleck detachment. From Bogart those same lines achieve a gritty tenderness consistent with his established persona. His nearest rival, Dick Powell, bestows what Charles Gregory calls 'a certain seedy charm' to the Marlowe part in Edward Dmytryk's *Farewell My Lovely*, but Powell lacks the humor and compassion which distinguishes Bogart.

Comparison between the two movies reveals several interesting parallels. The panchromatic seediness, treacherous dames, dissolute rich and complaining cops are all there, although Powell's detective is closer to Sam Spade both in motivation and temperament, an illusion compounded by its similarity of central theme, the grim tug-of-war for a priceless jade neckless between a cultured superthug and a languid murderess.

But Powell's feedlines are recognizably Marlowe. 'I don't like your manner,' snaps Ann Shirley, prefacing Bacall's 'I don't like your manners' by two years. Later on in Powell's film, hard boiled Claire Trevor remarks: 'I thought detectives were heavy drinkers,' a line that became 'I thought detectives were greedy little men snooping around hotel corridors' in *The Big Sleep*.

Marlowe's saucy repartee with Vivian throughout the film owes as much to *To Have and Have Not* as to Chandler. Here are the same two likable hard-edged characters squaring up where they left off at *Frenchies*, although the relationship in the later film never cements quite so successfully, due to a marked ambiguity in the Bacall character. Aside from being Bogart's straight man her function in the plot is relatively minor, although Hawks, who had her under exclusive contract, contrives to make it look a lot. Nevertheless her scenes with Bogart are exquisitely managed, and three in particular are outstanding.

There is that first barracking encounter at the Sternwood house, Bacall's ice-cool volleys contrasting nicely with a sweaty Bogart content for the moment to let her call the shots. (Vivian: Do you always think you can handle people like trained seals? Marlowe (nods): I get away with it, too.) A delicious little racetrack lunch scene has Bacall attempting to dispose of his services. The dialogue is scented with sly sexual innuendo. (Marlowe: You look like a slow starter. Vivian: It depends on who is in the saddle.) Later, in Marlowe's office Bacall telephones the police, changes her mind, and the receiver is tossed back and forth between Bogart and Bacall, while the desk sergeant on the other end tries to catch his breath. This is a delightful – and one suspects wholly impromptu – sketch, typically and irrepressibly Hawksian.

"Philip Marlowe" and Dorothy Malone in the 'Acme' Bookshop – [The Big Sleep] (1946)

As one would expect, his touch is everywhere. Bogart transforms into an effeminate bookworm in one scene not to be found in the shooting script, or in any of the other Marlowe movies it inspired. Apart from the Powell vehicle, these were disappointingly routine. Robert Montgomery's *The Lady in the Lake* strained credibility with its use of a subjective camera, a device that almost destroyed Bogart's *Dark Passage* the following year, and spiked Marlowe's inherent compassion with a hopelessly wooden narrative. John Braham's *The High Window* (filmed as *The Brasher Doubloon*) recalled *The Big Sleep* in its opening sequences of the detective approaching the prospective client's mansion, but thereafter fell apart, despite some genuine attempts to capture the reflective side of Marlowe's nature by George Montgomery.

James Garner's 1966 portrayal remained anchored to the forties in style and spirit, despite color, the presence of TV stars, hippies, go-go dancers, advertising men and other sixties phenomena. Already incarnated as TV's Maverick, Garner instilled Marlowe with the cowboy's soft center and roguish charm, his

biggest enemy being less the crooks as much as Stirling (*In the Heat of the Night*) Silliphant's pedestrian treatment. Robert Altman's *The Long Goodbye* with Elliott Gould as Marlowe, restamps him as a seventies flopout.

'You could squeeze the characters in *The Big Sleep* for days and you wouldn't get a drop of sentiment out of them,' commented the Daily Express. 'For 113 tense and thrilling minutes, they are all so tough that a trip-hammer would hardly put a dent in them.' Sunday Express thought it 'full of dark nights and darker implications, a stormy weather and stormier emotions.   .a bullet-riddled thriller in the *Laura* class.'

'Crime in excess, a spectacle I found neither edifying nor entertaining,' wrote one critic. 'Even glossier, more violent and more amoral than its predecessors.   .' commented another. 'There are murders by bullet and poison, blackmailing and personal violence of a type notorious in German concentration camps. And I have to admit, I enjoyed every minute of it.   .'

'Bogart makes his usual effective use of eyelids, cigarette butt, and seems to be branching out as a comedian, for he impersonates an effeminate bibliophile to the life,' observed Derek Griggs. 'He shows his quality, too, in the way he puts over the poker-faced repartee which has gained such a stranglehold on Hollywood dialogue. Often the performer is so anxious to seem sophisticated and casual that he gives the impression of a ventriloquist's dummy, but Bogart always suggests the emotion behind the machine-like wisecrack.'

Motion Picture Herald described it as 'a highly complicated tale that rivets attention to the screen for almost two tight hours.' Today's Cinema drew attention to 'its pace and excitement, plenty of violent action and exhilarating dialogue. Bogart plays Marlowe splendidly, making no false gestures or stepping out of the character for a moment. He is ideally suited to the role and succeeds in making it seem new despite the fact that he has played similar roles already. Lauren Bacall is chiefly notable for the wisecracks she delivers in the celebrated throaty tones.'

Kine Weekly decided it was 'by no means easy to follow, but even so, many big thrills emerge from its haze.   .its secret lies in its swiftness of surface action, its ability to create surprise after surprise. A Bogart beanfeast – or perhaps bloodbath is a more appropriate term.'

PRODUCTION BOGART

DIRECTOR

CAMERAMAN

SCENE

ON THE LIGHTER SIDE

TAKE 7

DATE

Humphrey Bogart was supremely qualified for comedy acting – he cut his teeth on a succession of frothy comedies on Broadway during the twenties, playing the kind of part James Stewart later adopted. Warners chose his trajectory for sound commercial reasons, and Bogart the all-purpose gangster was fashioned indelibly, leaving us with only rare glimpses during the later thirties of the kind of actor he might have been if Warners had been more imaginative in the way they developed their contract players.

United Artists borrowed Bogart in 1937 for a comedy part opposite his *Petrified Forest* co-star Leslie Howard. Based, like *Mr Deeds Goes to Town*, on a Clarence Kellard story, Stand In was a nicely judged lighthearted, incestuous view of Hollywood, that unlike the backstage sagas of Busby Berkeley and Mervyn Le Roy, mixed pungent satire with slapstick.

Wall Street bank executive Atterbury Dodd (Leslie Howard) is despatched by his apprehensive bosses to Hollywood to keep an eye on the bank's investment in the Colossal Film Company.

Atterbury, a shy accountant, is swept off his heels by starlet Lester Plum (Joan Blondell), a stand-in for glamor star Thelma Cheri (Marla Shelton). Miss Cheri is in league with Koslofski (Alan Mowbray) a Von Stroheim type director, and studio official Ivor Nassau (C. Henry Gordon) to swindle Atterbury's bank of its

investment by crippling the studio financially thereby encouraging the bank to sell out to them at a price considerably lower than its market value.

Unaware of their perfidy, Atterbury is being pressured by Miss Plum to engage her as his secretary (Atterbury: I've always had a male secretary. Miss Plum: I'll keep my voice and my emotions at a low register.)

Tacitly he agrees, but they quarrel when she discovers he plans to redeem the bank's interest in the studio. To appease Miss Plum, he enlists the help of producer-editor Douglas Quintain (Bogart), Miss Cheri's ex-flame, a cynical, bemused sub-playboy character over fond of the juice but non-corruptible, to stop the Koslofski-Cheri epic *Sex and Satire* from bombing out.

At the film's preview, Quintain genuinely needs a drink – it is, in his own colorful words, 'a turkey.' Asked which part of the movie they prefer, the audience unanimously declare, 'The End,' preferring also the gorilla to the star, Miss Cheri.

Quintain agrees to recut the movie, but the star has editing rights which can only be revoked if she is guilty of 'moral turpitude'. Atterbury takes her out on the town and they both end up drunk under a table, an indiscretion which costs her the editing rights. Nassau, meanwhile, impatient to cash in, appeals directly to the bank, over Atterbury's head, and wins the day, albeit temporarily, by persuading the bank to revoke its interest in the studio.

Stung by being seen off, and inspired by tough little Miss Plum, Atterbury fights them at their own game. Quintain completes a reworking of the film, turning the gorilla, previously applauded by the review audience, into the star, and editing down the glamor queen's part into a virtual walk-on. Result, the studio has a monster comedy hit on its hands. The conspirators are thwarted, Atterbury wins Miss Plum and Quintain recovers his self-respect plus the respect of his profession.

Stand In is a typical flashy, hard-driving thirties comedy, where nobody pauses for breath and only the pace of events makes remotely plausible their inherent absurdity.

Miss Plum's labored attempts to sophisticate the drab-minded Atterbury are very funny – a tango lesson finishes up with footprints chalked bewilderingly all over the floor. Later, gripped in his arms and gliding along she murmurs 'If only this could go on forever' while Atterbury, lest he

"Douglas Quintain" and Leslie Howard – [Stand In] (1937)

put a foot wrong, grimly chants the rhythm
'1-2-3-4. . .' into her ear.

Minor players in random moments
contribute unselfishly to the fun, like the scene
where the bank's crusty old founder is presented
with his birthday cake. Driven back by the heat
and the dazzle of the lighted candles, he exclaims
in horror, 'That looks like a forest fire!' Bogart
has a smallish role, but he dusts it off in a grand
manner, at one point wickedly sending up his
one-time Broadway image by brandishing a
raffish grin and a tennis racquet.

'A brilliant satire on Hollywood,' declared
the Monthly Film Bulletin. 'Helped by shrewd
and clever direction and a well-written scenario,
the audience is taken backstage where the
motion picture industry laughs at itself and with
the audience. Leslie Howard gives a brilliant
performance and is ably seconded by Joan
Blondell who puts over wisecracking dialogue
neatly and effectively. Humphrey Bogart as
Quintain and Alan Mowbray as Koslofski are
almost equally good, and there is real teamwork
from beginning to end.'

The London Spectator called it, 'a joyous
and nonsensical Hollywood fantasia. It reveals,
but not too closely, the more amusing features of
the studios and the chicaneries of film finance. It
allows Leslie Howard and Joan Blondell to
exercise their muscles, their acting abilities and
their personal charm, all of which were quite
considerable.'

According to the New Statesman, ' Stand In
amuses often but not continually. Jokes are
repeated, situations too lovingly dealt with, the
pace is lost.'

The Cinema complimented 'an amusing if
unpleasant study of Hollywood life' on its
'ingenious mixture of comedy, romance and
drama,' adding that 'Humphrey Bogart runs
Leslie Howard a close second for honors with his
interesting, sincere and truthful portrait of a
good producer too easily swayed by his
emotions.'

'Richly, savagely amusing,' observed Film
Weekly. 'Howard is superb. Blondell is
brilliant. . . Bogart is also excellent. . .a
virile lampoon that most filmgoers will receive
with joy.'

'Mr Bogart is found at the right side of the

ethical equation for a change,' wrote the Motion Picture Herald. '. . .The treatment is fundamentally, insistently and constantly humorous. A Hollywood audience sampling a picture about Hollywood laughed long, loudly and delightedly.'

Kinematograph Weekly thought it 'clever without being high brow. . .much of the humor is unavoidably technical but sufficient provision is made for slapstick and feminine demands to guarantee general appeal.' Film Weekly called it 'a film which America is now receiving with howls of delight.'

Swing Your Lady casts Bogart as Ed Hatch, an unsuccessful wrestling promoter who matches his 'Hercules' with a robust lady blacksmith in a backwoods Missouri town. Love smites the combatants before Hatch can get them on the canvas, so to speak, but the big lady's jealous boyfriend provides Hercules with a ready opponent, in a contest overbilled by the wily promoter as a grudge match. The boy friend loses in a knockabout contest, and Hatch, cheered by the news that the winner is to be offered a wrestling spot at Madison Square Garden, herds his troupe onwards to waiting glories.

It is difficult to understand the thinking behind *Swing Your Lady*, let alone be charitable about it. Even assuming that anyone might be mildly amused at the sight of oversize arrested adolescents mauling each other to win the favors of a big bird, the movie needs a sprightlier touch than director Ray Enright endows it with. Bogart wades around like a man with his feet in concrete blocks, sadly out of tune with the joke, if indeed a joke it is. *Swing Your Lady* was such a thorn in his side that later he would deny any connexion with it. The film marked a faltering debut by the fledgling Ronald Reagan.

Monthly Film Bulletin labeled it 'varied entertainment. . .the director has taken full advantage of an original story, unusual settings and a thoroughly competent cast. Humphrey Bogart's talents are wasted on a quite unworthy part. . .'

Men Are Such Fools, a Busby Berkeley comedy has Bogart, unbelievably, playing feed to Wayne Morris, the Aldo Ray of the thirties. Even

"Harry Galleon" and Priscilla Lane – [Men Are Such Fools] (1938)

the name of the character that Bogart plays
–Harry Galleon – is a crude anachronism.

The boss of a trendy New York ad agency,
Galleon has woman trouble, the ambitious
secretary (Priscilla Lane) whom he fancies is
married to Hill (Wayne Morris) an amiable
dumbhead. She plays them off against each other
to feather her nest, with Galleon coming off
badly, not only getting nowhere with her but
being knuckled to the ground by the vengeful
husband for taking an interest in the first place.

Men Are Such Fools represents the nadir of
Bogart's post- *Petrified Forest* film career, and
his discomfort is shared by others in this trite,
inept production based on Faith Baldwin's
Saturday Evening Post story.

'Bogart is wasted on the minor role of
lady-killer Galleon,' wrote Monthly Film Bulletin.

Picturegoer complimented him on being
'very good. . .the material is very familiar but
the dialogue generally has sparkle and polish.'

One of the several roles that Bogart won by
default – George Raft and John Garfield both
having firmly declined – was that of the fugitive
killer Chips Maguire in Louis Bromfield's
whimsical novel, *It All Came True* .

Maguire, a shady nightclub owner on the
run, forces his pianist/songwriter Tommy (Jeffrey
Lynn) who is implicated with him in a murder, to
shelter him in a decaying brownstone, co-owned
by his mother (Jessie Busley) and the equally
dotty MrsRyan (ZaSu Pitts). The boarding house
is infested with 'resting' showbiz freeloaders,
soon to be augmented by old Ryan's daughter,
songstress Sarah Jane (Ann Sheridan), Tommy's
boyhood romance.

With no visible assets incoming and the bank
hovering agitatedly in middle distance, Maguire,
who has his own stout reasons for not wanting
his hideaway to change hands at that precise
moment, suggests they make it pay for itself by
turning it into a ritzy nightclub. Against all odds
but with Maguire's midas touch, the venture is a
huge success, with Sarah Jane and Tommy,
literally resident singing star and accompanist,
making the grade, and the freeloaders happily
pressed into service. The only loser is Maguire,
whose cover is blown, but he accepts his fate
philosophically, having grown to like the old
bunch around him enough to absolve Tommy of
complicity in the murder before being led away.

Kine Weekly wrote: 'Ann Sheridan knows
how to put over a song number. Jeffrey Lynn is
much less effective, but Humphrey Bogart is a
tower of strength. His sureness of character and
sense of humor make the sob-stuff ring true. The
picture plays on the senses the easy, but
nevertheless sure, way.'

Monthly Film Bulletin thought Bogart was
'in his element, and so skilled an actor is he and
so sure his touch that he gets over his
sentimental sayings and doings without
embarrassment, apparently to himself or to his
audience. . .this rather naive and sentimental
story contrives to be, on the whole, surprisingly
good entertainment. It has a little of everything.'

'A personality who completely dominates,'
was how The Cinema summed up Bogart, adding
that Ann Sheridan 'acts with real verve' in the
somewhat 'fanciful story.'

In 1941, John Huston had rescued Bogart
from the mediocrity of Warners typecasting. Ten
years later he came to the rescue again, prising
Bogart away from his ill-conceived Santana
Productions, a venture that had made him a
millionaire but with one exception (*In a Lonely
Place*) had turned off all the creative taps.

As before, Huston diagnosed his friend's
trouble with little difficulty. Bogart was a poor
judge of his own material, artistically he was
overweight and out of condition. His Santana
films had been safe moneymakers, now it was
time for a spot of roadwork to get fighting fit
again, to sharpen that inherent sense of comedy
lying fallow since *Treasure of the Sierra Madre*
– a factor of all their collaborations is the grim
underlying humor that pervades.

The African Queen had been a breakthrough
in artistic as well as personal terms, after the
inertia of *Tokyo Joe* and *Sirocco* . By early 1954,
Bogart had been idle for nearly a year, following
Battle Circus and the birth of his second child,
Lesley, and was pugnaciously restless. Huston, by
then a European in spirit, felt it would do them
both good to change the locale and instead of
nibbling at comedy go all out for it. Huston knew
precisely what he wanted – to regale Bogart in
the off-beat and surround him with an array of
weathered characters, like himself, masters of the
faintly absurd. The story he chose, *Beat the Devil*
, from James Helvick's novel, echoed in outline
The Maltese Falcon but milked international
trickery openly for laughs instead of keeping the
humor nailed under the floorboards, as *Falcon*
had done.

Apart from Huston and Bogart, *Beat the
Devil* , the first of the three broad comedies that
Bogart made during the fifties and on which his

reputation as a comedy actor, such as it is, broadly rests, had several good things going for it, including a big name international supporting cast, exotic locations, grand scale larceny and clever dialogue. Huston assembled several ingredients which individually made stout box office sense, but which sadly, in the final analysis, made little or no sense at all to the audience.

Lacking the fast narrative and tight editing techniques which had distinguished the earlier film, *Beat the Devil* tends to ramble on in a fractured, ambivalent sort of way. A group of bizarre international tricksters led by Petersen (Robert Morley) are delayed on the Mediterranean coast while repairs are completed on the rickety old tub that is to take them to Africa.

The gang are peeved to discover their front man Billy Danreuther (Bogart) accompanied by his wife Maria (Gina Lollobrigida) also booked to sail without previous reference to them. They are joined by a third set of travelers, Harry Chelm (Edward Underdown) a finicky Gloucestershire squire and his boastful, scatty wife, Gwen (Jennifer Jones).

Suppressed suspicions, hostile distrust, and open treachery – even attempted murder – break loose during the short voyage, which terminates abruptly when the ship blows up, leaving the passengers to row ashore as best they can. Convolutions of plot add to the general confusion, but as with *The Maltese Falcon*, the focus is less upon the plot than on the interaction between thieves and intended dupes, and it is the engaging spontaneity of their actions that supplies the main source of the movie's elusive charm.

Individually, some scenes stand out, such as the interrogation interlude when Bogart feigns friendship with Rita Hayworth to win the admiration of a kinky immigration official. The eccentricities of the plot are too numerous to cope with in detail, but with Danreuther flirting with Gwen, Maria serving Harry breakfast in bed, and Petersen's ferret-bag of swindlers causing multiple havoc, and with the law in the shape of a tight-lipped Bernard Lee overhauling them as only a tight-lipped Bernard Lee can, Bogart's eventual declaration 'This is the end'

"Billy Danreuther" and Robert Morley – [Beat the Devil] (1953)

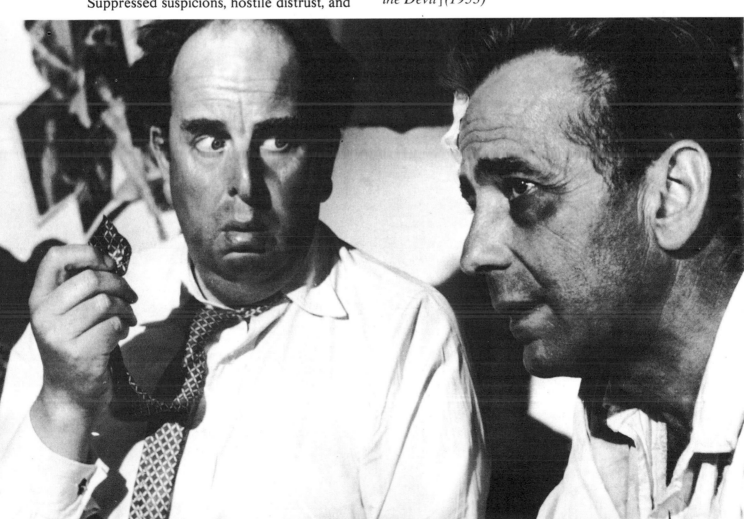

accompanied by the closing credits, comes not a moment too early.

The main irritation of *Beat the Devil* is that it promises everything and, sure enough, everything is there if only somebody would put it all together. The menu is extravagant but the kitchens cannot cope. Heavy handed direction is excusable in short bursts, but what is indefensible is no direction whatever, and what surprised most people was the way that Huston, a director who ordinarily imposes his articulate stamp and judgment on his work (there have been one or two other lapses) seemed to let go the reins and gamble on the diverse ingredients, admittedly powerful enough on paper, winning through.

The Cinema wrote: 'It is the satirical by-play dialogue which emerges as the entertainment backbone rather than any well-defined action. . .yet this summary is not to deny an occasional splurge of thrilling spectacle. . .charming light entertainment.'

'Unlike anything Mr Huston has yet done,' declared the Times. 'A comedy which seems to make itself up as it goes along. There are times when *Beat the Devil* seems to wait for its own wayward inspiration but it has the help of some amusing dialogue and it is refreshing to come across a film so unexpected and individual in its approach.'

The London Guardian complimented its 'wonderful collection of caricatures. . .the bits are funnier than the sum total, but then some of the bits are extremely funny. Mr Huston has always delighted in the use of extraordinary looking people in his films. The result is certainly hilarious and fanciful. . .nevertheless, the director might, in this instance, have done better had he ordered his fancy a little more.'

'As elaborate a shaggy dog story as has ever been told,' said Time Magazine. 'Bogart and Lollobrigida are a little too surface smooth with their lines suggesting sometimes that underneath the words they do not really know what they are up to. . .surprisingly, *Beat the Devil* turns out to be a sort of screwball classic.'

The Evening Standard wrote: 'The unsmiling Mr Bogart conveys the impression that he has lost interest in sin, and is not very excited about virtue. This somewhat limits his emotional range. I strongly recommend this Huston caprice.'

Trying to elicit what went wrong, one critic asked, 'Was the story overwritten or overplayed? Did Mr Huston, as a distinguished director, feel that this sort of thing was beneath him or old

hat? Or did he mean to make a thriller, find it wasn't thrilling and decide to play it for laughs? Whatever the explanation that's the way it turned out. The gifted players all work hard, but somehow it is neither exciting nor often funny.'

'Plenty of things to smile at though the laughs are rare,' concluded the Sunday Express. 'The really important fault is that Huston has cooked us a souffl'e just that much too long, and the edgy satire has turned on him with a rather limp and leathery look.'

'Is it a thriller? Is it a satire?' a confused Evening Star wanted to know. 'Morley is brilliantly Morley, Lorre is lethargically Lorre and Bogart, who had a hand in the production, is brashly Bogart. Clearly, he and Huston have enjoyed themselves on this film, but *Beat the Devil* is hardly the sort of film you expect from men of their achievements. There is an empty ring behind its laughter.' 'The dialogue is lively and literate,' wrote the New Yorker. 'I am not sure that Humphrey Bogart's acting is entirely attuned to the antic spirit of the piece, but he has his droll moments. While *Beat the Devil* becomes a bit choppy towards its conclusion it has too many estimable qualities for you to worry much about the ragged edges. Logic is hardly a requirement of a picture as carefree as this one.'

Variety thought that 'at times the action drags and the overall tempo could be heightened by more careful editing. Nevertheless the director sustains a bright and infectious atmosphere for the inconsequential yarn.'

'Urbane but without the heart which makes for universal appeal,' summarized Motion Picture Herald. Monthly Film Bulletin complained that 'no one has cared very much how the story developed, but that all the attention has been paid to incidental jokes. This inconsequential method might have resulted in an amusing film but the humor here is very intermittent, the excitements almost non-existent.'

Sight and Sound observed: 'The acting is at times inexpert and at times grossly unsubtle. *Beat the Devil* has the air of an expensive houseparty joke, a charade which enormously entertained its participants at the time of playing, but which is too private and insufficiently brilliant to justify public performance. The script has some good lines, but meanders hopelessly and badly lacks a climax.'

The review went on to describe Huston's style of direction as 'showy and over-emphatic. One is not asking him to repeat himself, but when one contrasts the pretentious strutting of this film, and *Moulin Rouge*, with the superb incisiveness and dramatic concentration of *The Maltese Falcon*, the conclusion is inescapable that here is a talent going sadly and seriously astray.'

Kinematograph Weekly considered the film 'actionful and snappy, it equals if not excels the continentals at their own game without sacrificing the popular British box-office touch.' The Financial Times wrote: ' *Beat the Devil* at first seems to bristle with cleverness and invention but afterwards things become curiously flaccid. . .it holds the promise of quality, rather irksomely withheld.'

Businessmen make unexciting movie figures, falling in step behind politicians as the kind of people nobody cares a lot about. Political subjects – *All the Kings Men*, *Advise and Consent*, *The Manchurian Candidate*, *The Best Man* – have on the whole been treated imaginatively in American movies, but the world of big business has been zealously avoided on the grounds, one suspects, that tycoons are difficult to identify with and boardroom intrigues even in the giant multis are insular affairs that excite no great public passions other than to reinforce distrust. Another important reason is, of course, they rarely make money.

Sabrina Fair, set in Long Island's millionaire belt, was conceived, initially, as a vehicle for Cary Grant, whose subsequent unavailability denied audiences an imaginative pairing – Grant and Audrey Hepburn. Bogart substituted at short notice and despite frantic rewrites, the character of the starchy, erudite tycoon who wrests the affections of a chauffeur's daughter from his flip, gadfly brother never quite added up.

Linus (Bogart) and David (William Holden) are joint heirs to the Larrabee fortune. Linus is the business brain and David the scatterbrain. Chauffeur's daughter Sabrina (Audrey Hepburn) is infatuated with David, but waist-high in top society glamorous women, he barely notices her, a realization that drives Sabrina to attempt suicide by closing the doors and revving all the motors in the Larrabee garage. An inquisitive Linus foils the attempt.

Despatched for her own good to a high-class Paris finishing school, Sabrina is transformed from a gauche hanger-on to a culture beauty whom David, at first, fails to recognize.

Not exclusively with Sabrina's interest at heart, Linus attempts to block developments between them, for his sights are set on David marrying the daughter (Martha Hyer) of a sugar cane tycoon to ensure a reliably cheap supply of sugar for a curious synthetic product he intends to mass produce. A lovers' tryst between David and Sabrina ends in disaster when David sits on two champagne glasses.

Unaware of his brother's true intent, David encourages him to see that Sabrina doesn't get too lonely while he is, literally, laid up – on a Larrabee patent plastic hammock – and the wily Linus obliges, masquerading as a genuine suitor, even though his tactics are comically out of date. 'It'll come back to me – it's just like riding a bicycle' he reassures his doubting father (Walter Hampden) as he departs on a river cruise with Sabrina, armed with a musty old gramophone and a selection of scratchy records from his college days.

Unhappily, his feigned interest in her is all to readily reciprocated, and on the pretext of joining her later, he inveigles her aboard a transatlantic liner that will keep her safely out of the way while David gets married. Staring at the departing liner from his executive boardroom, Linus realizes the fun that his life lacks, and springs madly up river, is hoisted aboard, right into the arms of Sabrina, prudently abandoning his homburg and rolled umbrella, along with his executive responsibilities, before they are reunited.

Sabrina Fair is a smart comedy with an authentic high society flavor, replete with lavish lantern-lit house parties, cooing servants, open-top fast cars and executive boardrooms with tuckaway kitchens, the sort of setting where William Holden, in a flashy white dinner jacket with patter to match, and Audrey Hepburn, sleek, gazelle-like in a Beatonesque ball gown looks elegantly at home. Cary Grant, too, were he available. It is, however, a long haul from Bogart's elected stomping ground on the other side of the tracks, and his doleful over-playing suggests that the incongruity of the situation got the better of him.

It is a competent performance that never aspires to be anything higher in a film redeemed as much by the comic relief of supporting players Walter Hampden, Nella Walker and Marcel Hillaire as by the all-pervading hypercosiness of the narrative style.

Holden's performance, on the heels of his Oscar winning supercad prisoner-of-war in *Stalag 17* disappoints in that the part calls for an underlying warmth which does not materialize. Throughout, he is the stock all-American chauvinistic smoothie, decorating rather than dominating the scenes he takes part in, and Bogart, even with three cylinders shut off, completely routs him in their scenes together.

Bogart's best moments are during the feigned courtship, abetted by scratchy recordings of 'Yes, We Have No Bananas,' the closest he can get to romantic background music, and while he retains a wry detachment from the relationships surrounding him – Sabrina and her father, Sabrina and David, David and Elizabeth, Larrabee Snr and David – moving through them, never quite one of them, surefooted and oracular, he gets close to his established persona without ever compromising the tone of the movie (a significant achievement in itself) but the moment he forfeits this palpable detachment, becoming the victim of his emotions rather than remaining their sole diviner, his hold on the movie evaporates also. Sabrina must have a lover, and David is plainly unworthy, so Bogart cannot escape the rigid dictates of the well-intentioned Cinderella script, but the lasting impression is of two hopelessly incompatible cardboard people sailing off into a contrived sunset. Not, as Sam Spade once said, 'the stuff that dreams are made of.'

The Observer noted that 'Bogart shows unexpected resources of quiet comedy as the businessman,' adding 'there isn't much substance in Sabrina Fair but in its slight way it makes for very pleasing entertainment.'

The Daily Sketch wrote: 'Only Humphrey Bogart rescues the picture from complete failure. Miss Hepburn matches his challenge. Their twenty minute sequence towards the end is the only good thing in the film.'

'Bogart hasn't the youth or the dash for Linus Larrabee,' quoted Saturday Revms of Sabrina, prudently abandoning his homburg and rolled umbrella, along with his executive responsibilities, before they to look at pictures of Audrey Hepburn, Sabrina is the album of your dreams. Unfortunately, it is little more.'

The Daily Telegraph thought Bogart 'too heavy for comedy such as this and past the age when he can make an acceptable Prince Charming. When we see Sabrina's affections transferring to this monument of humourless business efficiency, our feelings are of dismay and disillusion.'

'A gay trifle of a film,' wrote The Times, 'which chatters away without making a bore of itself. Mr Bogart is only too successful in considering himself past the age for romantic love.'

The New Yorker said: 'A really first-rate performance is turned in by Humphrey Bogart. . . there are, alas, quite a few lethargic stretches between the hugs and the chuckles.'

'It has everything,' said the Motion Picture Herald. 'The distinctive characteristic of this particular picture is the exact correctness of each player for the part assigned, the complete submergence of the personal identity of each in the role being portrayed. They never let you remember their past achievements while you are looking at their present ones, and when they have finished with them you wonder whether these may not have been their all-round best.'

Monthly Film Bulletin thought that Wilder had 'somewhat inflated the slight and engaging story. Finesse, in fact, is what this film ultimately lacks. Perhaps Wilder is too harsh and cynical a director for a story which has more elements of sentimental fantasy than smart comedy.'

Today's Cinema called it 'a delightful modern fairy tale. Humphrey Bogart is surprisingly effective in a part which is principally the lightest of comedy.'

'Scenes of hilarious buffoonery. . .interwoven with romantic passages that are fragrant with honeysuckle and glimmering with gossamer moonbeams,' panted the Hollywood Reporter. 'Holden as the playboy and Bogart as his tycoon brother share Wilder's genius for slipping expertly from gentle romantic moods to outright farce. . .every inch top-notch entertainment.'

Sight and Sound was less enthusiastic: 'The direction, unfortunately, does not match the material. Heavy, Oscar-demanding passages of 'production' are superimposed on the little story and at times completely swamp it – Humphrey Bogart, whose playing seems in the last year to have gained an added cutting edge, is subtly and touchingly funny as the grouchy tycoon.' The Daily Mail nominated it 'the comedy of the year. . .a witty, lovable film.'

Reunited with Michael Curtiz on We're No Angels in 1954, Bogart was on more familiar ground. Three tough French convicts led by Joseph (Bogart) escape from Devil's Island on Christmas Eve. Jules (Peter Ustinov) is a romantically-inclined strangler and Albert (Aldo Ray) a tame gorilla whose only item of luggage is a basket containing a viper. Refuging in the home of an addled shopkeeper, Ducotel (Leo G. Carroll), whose accounts are in a mess and who expects to be evicted along with his pretty wife (Joan Bennett) and daughter (Gloria Talbot) the moment his ruthless landlord-cousin finds him out, the three convicts are reluctantly drawn into their little drama.

Virtue had its own reward when, confronted with irascible cousin Andre (Basil Rathbone) and his snotty nephew Paul (John Baer) the convicts throw in with the family, using unsubtle techniques to dispose of the wolf at the door, twice. With the shop-keeper safely and permanently reinstated, and the family speechless with gratitude, the three convicts opt for a return to Devil's Island, disillusioned by all the criminal elements menacing the outside world.

We're No Angels has some elegant, if weighty touches, particularly towards the beginning as the convicts assert themselves within the Ducotel household. Most of the humor derives unashamedly from the fact that Bogart is the central invader, gently parodying the Mantee image, and prefacing his Glenn Griffin of *The*

Desperate Hours – in both other movies he is a violent jail-breaker with two murderous associatesterrorizing defenseless victims. Bogart's lines, funny in themselves, have an added twist coming from the actor who decisively cornered the slippery thug market many years before.

Learning that the prison guard he disposed of on his way to freedom, is still alive, he reflects ruefully, 'I must be losing my strength.' He is the last of the three to be softened by the Ducotels' kindness and concern, and even an invitation to share Christmas dinner with the family leaves him unswerved in his murderous intent. ('We'll bash their heads in, gouge their eyes out, cut their throats – after we wash the dishes!')

The film marked Ustinov's coming of age in Hollywood. Until *We're No Angels* he had never been considered a team performer. Already a gifted writer and non-conformist, ('The darling of the intelligentsia,' one reviewer called him), his appearances in *Beau Brummel* and *Quo Vadis* were flashy and flamboyant, the work of a spoilt-brat genius rather than that of a disciplined

"Joseph" and Peter Ustinov – [We're No Angels] (1955)

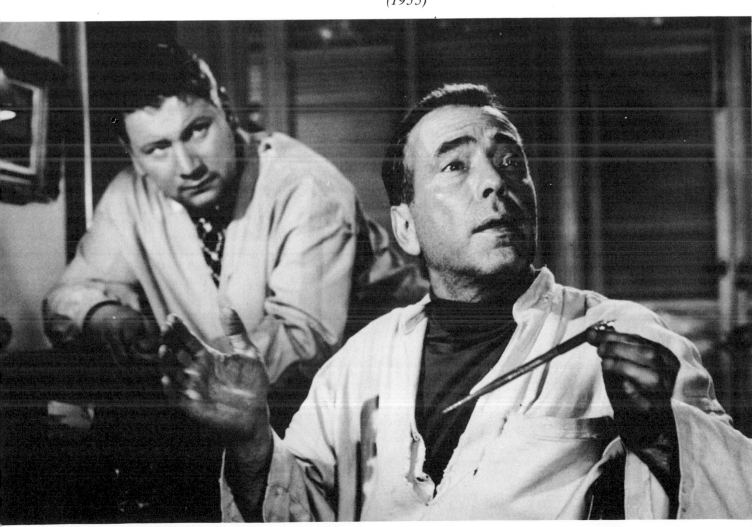

mature actor. When Ustinov went 'in extremis' his fellow actors ran for cover.

But in *We're No Angels*, he tones down the extravagances, dovetailing neatly and subduedly between the two conventional 'tough guys' and shrewdly stealing their gravelly thunder with quiet insistence. 'The last time anyone was nice to me was in 1891,' he laments, on the receiving end of unfamiliar kindnesses.

The underlying sadness of the three convicts counterpoints their ambivalent charm. Asked why he is taking an interest in the adolescent daughter's love tangles, Joseph explains 'She reminds me of the family I never had.' He had everything in terms of experience and self-assurance but no-one to share it with. All good pantomimes need a villain, but cousin Andre's intrusion breaks up the finely-woven atmosphere and from that moment the film surrenders its mellow surrealist quality.

The convicts have won us over by then, and we see them as through the eye of the grateful, bewildered family; not vicious, hardened criminals but tolerant, compassionate, resilient figures who understand the human predicament and have come to terms with their loneliness. A telling little scene shows them crouched on the roof, which they are supposed to be repairing, peering in through the skylight at the loving family below, eternal voyeurs in a world that, from the story's standpoint, has injudiciously boxed them out. Andre's arrival reverts them to type, and the gentle ironies of the previous hour give way to more or less a conventional scowling contest between the People's Champion and Snide Moneybags, with the inescapable heavy-handed outcome. The color camerawork of Loyal Griggs (who had won an Academy Award two years previously for *Shane*) is in perfect step with the shy, wistful texture of the material, and his use of warm colors set in a soft focus lends the film a visual beauty which the surroundings, and indeed the latter half of the film, is hard pressed to support.

The Daily Mail noted: 'Messrs Bogart, Ustinov and Ray are the most engaging trio of scoundrels who ever made crime seem a civilizing and comical way of life.' 'The fault would seem to lie in the slowness of direction. It is altogether too deliberate in making its ironic points, with a corresponding lack of wit in the acting,' cited The Times.

'All through, this comedy misses not only the Gallic touch of irony and paradox but the actual dexterity of the French language. While Mr Bogart is more in touch with the general idea as a forger and confidence trickster, he remains a citizen of a conventional Hollywood film.'

The Evening Standard called it 'very funny as long as we refuse to believe in it for a moment. Bogart and Ustinov, relaxed and easy but perfectly in step, strike sparks from each other and provide a firework display which it is always a delight to watch.'

'The playing of the convicts is an unbroken delight,' said the Sunday Times. 'Unpromising though the material may sound, on the screen it is extremely funny.'

Sunday Chronicle noted: 'The superb trio of convicts turn in a masterly piece of acting and gaiety that adds up to one of the most delightful and witty farces for a long time.'

Monthly Film Bulletin accused Curtiz' direction of retaining 'over much the tempo of the stage, taking some scenes at a pace altogether slower than they can stand. Humphrey Bogart gives a dryly accomplished performance as the resourceful Joseph. Peter Ustinov's performance suggests a determination to be funny at all costs; his over emphatic technique is out of gear with the tone of the film, at its most satisfactory when it resists the temptation to let comedy slip into farce.'

'From first to last, sheer entertainment,' observed the Hollywood Reporter. 'It is hard to describe the quality that makes Bogart's performances such a joy. He plays most of his comedy scenes straight, yet he endows them with a playfully satiric style that fits into the technique of the no acting 'school'. It can only come out of the good taste of the actor.'

Motion Picture Herald thought it 'a leisurely-paced comedy of many chuckles,' adding 'its dialogue is often bright and the characters appealing. The story, however, is the sort of extremely lightweight make-believe which requires more imaginative handling than has been afforded it by either script writer Ronald MacDougall or director Michael Curtiz. These two can thank their sextette of stars that the picture is half over before the audience realizes it is almost completely devoid of any action whatsoever.'

'At times proceedings are consciously cute,' wrote Variety, 'and the stage origin of the material still clings since virtually all scenes are interiors and characters are constantly entering and exiting. However, Michael Curtiz' directorial

pacing and top-flight performances. . .help
minimize the few flaws.'

Today's Cinema noted 'director Curtiz has
managed skillfully to reproduce the wry French
taste of the original, moving his cast constantly
through the business of a joke that in lesser
hands might have staled long before the
end. . .a hearty laughter-raiser for young and
old.'

'The lines have an occasional criminal wit,'
said Saturday Review, 'but instead of pacing its
dialogue swiftly enough to permit chuckle to
mount on chuckle, director Michael Curtiz insists
on waiting for the big laugh that just isn't there.
Of the cast, only Peter Ustinov reveals a true
feeling for this kind of comedy.'

'The charm seems sometimes thinned to
vanishing point' wrote the Financial Times. 'The
three rogues. . .look terribly hard put to it
having to be endlessly whimsical and droll. Mr
Bogart, favoring understatement, wildly throws
his part away.'

As one reviewer summarized: 'Mr Bogart
has criminal intentions but never convinces us
that he is more than trifling with what he can
bring off in grim earnest.'

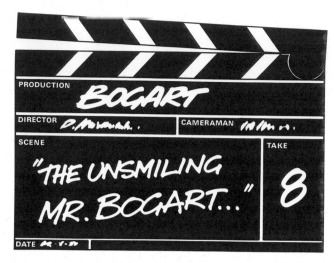

PRODUCTION **BOGART**

DIRECTOR *C. Bernhardt.*   CAMERAMAN *M Mr.*

SCENE

"THE UNSMILING MR. BOGART..."   TAKE **8**

DATE *M. 1. 50*

Conflict, directed by Curtis Bernhardt, put Bogart into the role of a man who kills for love. Having for long enough seen that he could kill, and since *Casablanca* known that he could love, it seemed inevitable that an overlap would occur, and on paper at least, his credentials looked sound enough to carry it through. On celluloid, it proved a different matter.

On his fifth wedding anniversary, Richard Mason's shrewish wife Katherine (Rose Hobart) confronts him with her knowledge of his infatuation for her younger sister, Evelyn (Alexis Smith) who lodges with them.

At a celebration party, hosted by the genial Dr Hamilton (Sydney Greenstreet, every inch as buoyant, garrulous and devious as in *The Maltese Falcon*) Evelyn is introduced to Norman Holdsworth (Charles Drake), a handsome academic. On their way home in the rain Mason's car crashes and although Katherine and Evelyn escape unhurt, he damages a leg. Confined to a wheelchair temporarily, he evolves a scheme to get rid of Katherine.

The plan centers on a vacation that never happens at a nearby mountain resort. On the morning of their supposed departure, Mason cries off on a pretext urging Katherine to drive on ahead, ambiguously promising to catch up with her later.

Which in fact he does, but rather earlier than she expects for as she negotiates the tricky mountain passes alone and justifiably

apprehensive, there he is blocking the road in a borrowed car, waiting to kill her.

Dumping her car along with the body down an obliging ravine, he dodges back to the house, climbs back into his wheelchair and solicits sympathy for the phoney pains in his leg. The sympathy he gets from family friend Dr Hamilton on the disappearance of his wife is short-lived. Listing for the police chief Egan (Patrick O'Moore) the items she wore when she left the house on the morning of the fake vacation, Hamilton overhears him mention a red rose in her lapel – not true since, unknown to Mason, his wife had called on Hamilton after leaving the house and the rose had been given to her then.

Very soon, odd things begin to happen. Katherine's ring is discovered on a pickpocket who describes her accurately. Vacationing with Hamilton and Evelyn, he gets a mysterious phone call from a lady who leaves her name as Mrs Mason with the receptionist. More than once he smells her perfume in the room, another piece of her jewelry and later her handkerchief turn up, both worn by her on the day she disappeared. Later a pawn ticket mailed to him in Katherine's handwriting redeems a locket, deposited by a lady whom, to Mason's deepening alarm, fits Katherine's description in every detail.

Everything points to Katherine being alive, so that after a graphologist has authenticated the handwriting and Mason, on a trip to town to buy some luggage, imagines he sees her, in his agitation he confides his fears to Hamilton, who hints that delusions such as his could stem from deep-rooted guilt feelings. Fearing for his sanity, and needing reassurance that she is truly dead, he returns to the wrecked car to find, not the body, but Hamilton, Egan and a squad of police skulking in the undergrowth. The psychic tricks were Hamilton-inspired, part of an elegant web woven by the flabby doctor to bring him to justice.

Conflict is an efficient little thriller that manages to lay some neat red herrings along the route to Mason's denouement. As the killer who thinks he has pulled off the perfect crime, only to discover that his victim will not lie down, Bogart is never totally convincing.

It is too dramatic a switch in style for ordinary digestions and the memories of Spade and Rick and Harry Morgan are too vivid. Audiences debating how the Bogart of *The Maltese Falcon* and *Casablanca* would have coped see how far off the target he has drifted.

"Richard Mason" and Sydney Greenstreet –
[*Conflict*] *(1945)*

Clearly he would never have married Katherine had there already been an Evelyn.

But had someone, anyone, needed getting rid of, he would have been cool and thorough. Far from being stung into a limp declaration of love for Evelyn by Holdsworth's proposal, Spade or Rick would never have rated Holdsworth as viable competition ('You despise me don't you, Rick?' – 'If I thought about you I probably would!').

He would never have become part of the drippy Hamilton set with their fey dinner parties and stale repartee.

The Rick of fond memory would have cut a deep swath through Hamilton and the other windbags, sailed to Cuba with Evelyn, opened a waterfront saloon replete with moribund Cuban pianist (Hoagey Carmichael?). When he was not harboring swarthy revolutionaries, or Devil's Island escapees, in the cellar, he might have got some light relief distributing stolen transit visas among homesick expatriate Americans, or if the price was right ferrying them personally ashore on the Florida mainland under cover of darkness.

Instead of this we have sweaty misfit Richard Mason, piling up his miseries like a demented squirrel storing winter nuts. Katherine makes his life a misery by marrying him – and even dead, she refuses to let him off the hook – Evelyn adds to his misery by not wishing to marry him, and the flabby doctor compounds his misery further by stitching him up in a bag and depositing him on Egan's doorstep.

In fact, everyone is so consistently nasty to him, that murder seems a well reasoned reaction, even though he got his motives confused, and our irritation at the end is balanced between suspended belief at Bogart taking such a role and a growing sense of disappointment at his failure to get clean away.

The bends in the distribution strategy didn't make any easier the acceptance of *Conflict*, having been produced prior to *Passage to Marseille* (1943) but not released until after *To Have and Have Not* (1944), a film that features Bogart at his toughest and most resourceful.

The London Sunday Times called it: 'Well written and skillfully directed, and as always, beautifully acted by Bogart. I should place it about the middle of the second class in the current output of well-constructed films about murder.'

'In *Conflict* Humphrey Bogart, Sydney Greenstreet and Alexis Smith waste some good acting on a melodramatic plot which is unforgivable in lacking both conviction and excitement,' noted the Spectator. 'Neither Mr Bogart nor his wife are unsympathetic figures. The psychological profundities of the plot aren't equal to the task of explaining why such nice people should find it necessary to become involved in an extremely unsavory crime.'

The Daily Mirror observed: 'In private life you couldn't meet a more charming individual than Humphrey Bogart. I spent hours in Hollywood chatting to this most retiring personality, who'd talk about everything except himself. Yet put this quiet self-effacing artist in front of the camera and he will put over the perfect interpretation of a brutal tough guy or murderer. In *Conflict* he has a role calling for skillful, restrained artistry and Bogart provides a perfect study of the scheming killer. . .a first class mystery thriller.'

'A first rate crime tale for adult intelligence,' wrote the Herald.

The Guardian noted: 'The tension never once falters after the scene of the faked death in the first ten minutes so it passes the simple test of a thriller with ease. . .Humphrey Bogart and Sydney Greenstreet play the major parts in a greatly contrived examination of the workings of a guilty mind.'

Today's Cinema called it a 'first rate thriller. . .quite the most absorbing melodrama that even Warners have ever given us. The dramatic build-up is indeed masterly. The role of the murderer sees Humphrey Bogart at his most dynamic, and the picture would be well worth watching if only for his vivid portraiture of a man driven daily nearer dementia by the inexplicable events which crowd about him.'

Kine Weekly applauded a 'tense drama staged in flawless atmosphere and with faultless detail. Humphrey Bogart contributes a masterly performance. The character he portrays has to take it as well as dish it out, and the agony of suspense is superbly illustrated in his acting. . .a classic and suspenseful thriller.'

Sunday Chronicle noted: 'When you see Bogart throwing adolescent sheep-eyes at his wife's sister (Alexis Smith) and vice versa (it never goes beyond that) you are expected to take it as grand passion, sufficient to fire him to

murder. Accepting a milk-and-water motivation, you will be slickly entertained, even thrilled by this movie, if you forget *Double Indemnity*, *Laura* and *The Maltese Falcon*.'

'A cleverly directed film of intelligence,' wrote The Times. 'Bogart has for once not to be so tough that he does not break under nervous strain, and he gives a competent enough performance within the nervous limits of his particular technique.'

'Bogart plays the unlucky killer with his usual proficient intensity,' said Time Magazine. 'There is enough talent and ambition involved in *Conflict* to make another *Double Indemnity*, which is roughly what its makers were trying for. But the picture is too ornate to be of genuine psychological interest, and too slow to be thoroughly exciting.'

'A consistently gloomy film in which Bogart efficiently reveals the crescendo of his tortured nerves,' concluded Monthly Film Bulletin. 'Good direction and acting maintain the interest of this depressing film.'

The Two Mrs Carrolls reprises Bogart's infatuation for Alexis Smith and casts him again as a man who murders for passion. The result is less than inspirational. The flaws – and the movie was riddled with them – lie not so much in Bogart's acting, admittedly on the heavy side, as in the conception of the central character and backgrounds. Madmen he can play anytime, but madmen who murder beautiful ladies who stand in the way of his marrying other beautiful ladies are simply not in his gallery.

In The Two Mrs Carrolls Geoffrey Carroll (Bogart) is an obsessive artist domiciled in England with invalid wife Christine (Anita Bolster) and daughter Beatrice (Ann Carter). Christine provides stability and inspiration for his work until, vacationing in Scotland, he meets Sally Morton (Barbara Stanwyck) a well-to-do beauty and they have an affair. Two years later Sally is Carroll's wife, after Christine has retired to bed and died.

Everything is beautiful between them until one day Sally's society lawyer friend Pennington (Patrick O'Moore) brings along to afternoon tea a dishy client, Cecily Latham (Alexis Smith), whose flirtatious attitude deeply unsettles him. Afraid of the consequences of falling for her, yet unable to stay away, Carroll's broody thoughts of how he might get rid of Sally are lent a new edge by Cecily's announcement of an impending South American trip.

Unlike the earlier Mrs Carroll, Sally is forewarned of his evil intent – a furtive visit to his sealed off attic studio reveals the grim state of his mind reflected in the ghoulish portraits – and a tension filled cat-and-mouse game develops. Thwarted in his attempts to poison her (when his back is turned she shrewdly pours the spiked nightcaps over the window box) and with Sally barricaded in the bedroom, urgency demands less fallible techniques. Shinning up a tree, he manages to break open the bedroom window, ripping the curtains apart and chuckling malevolently at the sight of Sally's soft, pliable neck like some out-of-town vampire looking for a spot to have a quiet drink.

Sally keeps him at bay with a revolver loaned by the faithful Pennington, who arrives on cue with the police. Sandwiched between two burly officers, he pauses at the door to offer them each a refreshing glass of milk. Wisely, they decline.

Tension is squandered when too early in the movie we are given too many glimpses of his instability. The murder of Christine is a callous affair, but we are not too shocked because she has no occasion to register. When he begins to poison Sally in anticipation of landing a third Mrs Carroll, the pattern of events is predictable enough, and the character of Sally opaque enough, to again inhibit our involvement. Viewed in considerable retrospect, neither woman seems worth killing for. Sally is limp and over-coy, Cecily cold and snooty, and we are left to wonder what delayed him until middle age before taking up such an absorbing hobby. Or is the second Mrs Carroll in reality his sixth or maybe his ninth victim?

The ease and speed with which Cecily's influence overhauls Sally's hints at a longer and more sinister maritial history than we have the time to share, which for many people, is plentifully long enough.

The film is forties melodrama at its creakiest, set in a wholly blasphemous rural England. Carroll's underlying dementia is far too crudely telegraphed by Bogart, disadvantaged as an actor by seeming the most rational of individuals when supposed to be totally out of his mind. When not playing himself the credibility gap between what he looks and what he is can be astounding, and as if sensing this, he risks at times over-compensation, never more annoyingly evident than on this outing.

In case anyone still imagines him just

benignly eccentric after polishing off one wife, Bogart trowels on the agony where the merest mention of insanity – even Van Gogh's – sends his temples pounding, his jaw sagging and his eyes wild. As the friendly doctor figure, obligatory in forties-style murder thrillers to establish class (in Hollywood terms, poisoners and wife stranglers were invariably upper-crust). Greenstreet is transplanted by Nigel Bruce, whose boozy half-wit contributes nothing whatever. The absence of Greenstreet's steely pragmatism, plotting or merely observing Carroll's crack-up, with sadistic candor is keenly felt, as indeed his presence had been in the earlier film.

Pennington, Sally's former suitor, is chinless from start to finish, and his intervention by loaning Sally a gun weakens the climax because we know what Carroll does not, that she is armed, and knowing it, the full horror of his assault loses its bite.

The contrived Englishness of it all – leafy lanes, cathedral bells, starchy maids, teas on the lawn – is insultingly hollow while the dialogue, at times as disconcertingly stiff and lifeless as any one of the earlier Mrs Carrolls, remains rooted in Burbank.

'Full credits to Mr Bogart and Miss Stanwyck,' wrote the Sunday Graphic. 'The plot, though ridiculous, has the force of its own convictions. The moments when the last wife gradually realizes that her ever-loving husband is trying to do her in are moments of genuine suspense.'

'Blazingly good,' noted the Star. 'Bogart with his grim and gloomy charm gives a good suggestion of growing insanity. Warners have been conscientious in suggesting our native atmosphere. Never was there so much quaint olde English architecture in one village, shop door bells tinkle as they have hardly done since Victorian days and it rains perpetually in what Americans fondly believe is the truly British way.'

The Daily Mail was surprised to find Humphrey cavorting around 'the English countryside. Mr Bogart wears a pained expression most of the time, and seems to miss his usual sparring partners (Lauren Bacall and latterly, Lizabeth Scott). He also seems to fret slightly under the restrained script which gives him no chance to pour out frozen streams of tough talk.'

The Times concurred. 'The characters Mr Humphrey Bogart normally plays are happier

"Geoffrey Carroll" and Barbara Stanwyck –
[The Two Mrs Carrolls] (1947)

knocking girls about than poisoning them in the intervals of talking about art, and as Geoffrey, he is equally unconvincing as artist, madman, and murderer. The setting is an English cathedral town as Warner Brothers imagine it, and a curious place it is, almost as curious as the failure of a film with an exciting idea to be in any way exciting itself.'

'Mr Bogart is here,' announced the Spectator. 'His haunted unsmiling face. . .rugged, expressionless and sad and his harsh nasal voice speaks as perfectly as ever. What it is that makes him so compelling I shall never know but he is irresistible for some reason, and I believe it is the dialogue which is too stagey to be alive, the picture hangs fire, but if you have the patience to watch the slow unfolding of Mr Bogart's insanity, you will be rewarded in the end.'

Time Magazine said: 'Once in a while audiences' spines register an authentic chill, but most of the show is a clutter of entrance and exit about as dramatically arresting as a game of in-and-out-the-window. Bogart appears uncomfortable. Violence and murder are old stuff to him, but madness and paint brushes are not quite his line.'

'Its direction ties it to a tempo so ponderous that it feels like an Edwardian drama bound in velvet,' declared Monthly Film Bulletin. 'One supreme touch however, is the sudden disclosure of a horrible portrait of Mrs Carroll – derivative of the similar moment in 'Dorian Gray' but much more shocking. With effective aid from camera and lighting, Bogart uses hands, eyes and distorted features emphatically to produce a portrait of a paranoic painter.'

'Strong feminine appeal and the big pull of Humphrey Bogart seal its obvious commercial success,' Kine Weekly noted. 'Bogart acts with conviction and considerable dramatic force as the cunning and deranged Geoffrey. . .intelligent thick-ear, or rather pocket serial that will have all the low- and most of the high-brows on the edge of their seats.'

Motion Picture Herald debated 'whether it will satisfy depends somewhat on the public's reaction to the change of style imposed on Mr Bogart as a demented intellectual addicted to poisoning his wives. It's quite a change for an actor who's always done his killing straight out and by manly means, but the picture's got considerable suspense to offset the possible objections. There is a good deal of killing and plotting to kill in the picture and only a dash, now and then, of sprightly dialogue.'

'A murder thriller of the very highest order, replete with crackling action with Bogart truly gripping as the demented, tortured killer,' said Today's Cinema. 'Humphrey Bogart and Barbara Stanwyck, giving their respective best, put this forthright murder thriller in the top bracket.'

'Bogart is better with arsenic than with art,' News Chronicle commented, adding that the film was 'an altogether disappointing version of a goodish story.'

London's Evening Standard noted: 'Mr Bogart has to hold his dramatic horses for three-quarters of the picture. If, as with the play, you are prepared to be patient during the long building-up process you will get your money's worth of excitement during the climax. Both artistes are excellent in the last half-hour.'

Dead Reckoning , directed by John Cromwell, whom Bogart had known since his early days on Broadway, echoes *The Maltese Falcon* both in atmosphere and storyline, with Bogart fearlessly tracking down the murderer of his Army buddy and sharing a brittle relationship with a shady lady who is not everything she pretends to be. ('You're going to fry,' he tells her, wrathfully. 'When a guy's pal is killed he ought to do something about it' – lines lifted bodily from the script of *The Maltese Falcon*).

Rip Murdock (Bogart), a hard boiled paratroop Captain, accompanies Sgt Johnny Drake (William Prince) on an official trip home, but during a scheduled train stop at Philadelphia en route to Washington where Drake is to receive a Congressional Medal for bravery (the purpose of his return home is not made known to either of them beforehand) the sergeant disappears. Murdock traces him to the small southern town of his origins, where newspaper files reveal why he baulked at being publicly honored. Drake was his assumed name, invented to conceal his involvement several years before in a sordid love triangle that had ended in murder of the lady's husband.

Shortly afterwards, Drake's body is discovered in the burnt out wreckage of a car, and Murdock, unofficially on leave to sort out the tangle, soon is embroiled with his pal's former lover, Coral Chandler (Lizabeth Scott) a husky songstress at the chic Sanctuary Club, run by Martinelli (Morris Carnovski) a fish-eyed mobster.

Drugged, beaten and menaced in a dozen ways, including waking up to find a warning corpse in the bed opposite, Murdock goes after Martinelli, whom he rightly suspects is the focal point of the mystery, but Coral's treachery delivers him literally into the hands of Martinelli's sadistic bodyguard (Marvin Miller), who nearly finishes him off. Later he returns the compliment, and solves the mystery.

When Drake had first known Coral, she was married to Martinelli (and still is) although bigamously married to Chandler, over whose violent death Drake had wrongly been hounded. Coral's fingerprints are on the murder weapon locked away in Martinelli's private safe to dissuade her from ever encouraging counter-bids.

Drake got through the cordon, and was subsequently murdered by Martinelli – inspired, in a fit of jealous rage to prevent Coral leaving with him. Escaping the burning building (Murdock had rigged the place with incendiaries to make the mobster talk) Coral kills Martinelli and when driving away at speed from the blaze she learns that Murdock has snatched the weapon with her prints on, she attempts to kill him, too, but instead the car goes out of control. Later in hospital, Coral dies, and Murdock returns to his unit equipped with the evidence and the murder weapon that will exonerate his dead friend.

Dead Reckoning beguiles on several levels. Its use of the narrative flashback is interesting although the persistent voice-over, helpful in setting the early scenes, begins to pall after we have picked up the threads of the story.

The beginning is shadowy and atmospheric. Bogart, fleeing from unseen assassins, takes refuge in a church where a sympathetic ex-army padre listens to the dramatic story why he is being pursued by the police and 'some pretty tough customers who'd like to get their mitts on me.' His long-winded confession becomes the voice-over narrative, the dark angular walls of the church giving way visually to the flash-back railway compartment where the story begins.

The voice-over becomes intrusive after a while, imposing as it must do Murdock's subjective viewpoint on everything, denying us the freedom to make up our own minds. Dancing with Coral, Murdock not only picks his moment to inform her that Drake, her lover, is dead, but describes the build-up with pitiless relish. ('Her whole body had gone soft as custard when I slugged her with it,' he drones, telling us nothing we cannot see for ourselves.)

As actress and *femme fatale*, Lizabeth Scott is definitely sub-Bacall, and when Murdock croaks across the table to her, 'I can see why Johnny loved you,' we do not share his clarity of vision.

Miss Scott is hard-faced and listless, attacking her part with the subtlety, but not nearly half the enthusiasm, of a truck driver, and though complimented by Bogart on the professionalism of her duplicity ('You're awfully good,' he quips, like some arrested adolescent who can't get *The Maltese Falcon* off his mind), she lacks Mary Astor's depth of register, and finding ourselves neutral to Miss Scott's charms we fail to see why everyone is killing and being killed around her.

Although the violence is more exaggerated here than in *The Big Sleep*, it is less stylishly executed. *The Big Sleep's* violence was central to the story and completely understated, but in *Dead Reckoning* it is flagrant and almost ritualistic. The villains never live up to their earlier threat that sends Bogart scuttling for cover like a church mouse. Morris Carnovski's sub-Greenstreet big shot is a seedy off-the-peg poseur of the kind that inhabits schoolboy yarns, while his sadistic henchman, wearing a let out version of Rick's discarded white tuxedo and black bow tie from *Casablanca*, seems unable to make up his mind whether he is a gorilla or a pansy or both.

But perhaps the most disappointing aspect of *Dead Reckoning* is the dialogue, which alternates between the superficially tough and the superficial. Bogart seems obsessed with the idea of sounding like Sam Spade, even to the point of pilfering several lines straight from his mouth ('I'll miss you, Mike'), while Miss Scott seems content to sound like a trombone, and between them they stack up some deliciously forgettable lines.

Murdock on the subject of women: 'All females are the same with their faces washed.' Discovering that a friend of Drake's who was delivering a vital letter has been murdered: 'I'm a guy who likes to get his mail.' When Coral plausibly evades his accusations of duplicity ('You think fast, don't you sweetheart?') she counters: 'I'm not the type that tears do anything to.'

The climax at Coral's deathbed is bewildering, as Murdock strives to reassure her that death,

which he has spent the entire film vigorously avoiding, is not so terrible after all. 'It's like going out the jumpdoor,' he croaks, unaware that most of us would prefer to die before allowing ourselves to be placed anywhere near a jumpdoor.

'Hold your breath,' he continues – a redundant piece of advice for the dying, surely – 'and just let go, Mike. Don't fight. Remember all the guys who've done it before you,' – presumably, held their breath? – 'You've got plenty of company, Mike. High-class company,' etc. etc. The funniest line of the movie belongs to Martinelli, preening himself while Murdock slumps in a chair about to be done over. 'Brutality has always revolted me as the weapon of the witless,' he coos before motioning his gorilla to smash in Murdock's teeth.

The Times commented: 'The director would seem anxious only to see to what lengths toughness and violence can go without defeating their own ends, but his experiment is not a success, and when the film is not ridiculous, it is incomprehensible. Mr Bogart, nonchalantly sardonic whether he is beating up other people or being beaten up himself, left to reflect that, after *Dead Reckoning*, there is nothing for him to do but change his course.'

'A characteristic Humphrey Bogart job which is probably commendation enough,' noted the Sunday Express. 'The action is exciting and the atmosphere fraught with sinister suggestion but the real virtue lies in the laconic, whiplash wisecracks. It is hardly credible that the same hand wrote the sentimental lines. Bogart needs more support in this kind of role, and he certainly gets little from Lizabeth Scott who still has to show me any good reason for being a star. Unless of course a husky voice, a curtain of hair and a strange mouth are qualifications enough.'

Tribune lamented: 'Hollywood quite clearly does not know any longer what to do with Bogart. A war story in the manner of *Casablanca* was all right in its day, and a Raymond Chandler thriller about highminded depravity on the Pacific coast is always pleasurable, but there can be no more *Casablancas*, no more villainous Vichyite policemen while even Chandler's invention must sometimes take a rest.'

Time Magazine listed the film's consolations: 'Leo Tover's crisp camerawork; Wallace Ford as a retired safe-buster; and the enormously proficient Mr Bogart who can just sit in a phone

"Rip Murdock" and Lizabeth Scott – [Dead Reckoning] (1947)

booth and make a long distance call to St Louis crackle with interest.'

'Columbia has given Lizabeth Scott an impressive role. . .but it is the slugging, grimacing performance of Humphrey Bogart that predominates,' wrote Motion Picture Herald. 'While the action is involved, it is tense and exciting every moment of the way even though some sequences would seem too facilely contrived for the satisfaction of the critical.'

Today's Cinema noted: 'The dynamic personality of Humphrey Bogart dominates the whole picture, and his playing in the leading role is a fine example of the value of dramatic under-emphasis and intelligent modulations in voice and expression. The basically melodramatic plot has been treated with such skill by the director that its tricks and turns lose their intrinsic implausibility and take on an air of absorbing realism.'

'Bogart blasts his way through the film. He has no peer in lusty he-man roles,' said Kine Weekly. 'It goes on a little too long and is somewhat vague even when it does end, but the fascinating vigor of Humphrey Bogart's acting and its many hair-raising thrills amply atone for penultimate flabbiness. Whatever you may think, Bogart and bombs represent an invincible box-office combination.'

'Exciting and full of action and dramatic surprises,' noted Monthly Film Bulletin. 'Towards the end there seems to be so many conclusive sequences that one has a feeling of anticlimax, and it is only in retrospect that one realizes that the final dramatic twist is the logical ending to the story. The part of Murdock is 'made-to-measure' for Bogart.'

Daily Graphic wrote: 'Mr John Cromwell is a director who knows his job and there are touches in *Dead Reckoning* so sure in telling that one is utterly confounded when, at the very end, he abandons the good, hard cynicism in favor of drooling sentimentality.'

Sunday Chronicle's cryptic comment was: '*Dead Reckoning* contains so many corpses (some actually stacked in filing cabinets) that being unable to reckon its dead, I merely commend it to the living.'

Dark Passage was Bogart's third, and most thoughtful, picture to be released co-starring his wife Lauren Bacall. Vincent Parry (Bogart), a convicted wife-killer, breaks out of San Quentin jail and hijacks a passing motorist, but a radio bulletin establishes his identity and Parry, to cover his tracks, knocks the driver senseless. The incident is witnessed by Irene Jansen (Lauren Bacall) a successful artist, who coolly intervenes and spirits him away, past several police road blocks, hidden among some canvasses in the back of her station-wagon. Puzzled why this liberated soul should come to the aid of a total stranger, and a fugitive from justice at that, Parry learns that her wealthy father had died in San Quentin, convicted of murdering her stepmother on purely circumstantial evidence, in fact, a case identical to Parry's. Now powerless to help her father, she is repaying the debt society owed him by helping someone in similar circumstances.

To take the heat off Irene, he moves to the apartment of a trumpeter friend George, who fingers a lady named Madge Rapf for the killing of his wife, before he too is beaten to death with his trumpet. An amiable plastic surgeon alters the shape of Parry's face so that he can pursue the real killers without much interference from the police, whose expressed theory that the runaway killer murdered George for refusing him sanctuary seems too rudimentary by far.

Madge Rapf (Agnes Moorehead), the lady George had suspected, was one time close friend of his dead wife and the chief prosecution witness at his trial. She re-enters the picture along with her limp ex-fiancé Bob (Bruce Bennett), who twitches after Irene.

Pursuing George's theory, Parry makes some interesting discoveries that clinch Madge's guilt and establishes her beyond doubt as the murderer of his wife and of poor hapless George, whose killing was a callous and, as it turns out, futile attempt to intensify the police effort to nail him. Armed with his findings but no witness, and sporting a plastic face that Madge cannot possibly recognize, he calls on her, masquerading as a friend of Bob's and bluffs her into a wild admission of guilt, but before it can be authenticated Madge takes a tumble out of the window, killing herself in the multi-story fall.

With Madge, and his last hope of a pardon gone, Parry vanishes to Peru, and to a secret rendezvous with Irene after a prudent delay places her above suspicion.

The diverting love affair between the two tough central characters, set against equally tough, uncompromising backgrounds is what gives *Dark Passage* true depth and breadth. One of the great atmospheric thrillers of the forties, unfairly half-hidden by the bluster and ballyhoo of earlier Bogart-Bacall collaborations, this one gets closer to laying bare the heart of that robust partnership than practically anything else they appeared in or subsequently had written about them.

In *To Have and Have Not* and *The Big Sleep* Bogart dictates the terms of their relationship, forcing the pace, toying irreverently with her when the fancy takes him in the way that a well-fed cat paws at a cheeky mouse, building her up and taking her apart, sympathetic to her moods but never to her ego, giving her no space to move into that is exclusively her own. Although lacking the sparkle and wit of the earlier productions (to be fair, most of the sparkle and all of the wit had been Bogart's) *Dark Passage* captures a new dimension of tenderness between them, not merely because the Bogart character, a fugitive whom she is hiding out, has more dependence on her loyalty and judgment than previously, but because for the first time they dominate the film as equals, and she has space of her own.

Irene Jansen is the most complete realization of Bacall's screen personality, just as Rick or Harry Morgan are arguably Bogart's. Cool-headed, resilient, competent, off-beat, taking the initiative when slack occurs, decisive in a crisis, shielding a somewhat checkered past and brazenly uncertain about the future – in other words, she is the near perfect embodiment of the hard, worldly Bogart in female form. ('I like a dame with guts, real guts,' he tells Martha Scott in *The Desperate Hours* , summarizing unequivocally the quality he demands in a soulmate.)

In *Dark Passage* she displays guts true to form, but more importantly, she displays maturity, and tones down the resilience and cool-headedness, yet keeping it mindfully in focus, with a deepening tenderness that contrasts the harshly lit, menacing world outside her apartment. Urging the fugitive, a total stranger, to bathe and shave while she pops out to buy him a suit sounds as natural as if she was back in their real home. The background music, 'Too Marvelous For Words,' summarizes an indebtedness he is unable to express verbally. Their dialogue is brittle-smooth without being flip ('Right now, I'm letting myself in for a broken jaw' – 'What d'you mean, a broken jaw?' – 'You're all set to clip me one aren't you?') with only a taste of the elaborate verbal foreplay of their earlier encounters ('When I get excited about something I give it everything I have, I'm funny that way!') the real warmth is not so much in their repartee as in the countless beguiling glances and spontaneous turn-ons that radiate between them.

Irene's apartment represents sanctuary from the impinging reality of the alien world outside, her soft lights and sweet music counterpointed by the metallic discord of a hostile city baying for his blood – the grimy, dark alleys and cheap rooming houses riddled with thugs, nosey cops, schizoids and petty grafters, all waiting to pounce.

The night people are cunningly sketched, lending the urban shadows an added starkness and realism. There is a tough-egg cab driver charitably disposed towards our hero (a switch on the more conventional tart-with-a-heart), a wise-owl plastic surgeon, proud of his ability to adjust people's faces to resemble 'bloodhounds or monkeys' (his skills making Parry a gift of Bogart's bleak face, a raffish compromise); the blackmailer who appears corrosively ambivalent at first, later reduced to whimpering anxiety when the victim retaliates untypically.

The narrative suffers through underscribing the role of the jealous murderess Madge Rapf in order to exploit to the full the Bogart-Bacall teaming. We see her only through the results of her tested actions, never until the death scene confrontation as the evil, tormented woman she is, because one suspects Warners could not have her stealing Bacall's thunder. Apart from the killer's role being a potentially stronger one on paper than that of the artist-benefactor, it is played by the superb Agnes Moorehead, against whom Bacall would have stood no chance, so rather than disappoint the fans, Moorehead's part was pitched at a level where it could in no way compromise the star. This was fine for the box-office but led to confusion on the screen, as her relationship with Parry prior to the murder – a pivotal element in the story – is never

"Vincent Parry" and Bacall – [Dark Passage] (1947)

explored other than fleetingly and then, like most of the movie, only from Parry's subjective viewpoint.

The first-person camerawork up till halfway through the film is again a concession to the Bogart-Bacall partnership. A photograph of Parry before the plastic surgeon adjusts the contours of his face to look like Bogart shows a younger man, bright-eyed, handsome even. Clearly since the object of the operation is to deceive the police, the change needs to be fundamental, and also since it is the updated Parry that Irene settles down with, Bogart needed to play him after the operation.

To have Parry prior to the operation played by a different actor would have seriously imbalanced the chemistry between Bogart and Bacall later since the early, mutual-assertion period of the relationship is the central bulwark of the story.

Subjective camerawork, where the camera lens becomes Parry's eyes for the opening 40 minutes of the film, solves some problems but creates others, the prime one being that it imprisons us within Parry's consciousness, so that we see only what he does, which for a relatively complex story such as this one, is not half enough. When he attacks someone, disembodied arms, purportedly ours though we cannot control them, flail the unfortunate victim from each side of the screen.

Likewise, characters addressing Parry talk directly at us and a robot voice replies on our behalf. It's a device which becomes less certain of itself once the novelty wears off, that slows the action to a crawl and makes the simple action of walking upstairs and dodging inside an apartment door an incredibly laborious and even crazy thing to do.

'Plain melodrama in a style which we have, I trust, outgrown,' wrote the Observer. 'The very tricks by which the director has striven to give the film originality show up the fundamental bareness of the plot. For several reels the hero's face is not revealed at all. At last the great moment comes. The triumph of plastic surgery is to be unveiled. Portentiously, gingerly, proudly, Miss Bacall rips the bandages away and, blimey!, if it isn't just Humphrey Bogart!'

The Sunday Despatch noted: 'It turns out to be an absorbing yarn, neat, tense and extremely

"Duke Mantee", Bette Davis and Leslie Howard – [The Petrified Forest] (1936)

well told. Or rather, neat and tense because it is so well told following an unfamiliar channel.'

'A suspenseful and surprising melodrama,' said Motion Picture Herald. 'Bogart commits many a killing although charged with three, while Miss Bacall portrays a wholesome if venturesome young lady with a heart of gold and $200,000. This pairing of them is no mere repetition of past performances.'

Monthly Film Bulletin marked it down as 'an overlong and at times rather tedious thriller, propped up throughout its entire length by a remarkably capable team of supporting players. Humphrey Bogart as Parry lacks something of his customary vigor. One is bound, however, to express one's admiration for the studio surgeon who remodels Mr Bogart's face without leaving as much as a scar.'

'The already compelling development is emphasized by the tense portraiture of Humphrey Bogart presenting another of those studies in baleful concentration,' noted Today's Cinema. 'Though fanciful as to its coincidental twists at times, this crime melodrama is an expertly tailored specimen of its own violent type, and its blend of action, suspense, thrill and dynamic characterization effortlessly registers as first rate entertainment of the devotees of the species.'

The Times said: 'Hard luck on the admirers of Mr Bogart's face, and hard luck indeed on Mr Bogart, for in this film he is visited by one misfortune after another. Dark Passage abounds in violence and it is no absorbing labyrinth; rather an old, old trail that has been covered many times before.'

'Vintage Bogart,' noted Kine Weekly, 'He sinks his own personality into his part and seldom pulls his punches as the roughly handled Vincent. It's definitely worth its salt except for the last ten minutes.'

'Thirty minutes of Dark Passage has to elapse before the audience is vouchsafed its first glimpse of the sad, haunted, rugged beauty that is peculiarly Mr Bogart. From then on, it is the familiar tale of overcoming insuperable odds and weeding out his foes one by one,' wrote the Daily Mail. 'The lovemakings are also in accordance with custom. Mr Bogart is a lover who snarls like a blast furnace, and his woeful ballad mostly takes the form of grunts from public callboxes. While Miss Bacall responds with the monosyllabic mating call that is her special contribution to the art of acting.'

'I enjoyed the suspense and the playing. By ingenious camera treatment Mr Bogart's face is not seen until the picture has run for an hour,' noted the Herald, adding waspishly: 'One or two other stars might try this.'

The London Daily Telegraph commented: 'With Bogart's new look, Lauren Bacall's help and at least one escape explicable only by levitation a wildly improbable story is brought to a tame, unsatisfactory end.'

PRODUCTION BOGART
DIRECTOR D.Nnaah.
CAMERAMAN MMn.
SCENE KING RAT
TAKE 9
DATE

First impressions, they say, last longest. The first impression that moviegoers had of Humphrey Bogart was that of a sullen, moronic killer, eyes dulled but restless, set in a face molded for striking matches on, a man who has long since stopped functioning on either social or emotional levels, in his own words 'a candidate for a hanging.' That was Duke Mantee, playwright Robert E. Sherwood's semi-neanderthal creation in *The Petrified Forest* brought chillingly to life by Bogart in both the 1935 Broadway production, and Warners' atmospheric movie of the following year.

The action centers around a beguiling collection of misfits whose paths cross at the Black Mesa Filling Station and Bar-B-Q, a rundown garage-diner on the rim of the Petrified Forest area of Nevada. Gabrielle Maple (Bette Davis) is the daughter of the owner, an impressionable, imaginative girl with her sights on Paris – her mother's birthplace – and a career in art. Hertzlinger (Dick Foran), a dull-witted footballer-handyman who thinks he is her boyfriend, pads out a tiny square of her vacuous existence, so there is ample room for interest in Alan Squier (Leslie Howard) an egghead dropout who comes up with a plausible line in patter instead of hard cash to pay for his hamburger sandwich.

Squier is cultured, articulate, charming and in a different way to Hertzlinger, immodest ('I belong to a vanishing race – I'm one of the intellectuals'). He laments the emptiness of his life ('I've been looking for something to believe in. . . .something that's worth living for') and identifies immediately with this lonely, talented waif apparently doomed like himself, to a life of unfulfillment.

More accustomed to the kind of articulacy that goes with ordering beef sandwiches, Gabrielle is mesmerized by his tardy eloquence ('Nature is hitting back at the intellectuals with strange instruments called neuroses. She's deliberately inflicting mankind with the jitters, taking the world away from the intellectuals and giving it back to the apes.').

One ape who seems determined to plunder more than his fair share is escaped convict Duke Mantee (Bogart) who, along with two other fugitives, massacres eight prison guards in the breakout. They burst into the diner demanding food, his burly accomplice making the introductions ('This is Duke Mantee, the world-famous killer, and he's hungry'). It soon becomes evident why Mantee employs a spokesman; his idea of varied conversation is to stare unblinkingly ahead and grunt, identifying himself clearly in Squier's 'ape' category.

Others litter the drama but inconsequentially. The main interest arises from the squaring off between the intellectual and the killer, who is impervious to the former's blandishments.

Saluted as 'the last great apostle of rugged individualism,' Mantee remains unmoved, slouched in his dais chair with a shotgun across his knees, observing the hostages in the way some medieval despot king might observe the remains of an afternoon's sport in the bear-pit. 'Maybe you're right, pal,' he snarls, impassively refusing to be drawn.

Grandpa Maple's (Charles Grapewin) nestegg, a mini-fortune (comparatively) in Liberty Bonds wasting in a Santa Fe vault, irks Squier when he considers how it could be used to help Gabrielle fly the coop. 'Why in God's name don't you die and do the world some good!' he bawls at Grandpa, who ignores the appeal. Nevertheless, it gives Squier the thought, 'if not Grandpa why not me?' and assigning his life insurance over to Gabrielle, barters with Mantee, now becoming increasingly nervous at the failure of his girlfriend to show, to kill him. ('I'm planning to be buried in the Petrified Forest. That's where I belong and so do you, Duke').

Mantee, noncommittal about his own funeral arrangements at this stage – although to the law,

amassing in strength outside, it is a priority item
– is reluctant to kill Squier, but in the mad
scramble to escape, when Squier recklessly bars
the exit, Mantee obliges. Minutes later, the gang
is apprehended – we don't actually see the
shootout – and Squier dies in Gabrielle's arms,
relieved that the insurance money, now hers, will
be put to practical use.

Over forty years on, *The Petrified Forest* is
incscapably a museum piece, but taking into
account other mid-thirties melodramas, it holds
up against them fairly well. Shot in the days prior
to location filming – the perceptively
handpainted sierras in the background take a
little adjusting to – nevertheless the stifling
living-dead atmosphere is nicely contained, the
arid, dustbowl surroundings reflecting the equally
arid fate awaiting Squier and Mantee.

Squier is to Gabrielle what the pull-in is to
the desert, a light beckoning out of the barren
wilderness, assurance that civilization, and
chivalry, are not totally extinct.

Mantee is a nowhere man, fodder for the
intellectual, contemptuous of word games,
imprinting his gloomy presence on event with a
rigid economy of words. Asked for details of his
past, he replies: 'I spend most of my time since I
grew up in jail and it looks like I spend the rest
of my life dead.' Growing up, jail, death –
personal horizons, as empty as Gabrielle's future
before Squier's sacrifice.

The clash of styles and characters is
interesting here, not only because it represents
the classic confrontation between idealism and
anarchy, but because it illustrates how far our
sympathies have slid in nearly half a century
towards the latter.

One can imagine yesterday's audience rising
to the intellectual dropout, then something of a
rarity. Today, one is never conscious of being in
the presence of a Great Thinker. The experience
is more like being trapped by the dinner party
windbag who has read two books on The
Purpose of Life and who feels he must share his
discoveries with you. By comparison, Mantee's
raw ferocity has lost little of its edge. Warners'
prototype anti-hero, canonized and reprocessed
down the years for us by Marvin, Eastwood,
Bronson, Hackman and others, remains central to
the world we live in, whereas Squier, the prisoner
of a ludicrously outdated moral code, cocooned
in a pre-Munich mentality can justify only to
himself the wan delusion that clever words have
some kind of chance against brute force.

Allowing for the dilution of impact that
nearly half a century occasions, one can see how
audiences of 1936 must have responded to the
sight of Bogart, hunched and wolverine, with a
voice like broken glass, Dillingeresque in looks as
well as in essence, the compendium of several of
urban society's worst nightmares.

Film Weekly noted: 'Bogart's study of Duke
Mantee, the killer, is a remarkable piece of
acting, underlining without exaggeration the
animal-like mentality of a professional murderer.
There are indications that this unusual drama,
adapted from a play by Robert Sherwood,
started out with every intention of being a
penetrating psychological study of the impact
upon one another of various sharply contrasting
characters, but unfortunately the psychology
seems to have had its sharp edges blurred in the
process of translation to the screen. An
interesting but patchy picture.'

'A splendid character gallery comes to life
under the canny but respectful direction that
Archie Mayo has given to Mr Sherwood's play,'
wrote the New York Times. 'Static scenically the
picture may be, but it is animate and vital,
nevertheless, under the goad of thoughtful
writing and the whiplash of melodrama that its
author cracked over the back of a conversation
piece. There should be a large measure of praise
for Humphrey Bogart who can be a psychopathic
gangster more like Dillinger than the outlaw
himself.'

Kine Weekly thought Bogart 'curiously
impressive as the dumb killer. Dialogue
frequently takes precedence over action but it is
so rich in observation and repartee that this in no
way impairs the fullness and quality of the
sensitive, imaginative play.'

Monthly Film Bulletin listed 'excitement,
tense situations, humor, romance, witty and
brilliant dialogue,' among its plusses. 'Practically
all the action takes place in the lunchroom of the
gas station, but consciousness of the weird
surroundings is never lost though never obtruded.
The acting reaches an equally high level. Where
all are so good it is almost invidious to name
individuals but mention must be made of a
remarkable performance by Humphrey
Bogart. . .'

'A story that is right out of the ordinary and
full of brilliance and depth that inspire not only
pleasure at the time but thought afterwards,'
noted Picturegoer. 'Humphrey Bogart acts with
such understanding that one pities the man as

much as one detests the crime he commits.'

Kine Weekly called it 'a film of arresting and thought provoking entertainment.'

San Quentin is a fast-paced prison melodrama, with Bogart cast as 'Red' Kennedy, a violent society-hating criminal lodged in San Quentin. Sneering and disparaging, he resists the corrective overtures of his sister May (Ann Sheridan) and Jameson (Pat O'Brien), the sympathetic prisonyard officer who takes an interest in him through May. Kennedy respects a steely nerve so that when Jameson risks his life to wrest a machine gun from a deranged prisoner, thereby saving the lives of other prisoners, he is impressed to the point of grudging respect – a feeling that quickly evaporates when malicious tongues put the wrong inference on the love affair between Jameson and his sister.

With another lag and armed with a gun, Kennedy breaks out, furiously confronting the prison officer later in his sister's apartment and managing to get off a shot at him before the level-headed May can put him straight on a few pointers. Acknowledging his mistake, the convict attempts to return peaceably to prison, but he is shot dead en route, taking care to linger on till he has solemnly lectured his fellow prisoners on the fair-mindedness of Captain Jameson, and exhorted them, with drooping eyelids, to be better chaps in future.

San Quentin is a slight film vigorously bashing away at a favorite Warners theme of the thirties, that of the regenerative effects on the criminal mind of familial concern. Criminal-brother good-sister relationships were stable ingredients in the sociological dramas of the period, and the brother-sister angle occurs repeatedly in the work of Bogart, as well as others, down the years.

Edward G. Robinson is drawn into the final shootout with Bogart in *Kid Galahad* through overzealous regard for his sister. In *Marked Woman* Bette Davis comes over to Bogart's side and turns State evidence after the thugs have murdered her sister. Tearaway Billy Halop's regeneration occurs in *Crime School Dead End* and *You Can't Get Away with Murder* in response to dramatic sisterly appeals and conversely it is Bogart's terse rejection by his mother (Marjorie Main) in *Dead End* that regenerates him totally. George Raft reverts to crime to keep his brother straight in *Invisible Stripes*, and gets sucked into Ida Lupino's

amorous web in *They Drive by Night* to pay his married and crippled brother's (Bogart's) bills. Morbid jealousy of his sister is what ultimately destroys Bogart in *The Wagons Roll at Night* and it ought to be noted that other people's sisters have featured prominently in Bogart films – most notably in *Conflict* where love for his wife's sister cooks his goose and in *Key Largo* where love for his dead friend's sister (Lauren Bacall) snaps him out of his complacency. Brothers and sisters are also central to the plots of *Sabrina Fair* and *The Big Sleep* respectively.

Motion Picture Herald described *San Quentin* as 'essentially a character romance which necessitates the sacrifice of two lives to prove a humane point. It presents good actors handling a dynamic subject in an impressive style.'

'Thoroughly efficient,' noted Film Weekly. 'A routine prison drama rather more than capably acted, competently directed with some real thrills. Humphrey Bogart, as usual, makes a sympathetic and impressive figure of the tough "Red".' Under Lloyd Bacon's direction, in a screenplay co-authored by Robert Rossen, Bogart appeared in *Racket Busters* as Pete Martin, a Mafia-style gangboss who imposes a protection racket on New York's uptown trucking association. Opposed initially by an amalgam of small truck owners, Martin subdues their leader Denny Jordan (George Brent) with a token roughing up and sinister threat to his pregnant wife. Angered by Jordan's apparent cowardice, the truckers close ranks against him but nothing, not even the callous murder of a close friend nor the fiery derision of his colleagues, will induce him to risk harm to his family. To compound Jordan's troubles, even his wife begins to think he is a coward who is using her as a convenient excuse, and the police detain him on a charge of withholding evidence.

The climax occurs when Martin engineers a wholesale truck stoppage, cutting off the city's vital food supplies. The crime-busting D.A. (Walter Abel), shrewdly assessing Jordan's ability to rally a crowd, turns him loose, and the strategy works and with the truckers' roared approval, he leads them back to work and Martin's grim hold is broken.

Like *On The Waterfront*, *Racket Busters* is a realistic tale of worker coercion by strong-arm tactics and like the Elia Kazan film which it prefaces by fifteen years, the story centers on how one man's middle-of-the-road attitude hardens against persistent thuggery.

Racket Busters is an efficient minor-league thriller that neither takes sides nor presupposes sociological arguments, but paces its story well and attains the correct mood and atmosphere without any obvious tricks. Like *On The Waterfront*, it's a man's world, and appropriately the final confrontation between the mobster and the people's champion is a bold physical statement in which words, and reasons, are simply an intrusion. Brent is no Marlon Brando but Bogart is cold, cunning and remorselessly vindictive in a way that Lee J. Cobb could never be, and whilst Cobb is broken at the end of the Kazan film, for Bogart it is merely a lost battle in a continuing war. Coldly denounced by the Judge before going down, Bogart stares emotionlessly ahead, already drawing up, one suspects, the next set of battle plans.

'The story is told tersely and forcefully,' noted Film Weekly. 'There is a strong element of suspense all through, although it is obvious that the law will triumph in the end. In view of that certainty, the many scenes which keep you on the edge of your seat are testimonials to expert direction. Bogart and Brent play their parts with their usual competence. If you're not completely tired of gangster stuff, you'll enjoy this film. It has pace, realism and vigor.'

Cinematograph Weekly called Bogart's performance 'thoroughly convincing' in a film that 'can be described with equal correctness as either a man's film with the feminine touch, or a woman's picture firmly embossed with masculine essentials.'

Lewis Seiler directed Bogart in *King of the Underworld*, a pretentiously-titled thriller where he, again, played a rat with Napoleonic delusions of grandeur. This time, as gang boss Joe Gurney, he suckers a surgeon loaded with gambling debts to join the gang, but shortly afterwards, in a police raid on the hideout the surgeon is killed. Implicated, although innocent, is his wife Carol (Kay Francis), whose own career as a surgeon suffers even though in a controversial trial she is acquitted.

Determined to restore her good name, Carol begins to work on Gurney's aides, with the help of a novelist whom she restores to health after being cut down in a gun battle with Gurney's men, and eventually traps the mobster with the help of some eye-drop solution which temporarily blinds him while police surround the gang's hideout.

Mortally wounded in the shootout, which he recklessly starts without being able to see what he is shooting at, Gurney senses that his Napoleonic ambitions will exit with him when word gets out that a woman crocked him, and implores the police with his dying gasp to suppress the truth for the sake of his image.

King of the Underworld was a remake by Bryan Foy of the W.R. Burnett thriller, *Doctor Socrates*, in which Paul Muni, as a doctor, traps a gang of hoodlums. The Bogart film gave Muni's part to Kay Francis, the only positive visual relief in an unsure production. Bogart's egocentric gangster, fired with the notion of being a legend in his lifetime and committing his vision of himself to the pen, is just plain silly, but no sillier than the climax, as, temporarily blinded, he lurches around like a headless chicken, popping off shots at people who aren't there.

'Bogart as a "gorilla" chief adds another portrait to his gangster gallery,' wrote Motion Picture Herald. 'Lewis Seiler's direction has paced the story in a rapid mounting stride to a finish that reaches a high in ingenious and suspenseful action.'

Kinematograph Weekly noted: 'Here is one that breaks new ground. The picture as a whole is thoroughly convincing and the director keeps one continually interested in the fate of his characters, they are flesh-and-blood creations. Humphrey Bogart gives another of his arresting studies of criminals, and in this case makes it extremely interesting.'

'Well acted, exciting and humorous,' said Monthly Film Bulletin. 'The settings and photography are effective and pleasing, and the plot works itself out consistently and provokingly until the culmination when it degenerates into sensationalism and sentimentality. Humphrey Bogart plays the ruthless though disarming gangster, who has Napoleonic complexes and a comically ingenious respect for culture, with his usual finish.

The conveyor belt was oiled again for *You Can't Get Away with Murder* (1939) directed by Lewis Seiler, where Bogart, as small time crook Frank Wilson, reunites with former Dead End Kid Billy Halop. Wilson influences footloose slum kid Johnny Stone (Halop) into participating in minor raids which, when she discovers it, antagonizes Johnny's sister (Gale Page) and her fiancé Burke (Harvey Stevens). Borrowing Burke's service revolver without his knowledge, Stone is an accessory to the murder of a

"Joe Gurney" studio pose for [King of the Underworld] (1939)

pawnbroker whom Wilson shoots, with Burke's gun, during a robbery.

Burke is pulled in and convicted of the crime, while Wilson and his accomplice go down on a lesser unrelated charge. Wilson's problem then becomes one of keeping Stone quiet about the killing after Burke's appeal against the death sentence is denied. Shocked at finding himself an accessory to the legal murder of the man his sister loves and pressurized by both his sister and Burke's lawyer (John Litel), Stone scribbles a confession but Wilson intercepts it, and following a prison breakout, shoots the youngster while they are refuging inside an abandoned freightcar.

He conceals the written confession he took from Stone inside the boxcar before submitting to the police, confident that Stone's death will be ascribed to police bullets and that Burke, a patrolman whom he despises, will 'fry' for the earlier killing. Stone however, is not quite dead, and manages to retrieve the confession, which along with his gasped testimony, saves the innocent man from the electric chair and deposits the guilty one in its shadow.

You Can't Get Away with Murder was a play-safe prison melodrama, the sentiments of whose title being strangely at odds with what Warners were doing to Bogart's career. Within the limitations of the material, he performed well as the brutish felon wearing the same black shirt he had on in *The Amazing Doctor Clitterhouse* and *King of the Underworld* and the same natty striped suit (when not in prison grey) that appeared on him also in *The Roaring Twenties*, *Invisible Stripes* and *The Maltese Falcon* – useful when, as often happened, he was working on two, sometimes three, films at once. Like his dress sense, however, there had emerged a weary predictability to the roles Warners were assigning him – ten times during 1937-1939 he played the same part – and the qualities about his performance, and his personalities, that had rivetted audiences in the early days were clearly on the wane. In Bogart's case, although he was by no means exclusive in this way, the studio seemed to favor a strange dichotomy where, on the one hand, it acknowledged that repetition and over-familiarity were weakening his impact at the box office by floating bigger star names in front of his (in twenty of the twenty-eight films he made between *The Petrified Forest* and *High Sierra* he was secondary, and lower, in the credits), but on the other hand, it did nothing to nurture fresh impact. Bogart often referred to Warners as 'the factory', and the botched-up production line look about many (such as *You Can't Get Away with Murder*) of the products seems to support the accusation that artistic merit came after volume output as the studio's main preoccupations.

Monthly Film Bulletin noted: 'A familiar type of film but one rich in dramatic content and emphasizing human problems rather than horror. The central theme of the youth's dilemma between loyalty and fear is developed with dramatic intensity. The action is swift and the story is worked up with clarity and force to a dramatic climax. Humphrey Bogart gives a strong performance in the role of the crook and Billy Halop, in presenting the tortured mind of the misguided youth, gathers strength as he goes along.'

'Both melodramatic entertainment and a gripping moral document,' said Motion Picture Herald. 'It preaches that crime doesn't pay and does so grimly, forcefully and in a way which teaches a powerful moral lesson. The picture features Humphrey Bogart and Billy Halop in vivid roles which they play for all the parts are worth. Grim but not gruesome, while potent in its picturization of desperate men bent on dangerous missions, the story carries a strong human interest appeal. It was evident that the patrons (at the Hollywood preview) were impressed.'

Kinematograph Weekly thought it 'sternly protracted and a trifle grim in places, but its stern message is nevertheless firmly driven home. The powerful all-star cast sees to that. There are a few loose ends but otherwise the play bears the grim yet entertaining stamp of authenticity. In brief, it delivers the goods.'

Film Weekly commented: 'Though it contains nothing new, it is all done with a grim realism that carries conviction. Acting is above the average, with outstanding performances from Humphrey Bogart and Billy Halop. See it, if you like strong stuff.'

Invisible Stripes directed by Lloyd Bacon is strong stuff, too, the first and least memorable of two teamings with George Raft, here seen as the familiar good-bad guy putting family considerations before personal honor. Raft and Bogart are two paroled toughies who revert in their individual ways to armed robbery. Cliff

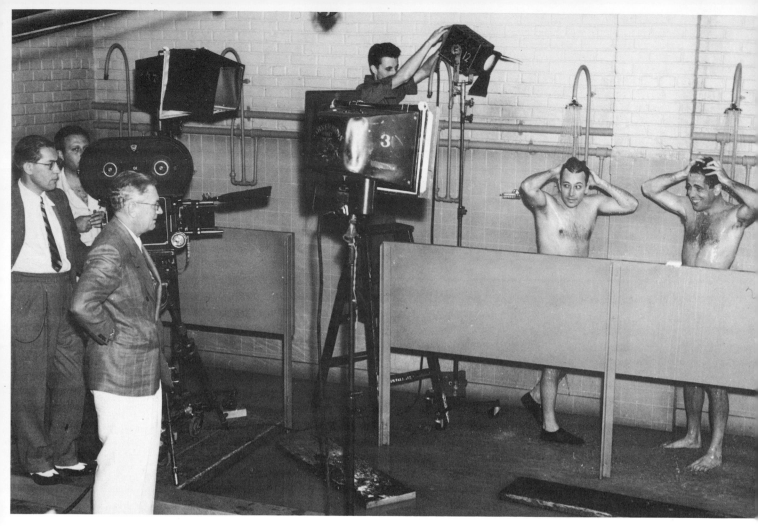

"Chuck Martin" with George Raft, Director Lloyd Bacon and crew on the set of [*Invisible Stripes*] (1939)

Taylor (Raft) has no relish for crime, but society is less than open-armed about having him back. Jobs are scarce, and there is his disillusioned bull-headed younger brother Tim (William Holden in an early role) to contend with.

Struggling to make enough money to get married, Tim is already a minor criminal, poised on the threshold of worse things, but Cliff, anxious to divert him back to the straight and narrow, realizes that in his frame of mind conciliatory words are insufficient. The only answer to Tim's predicament is 'dough', so Cliff surreptitiously throws in with his former prison buddy Chuck Martin (Bogart), a sour-faced heel actively engaged in robbery. Their partnership prospers, and when sufficient money is in the bank – presumably one not on their raid list – to set his brother up in a garage business, Cliff defects from the gang, a move that alienates him from several members, notably Kruger (Paul Kelly, a close friend of Bogart's from their Broadway days, in a role similar to the one he had in *The Roaring Twenties*).

Tim's garage is implicated when, following a subsequent robbery in which Martin is wounded, the gangster hides there for safety.

With his injured pal hidden in Tim's fiancée's apartment, Cliff accompanies his brother to the police station for questioning, exonerating him of any involvement. He is spotted leaving by the Kruger faction who, presuming that he has informed on them, tail him to where Martin is hidden. In a gun-happy showdown, both Martin and Cliff are killed before the police can intervene.

Warners' armory of grainy supporting characters, plus its brisk narrative, makes *Invisible Stripes* watchable today. There is little else to commend it. Raft makes heavy weather of the central role, the handling of most of the relationships is rather sloppy, and in making too many concessions to the Hays Office by insisting that both ex-convicts die, the story loses more teeth than it can afford.

With a line-up, however, that includes, in addition to the cold-eyed Kelly, Marc Lawrence (the guffawing Ziggy of *Key Largo*), Joe Downing (*Racket Busters* , *Angels With Dirty Faces* , *You Can't Get Away With Murder* , *The*

Big Shot), Henry O'Neill (*The Great O'Malley* , Marked Women , *The Amazing Doctor Clitterhouse* , *Racket Busters* , *They Drive by Night*), and Leo Gorcey, the Dead End Kid later to flower as the inestimable Slip Mahoney of Bowery Boys fame, the movie, dying like Bogart's gangster on its feet, offers a robbers' roost of minor compensations, as well as one surprise, Britain's Flora Robson, unwisely remaining in Hollywood after *Wuthering Heights* , looking a trifle fraught (as well she might) as George Raft's mother.

Motion Picture Herald observed: 'No studio produces a gangster picture quite so expertly as the Warner plant, where, under executive producer Hal B. Wallis' gifted tutelage the business of proving that crime doesn't pay has been reduced to the status of an exact science. . .Raft plays with the usual Raft solidity. . . Bogart makes a less noble gangster type more credible. . . The picture winds up in a hail of lead quite as spectacular and lethal as any studio has turned out.'

Kine Weekly called Bogart 'every inch the ruthless gangster,' in a 'powerful if stereotyped story. Its evidence and conclusions are obvious, but thanks to powerful acting, good production qualities, the human touch and a terrific climax, it nevertheless makes cast-iron mass entertainment.'

'The film is moving, tense and holds the interest,' noted Monthly Film Bulletin. 'George Raft gives an excellent performance and is strongly supported by Humphrey Bogart.'

Coming several months after *The Maltese Falcon* , *The Big Shot* , directed by Lewis Seiler, illustrates the patent inflexibility and unfairness of the Warners system which so frustrated their stars. To keep the factory going, routine projects could be earmarked for contract players months in advance with no account taken, in the short term, of audience reaction to recently released work. Incredibly, while the world raved about his performance in *The Maltese Falcon* , Warners could find nothing more substantial for him to do than play *The Big Shot* , an insipid prison melodrama that looks like an amalgam of left-over material from a dozen earlier Bogart films, joined up inexpertly to cash in, as the title suggests, one last despairing time on a dying genre.

Bogart plays Duke Berne, onetime public enemy reduced to supping in cheap cafés, where against his better judgment, he consorts with minor villains. Invited to participate in a robbery, Berne consents, having been assured that a leading criminal lawyer Fleming (Stanley Ridges), whose wife Lorna (Irene Manning) he knows from the past, is attending to the arrangements.

On the night of the robbery, Lorna detains him, at gunpoint, and the raid misfires. Mistakenly identified by a flustered witness whom the police pressurize, Berne is sent for trial, but unable to reveal his whereabouts at the time of the robbery without implicating Lorna, he invents an alibi which Fleming, needled by the knowledge of his wife's affection for the gangster, destroys in court, leaving Berne, unjustly, to take the prison rap.

With another prisoner he hatches a daring escape plan, which though successful, results in the death of a prison guard. Reunited with Lorna, they enjoy a brief idyllic interlude in a mountain hideaway before the peace is shattered by the news that his friend on the inside has been given a death sentence for the prison killing.

Berne decides to surrender himself but on the way back, the police, acting on a tip-off by Fleming and unaware of Berne's intentions, intercept them, and in a thrilling car chase sequence through winding mountain passes (not only reminiscent of the robbery getaway sequences in *High Sierra* but using several of the movie's long shots) Berne escapes although Lorna is killed by a hail of police bullets.

Bursting in on Fleming, whose part he establishes in Lorna's death, and having telephoned the prison to rescue his friend from Death Row, Berne ignores the lawyer's pitiful pleas to spare him.But with Lorna gone and only the electric chair to look forward to, Berne is purposefully slow on the draw, giving Fleming a momentary advantage to save the state a little electricity.

The last of Bogart's 'King Rat' portrayals was as Glenn Griffin, the bitter, unshaven escaped convict of *The Desperate Hours* , William Wyler's moody setpiece of 1955. Previously a Broadway play by Joseph Hayes starring the then up-and-coming Paul Newman, the author's screen adaptation cleaves very closely in spirit and feel to the stage original, and despite the additional exterior shots, mostly atmospheric night shots as the police net tightens on the three suburban terrorists, the film suffers from the same lack of mobility which nineteen years previously marred *The Petrified Forest* , whose plotline it recalls.

Jail-breaker Griffin, accompanied by his younger brother Hal (Dewey Martin) and a podgy psychopath named Kobish (Robert Middleton) takes over the house of Dan Hilliard (Fredric March) an Indianapolis business executive whilst awaiting the arrival of his Pittsburg girlfriend Helen Miller, with money for their getaway. It is a typical middle-class American suburban house, chosen by the thugs because the child's bicycle, lying on the lawn, implies vulnerability. The rendezvous with Helen is intentionally Pittsburg because Griffin has a score to settle with the local sheriff, Jesse Bard (Arthur Kennedy) who had broken the criminal's jawbone during his arrest.

Griffin is explicit about his intentions if the family resists ('If you pull anything, Hilliard, I'll let you watch me kick the kid's face in'), but son Ralphie (Richard Eyer) resents his father's tame attitude towards the intruders, and almost effects an escape which earns Griffin's surly regard.

The insular family atmosphere and unfamiliar comforts unsettle Hal, who counters Griffin's boast, 'I taught you everything,' with a scornful 'Except how to live in a house like this!' Later, promised that he will get what he wants, Hal responds grimly, 'I doubt it, Glenn. I doubt if I

"Duke Berne" and Irene Manning – [The Big Shot] (1942)

ever will.' The showdown between the brothers occurs after Kobish's murder of an inquisitive housecaller, and Griffin's melodramatic postulating ('I laugh when I feel like it and you ain't got nothing to say about it!') – that, plus a deepening sense of doom ('What good is the dough going to do you in the death house?') prompts Hal to strike out for himself. His nervy response to a uniformed policeman, innocently waiting his turn to use a phone booth, however, gets himself killed.

A delay over the cash – it is mailed to Hilliard's office and he is despatched to retrieve it – buys the executive thinking time, but intercepted by the police as he returns home with the money, to their astonishment, Hilliard devises a simple but risky plan to disarm Griffin. He will return to the house with an empty gun, which the convict is certain to discover and remove for his own use. Hilliard gambles, rightly, that Griffin will skip the precaution of checking it for bullets. Thus, the villain is cornered, but he decides against peaceful surrender and dies, defiantly brandishing the empty revolver, in a savage burst of machinegun fire. The movie ends silently as the cameras track back from the family home, with police, newsmen and assorted wellwishers crowding round to toast returning normality.

The Desperate Hours is a flawed but gripping essay, and it is entertaining to see Bogart storming around ramming guns into people with all of, although not visibly exceeding, his former menace and swagger. It is a complex, demanding part with no let-up or easy passages for him and he had to touch deeper chords in his repertoire of sadistic killers than ever before – a feat he accomplished with consumate skill. Nevertheless he is plainly too old for the part, and the father-figure hatred of the urbane, affluent Hilliard by Griffin, so ably expressed by Newman on stage and central to understanding the violent interplay between them, is abandoned totally. In the movie version, we are given no insight into why Griffin taunts and mauls Hilliard so badly if, as the story suggests, he is merely lying low for a few hours to make a connexion. After Hal's

"Glen Griffin" and Frederic March – [*The Desperate Hours*] *(1955)*

defection, Griffin makes his point, that Hilliard reminds him of 'smart-eyed' parole board freaks ('Throw us back in the cell. We ain't fit to live with decent folk') but the explanation comes too late and, anyway, his argument is dulled by a conscious lack of disparity in their ages, making the gangster as old, if not older, than the people sending him down, and coming across as a rather senile all-time loser, not the anti-social firebrand of the original play.

Wyler sets his moods with biting effect; the getaway car invading suburbia at the start, cameras searching hungrily out the driver's window before picking out and zooming gleefully onto the discarded bicycle.

Low angle shots inside the Hilliard house, emphasizing the acute claustrophobia of its trapped occupants, contrasted by the open, deserted streets at night as Hilliard returns with the retrieved money. The imaginative use of lights to signal the end of the criminals' dark reign – Hal caught in car headlights before he is killed at the truckstop, and Griffin pinioned on the verandah by police searchlights, one of which he symbolically shatters by throwing his empty

gun before the bullets cut him down.

Wyler uses subsidiary characters cleverly too: the intrusive boyfriend, the politically motivated police chief, and inquisitive neighbor, all contribute to the drama without hiving off any of the interest. Gail Kubik's music is nicely paced, giving us plenty of expressive silences, and it is a compliment to the discreet camera work of Lee Garmes (*Duel in the Sun* , *The Secret Life of Walter Mitty*) that we are not aware of having been voyeurs on a private tragedy until he pulls us back from the brink at the very end.

The London Evening Standard declared: 'Bogart as the hoodlum leader gives one of the most unsympathetic and compelling performances of his career. With that scar-tissue face, which is as crumpled, stained and badly sewn as his prison shirt, he almost smells of crime. Matched against him is Fredric March as the husband. His haggard, handsome Roman mask is fissured with anxiety, and every tense, vulnerable movement of his body turns the screw on our nerves.'

'Bogart looks like an elderly, thin-lipped monkey, uses a voice of unvarying venom – and is right back at the top of the form that made him famous,' said The Daily Herald. 'Almost all the acting is Oscar-worthy.   . .it should be in the top three films of the year.'

Tribune noted: 'Breaking and entering is one of the numerous things at which Mr Bogart excels. As I remember, the first thing he ever did on the screen was to walk into somebody's place and take it over. He still does it very well.'

Time Magazine called it: 'A thriller that jabs so shrewdly and sharply at sensibility that the moviegoer's eye might feel that it has not so much been entertained as used for a pin cushion. But for melodrama fans, it may prove one of the most pleasurably frustrating evenings ever spent in a movie house. Director Wyler has subordinated his actors with unusual severity to the pace of the plot, and most of them have taken to the rein like the thoroughbreds they are. Bogart gives a piteously horrible impression of the essential criminal.'

Film Daily said: 'All the superlatives can be rolled out to summarize this one. Individual praise can be accorded each and every player but it is the perfection of the cast, as a whole, which leaves the lasting impression. Each player had in his or her own way contributed a share to the film's overall quality.'

'Bogart has the honesty to meet his death

scene as a small beaten man without any of the false movie bravado that sometimes glorifies crime. It is one of his greatest performances,' wrote Hollywood Reporter. 'Both a money picture and an artistic picture, it is played by a distinguished cast so thoroughly integrated by William Wyler's excellent production and direction that all the actors seem to be unified in one all-encompassing stellar performance.'

Motion Picture Herald called it 'simple in outline, explosive in effect and lasting in memory. By the time March makes a desperate decision and delivers his family to safety, the audience will not have a nerve left.   . .a superbly told story.'

Monthly Film Bulletin criticized 'the film's tendency to over inflate its material. The controlled but rather heavy and impersonal craftsmanship that now characterizes much of Wyler's work,' and Joseph Hayes' script failed 'to give the characters the kind of individuality that might have made the film more than a solid, deliberate and long drawn-out exercise in the mechanics of suspense.'

The Times called it 'a powerful, heavyweight film, and in its class it is a reigning champion.'

The London Observer summed it up as 'a very formidable piece of frozen savagery.'

During the thirties and forties, Warners had an overriding production rule – never ditch a winning formula until it dies of exhaustion. Their movies were explosive and inventive, certainly, but like good choreography, nothing was left to chance. Conveyor belt theatrics it might have been, with little or no concessions towards high art, yet artists were at work there, fashioning grainy images which have survived the test of time.

Between *The Petrified Forest* and the launch of his Santana production company in 1948, Humphrey Bogart made over forty films for Warner Brothers, and, incredibly, around two-thirds of these were made during the first five years, with Bogart supporting a bigger name during this frantic period in all but seven of them. Warners have been severely censured for having failed to recognize Bogart's talent earlier than they apparently did, but the real culprit was not their lack of judgment – a company which broke the line to pioneer sound could hardly be accused of that – but the system they operated, which made it extraordinarily difficult for featured players to come up through the ranks.

By the time Bogart arrived, a triumvirate was already established in the gangster field – Cagney, Robinson and Raft – with strong appeal at the box-office and, generally speaking, they continued in control until the genre died around the outbreak of World War II, primarily due to Warners rigid insistence on never tampering with

success. The formula – working class musicals, adventure yarns and melodramas, harsh, hard-hitting monochromes about people, and cities, in conflict – plus their patented sound system, lifted them from dire financial straits in the late twenties to buoyant solvency in the mid-thirties. The formula dictated everything, with directors and actors held in fairly tight subjugation: paid little, worked blind and quite often (as in Bogart's case), their talents wasted for short-term ends.

Not always did the contractees succumb willingly, and frequent court battles, feuds and suspensions ensued, with Cagney, Flynn, Tracy and Bette Davis among the headline rebels. Warners let nothing – and no one – stand in the way of progress; when a recalcitrant star refused a role, providing the planned property met all the criteria for success, it was simply passed down the line, on a horses for courses basis, occasioning a minimum of adjustment and delay.

Fortunately for Bogart, the public did not always agree with the stars on the question of choice, *High Sierra* and *The Maltese Falcon* being rebound classics of their type, and once he had found the gap, the horse for that particular course never lost sight of the winning post. But it was a long hard gallop, with minor classics and routine features riding shoulder-to-shoulder with some of the worst movies ever made.

China Clipper, directed by Ray Enright, had Bogart fourth in the cast behind Pat O'Brien, Beverly Roberts and Ross Alexander, as Hap Stuart, a World War I flying ace who, during the post-Lindberg period, teams up with a friend Dave Logan (Pat O'Brien), head of a small airline consortium determined to set up a trans-Pacific air service. Logan is obsessive about succeeding, jeopardizing his marriage and friendships in the fulfillment of his dream. But tolerance prevails and the Clipper struggles on to China with Stuart piloting, literally clipping the deadline and insuring happiness for everybody except the firm's gnarled old designer who succumbs to a heart attack amid the excitement.

An undistinguished, rather chauvinistic soap opera – the ladies are either dumb, outraged or decorative – *China Clipper* could wave topicality as a plausible line of defense at its critics in 1936.

Certainly audiences of the period would have enjoyed the authentic, cleverly edited newsreel shots of real clippers in flight. It is O'Brien's film, and his entrepreneurial airline boss is full of O'Brien devices – firecracker voice,

"Val Stevens", E. E. Clive, Donald Woods and
Margaret Lindsay – [Isle of Fury] (1936)

steamroller manner, gruff humor – which for
O'Brien fans, if any survive, is probably enough.
Bogart's Hap Stuart supports and heckles
agreeably, and in one redeeming scene biffs the
clippermaniac to the ground, forcing him to
pause and reflect.

. There are some genuine moments of
excitement as Bogart nurses the plane across
thousands of miles of hostile weather conditions
and other hazards, but alas the film's heart
remains grounded, in more ways than one,
over-emphasizing O'Brien's haggard vigil and
dreary punctured romance.

'The treatment results in an honest, almost
documentary subject free of exaggerated
glorification,' said Kine Weekly. 'The movement
of the story is smooth and deliberately paced
working to a thrilling climax././.comedy is nicely
balanced with pithy dialogue adding punch to the
tale.'

Monthly Film Bulletin noted: 'Some of the

drama inherent in the actual achievement is lost
in the manufactured drama of the fictional plot.
Nevertheless, vigorous direction with
considerable emphasis on close-up work smooths
over these failings and the flying in general is
quite exciting. Excellent entertainment.'

Isle of Fury, based on a flaccid Somerset
Maugham novel, *The Narrow Corner* (filmed
earlier in 1932), is a good example of what
boredom and ineptitude can achieve when they
meet. Fugitive Val Stevens (Bogart) lives in the
South Seas in hiding, where he marries Lucille
Gordon (Margaret Lindsay). As the ceremony
concludes, a ship founders off a nearby reef, and
Stevens plunges off to rescue Eric Blake, (Donald
Wood), a cop hot on Stevens' trail – neither at
this point aware of who the other is. Blake
returns the compliment later, on a pearl-fishing
expedition, when Stevens, demonstrating his
invincibility to a group of popeyed natives whose
colleagues have failed to surface, is pinned to the
ocean floor by a randy octopus.

Amid all this life-saving Blake and Stevens
become friends, although Blake's real interest is

in Lucille, who responds with a beguiling mixture of 'stay back' and 'come on'. Alerted to the fact that Lucille might be carrying on behind his back, Stevens confronts them, but is once more saved by Blake, this time from a bounty-hunting sea captain who has rumbled his dastardly secret. Impressed by Stevens' demeanor, and not wishing to cause Lucille unhappiness, Blake returns to the mainland with a concocted story, leaving the newlyweds free to caper under the palm trees.

Isle of Fury seems an incredible assignment for Bogart so soon after *The Petrified Forest* (made earlier the same year) when his presence as Duke Mantee was still enormously vivid and with the earlier movie still going the rounds. It was a step backwards off the pier for Bogart, who later denied ever having made it, but blame cannot be shrugged off too easily and the evidence survives, although mercifully it is never shown.

Monthly Film Bulletin observed: 'The center of interest shifts so often that the film lacks coherence and the ending is surprising. Humphrey Bogart makes Val a credible character, physically brave and with a careless charm which Eric, as played by Donald Woods, lacks; he is dull and wooden by comparison. Margaret Lindsay is attractive as Lucille, but her acting is self-conscious and varies in effectiveness.'

The Great O'Malley, directed by William Dieterle, sees Bogart as destitute family man John Phillips, supporting Pat O'Brien's martinet cop of the title in the second of their four-film association. En route to a job interview in his scrappy motorcar, Phillips is detained by the officious O'Malley on a minor traffic infringement long enough to miss his job opportunity. Frustrated and resentful, Phillips is obliged to pawn his war medals to support his wife (Frieda Inescourt) and his crippled child Barbara (Sybil Jason) but after an argument with the pawnbroker, whom he knocks out in desperation, he snatches money from the till and is promptly arrested by O'Malley – not for the robbery, but, ironically, for the same silly traffic infraction.

Aware that his officer's overzealous, inflexible attitude is bad for community relations, O'Malley's chief switches him to point duty where, on patrol at a school crossing, he witnesses a lame child being run down by a car. Assisted by the child's teacher, Judy Nolan (Ann Sheridan), O'Malley delivers the child home, and

only then does he discover she is Phillip's daughter Barbara, and learns the full extent of the family's tragic circumstances.

Anxious to make amends, and without Phillip's knowledge, he arranges for an operation for the child, and pulls strings to re-schedule the job interview he caused Phillips to miss in the first place, as well as making representations to the parole board to secure the prisoner's earliest possible release.

Phillips, however, whose bitter hatred of the cop has festered during his term inside, has only one thought on his mind when eventually freed, to shoot O'Malley. He does, though not fatally, at the first opportunity. Wise now in the ways of commonsense and compassion, O'Malley passes off the damage as an accidental gunshot wound, and restores the apologetic Phillips – for whose erratic actions he feels partly to blame, anyway – to his grateful family.

A whimsical morality tale with just a whiff of Irish blarney, *The Great O'Malley* did nothing whatever for Bogart's career. Never wholly convincing either in pain or overtly conscious-striken, he seems unnerved by all the woes dumped on him in this picture, and occasionally his eyes take on the wistful look of a man who would like to be back in a desert-diner behind a shotgun, away from all this febrile baloney.

Not so much a good guy as a weak one, and not so much a bad guy as a soppy one, Phillips flits worriedly from poverty to violence to theft to jail and out again, the sole author of his misfortunes. His resentment of O'Malley who, like the man behind the social security counter, is only doing his job, seems an evasion of personal responsibility and inhibits us identifying with his character, or his predicament. O'Malley's switch from bully boy to kindly uncle happens too quickly, on a threadbare motivation, and we tolerate it only because it is Pat O'Brien, an actor famed for sudden, implausible changes of heart.

Marked Woman was social drama lifted from the headlines with Bogart as David Graham a crimebusting district attorney, modeled on Thomas A. Dewey. Graham is determined to wipe out a high-class prostitution racket run by vice czar Vanning (Eduardo Cianelli), but misplaced trust in Mary (Bette Davis), one of Vanning's spirited hostesses whose evidence deliberately wrecks the case, puts him right back where he started. Convinced that Mary will come round, he bides his time, and the opportunity occurs when Mary's younger sister, duped into attending one of Vannings lavish house parties, meets with a fatal accident whilst escaping an amorous guest. A witness to the killing disappears, while Mary's face is slashed in an attempt to dissuade her from giving evidence. But Mary is undeterred, and urged by Graham, rallies the other frightened girls out into the open to testify against Vanning, effecting the collapse of his corrupt empire.

Viewed now, *Marked Woman* is vintage courtroom melodrama, with Bogart's relaxed, competent performance attributable in part to the presence in the film of his current flame Mayo Methot (he always seemed to give that little bit extra concentration when his favorite woman shared the billing).

Bette Davis is excellent as the spunky, high-class hooker, calling people 'suckers' and scoffing up her sleeve at the law's ineffectual attempts to smother the rackets, later volunteering those same energies to nail her boss.

The flowering of trust between the Bogart and Davis characters against this violent backdrop is deftly handled by director Lloyd Bacon, and Bogart's gritty determination to clean up the city, climaxed in a decisive courtroom speech (prefacing his memorable courtroom oratory in *Knock on Any Door* twelve years later) is advocated with a clear head full of cold, arbitrary logic.

Moral-conscious Americans expected to be shielded from words like 'prostitution' – the real nature of the ladies' services blanketed, as it were, by calling them hostesses – but Warners publicity hounds went over the top on the 'frankness' theme, as if prostitution was something only they had stumbled across.

For two weeks prior to the movie's opening at the Strand Theatre in New York in March 1937, a five-foot high foyer display, under the chilling headline 'To Every Woman Sheltered by a Good Name', shrieked: 'To every mother who fights her daughter's yearning for gay night life; to every sister and sweetheart – and the men who love them – we believe *Marked Woman* is the most significant drama of life filmed in the past decade. Some women may be offended by the bold reality./././.some may be shocked by the honesty of a fearless story./././.but none will deny that they have been spellbound by the powerful portrayal of life that sheltered women never see!'

Motion Picture Herald admitted pious bewilderment. 'Trying to gauge previous audience opinion did not get the writer any place,' it confessed, dutifully avoiding that word 'prostitution' with an oblique reference to the vice czar as 'a ruthless trafficker in women's bodies' and to the ladies in question as 'unpleasant persons,' and ending on a note of stern rebuke: 'This film will undoubtedly find its best reception in the minds of sensation seekers.' Film Weekly said: 'The story is told vigorously and at times crudely with that terseness, punch and excellence of acting that is common to most good American pictures of this type. Its merits are vivid portrayals, a few really striking dramatic moments and unquenchable vitality. Bette Davis is as sincere and energetic as ever, but there are occasions when she overacts badly. Humphrey Bogart in a sympathetic part for once, makes the attorney too real a figure to be dismissed under the label "hero".'

'A powerful story,' noted Kine Weekly. 'The picture, as complete a portrait of inhuman cruelty, viciousness and brutality that the mind of man could possibly invent, let alone borrow from real life, is sheer sensationalism, but so magnificently is it portrayed by an outstanding cast, and so realistically presented that with all its horrors, it makes gripping entertainment for those who can stomach strong meat.'

Monthly Film Bulletin called it 'a sordid and powerful melodrama, tellingly presented.' Variety's view was that ' *Marked Woman* is a strong, well-made underworld drama.'

Dark Victory , directed by Edmund Goulding, was not really Bogart's cup of tea, but his role was non-pivotal and all he had to do was act brash and be buoyantly sympathetic to the heroine Judith (Bette Davis) who is dying of a malignant brain tumor. Judith, a liberated blue-stocking with a tidy inheritance and a string of horses, is aghast when she learns the awful truth but maximizes the time she has left by promptly marrying her doctor-boyfriend (George Brent) and quitting the Long Island high life for a quiet, hideway farm in Vermont.

Poignantly she fills her days with simple pleasures, like warm sunlight and woodland walks and visualizing next year's flowers that she is destined not to see, encouraged and sustained throughout by the devotion of her husband displaying calmness and fortitude when the end comes. *Dark Victory* is fundamentally a weepie in time-honored tradition (remade as *Stolen Hours* in 1963 with Susan Hayward in the Davis part) and the wasting away of one pair of lovers

is undeniably good box-office (remember Ali McGraw in *Love Story*). Bette Davis is superb as the flightly heiress who crashes down to earth, beguiling and kittenish to begin with, and at different times, sober, withdrawn, tender and defiant, chilled yet oddly mesmerized by the contracting spirals of her life.

As the tender doctor, George Brent registers well, but Bogart, as the oddball Irish groom with quiffed hair and an affected Irish accent, looks like someone adrift in the wrong picture, possibly an escapee from something by John Ford. Not for a moment can we believe in what he says or the way he says it and only in the later moments of the film when Davis becomes the genuine object of our sympathy, does *Dark Victory* inherit real style.

'First, last and always a Bette Davis performance,' said Motion Picture Herald. 'A straight telling of an essentially sad story with only minor moments of comedy to relieve the tension. The narrative affords Miss Davis ample opportunity for demonstration of her histrionic talent.'

Film Weekly noted: 'Full of deeply moving but not harrowing passages, and its cumulative

effect is inspirational. Miss Davis, with her unique blend of sure technique and spontaneous emotional vitality, makes a magnificent, complex character of the heroine. She is consistently impressive. Bogart, too, is very good. A film you must not miss.'

'Entertainment that must appeal to all who see, hear and think,' announced Kinematograph Weekly. 'Purposefully and intelligently written./. /.drama that mirrors faithfully both the light and shadow of human existence.'

The Return of Doctor X (1939) directed by Vincent Sherman, was an attempt to capitalize on the studio's earlier *Doctor X* (1932), rated by John Baxter in *Hollywood in the Thirties* , (Zwemmer Barnes 1968) as 'one of the greatest of the classic horror films, incorporating most of the key Germanic elements: necrophilia, dismemberment, rape.' The sequel is literally a pale shadow of the original, with Bogart cast as Doctor Xavier, a modern day vampire terrorizing New York City, who also survives by draining blood from victims of the type one blood group. His existence, or rather second existence, having

"Marshall Quesne" lies prostrate – [The Return of Doctor X] (1939)

previously been electrocuted for letting a baby die during an illegal experiment – comes to light after Barnett (Wayne Morris), an ambitious newspaperman, is fired for reporting a murder which apparently never happened, for next day the lovely lady victim barges into his editor's office and files damages. Puzzled by what he saw, Barnett traces her to Dr Flegg (John Litel), a brilliant haemotologist, whose assistant Rhodes (Dennis Morgan), a friend of Barnett's, agrees to help the baffled reporter find some answers.

Clegg is ahead of his time with experiments into human survival on synthetic blood, but his work has created a breed of awesome vampire-like creatures like his lab assistant Quesne (Bogart), an alias for the notorious Doctor X, whom Clegg has restored to life.

With his latest victim (Rosemary Lane, sister of Priscilla who appeared with Bogart in *The Roaring Twenties* and *Men are Such Fools*) trussed ready to be siphoned off, the fiendish Xavier is rumbled, and ceremoniously disposed of.

Despite the moments of genuine horror, *The*

Return of Doctor X shows signs of desperately trying to catch up with the Lionel Attwill version. Warners' depth of faith in the project is graphically evidenced in the movie's undistinguished line-up: no major stars and a telling paucity of top supporting players. Bogart, leering evilly but self-consciously behind his Marcel Marceau complexion and two-tone crew cut, like a banshee amusing himself between funerals.

Monthly Film Bulletin said: 'This lightly coloured and sensational story is full of improbabilities but it is effectively put over by a highly competent cast. Backgrounds contribute to the eerie and creepy atmosphere.'

Motion Picture Herald applauded its 'good direction, good acting, pace, suspense, and that touch of the weird which many humans find so fascinating. Bogart, with a streak of silver in his hair and a face of marble pallor is the sinister stalker of Type 1 blood group victims. A very good picture of the eerie type of melodrama.'

'A successful exploitation of the macabre,' noted Kine Weekly. 'Responsible for many thrills, yet ever conscious of the need for appropriate light relief././. Humphrey Bogart puts over quite a good Frankenstein act.'

Putting Bogart in a movie with Errol Flynn and Randolph Scott was an odd decision even for a studio noted for artistic illogicality. In *Virginia City* (1940), directed by Michael Curtiz, neither Flynn nor Scott were actors that Bogart had much enthusiasm for – Flynn expecially – but for the sake of peace he concealed his animosity although his good behavior did nothing to dispel the incredulity of seeing him uncomfortably astride a horse playing a mustachioed Mexican guerrilla during the American Civil War.

Flynn and Scott play opposing officers in the Union and Confederate armies respectively, upstaging each other in a spectacular game of cat-and-mouse to keep control of a five-million-dollar gold shipment en route in covered wagons from Virginia City to assist the Confederate cause. Bogart is enlisted to effect a small diversion at the Union garrison, allowing the gold to be moved, and having agreed a fee, rides off in pursuit of the wagons intending to palm off the rest, but out in the foothills he encounters the combined energetic resistance of Flynn and Scott, each of whom still wants it for his own cause and is vigorously opposed to bequeathing

it elsewhere.

Bogart is killed by Scott, and Flynn avoids execution as a spy when peace is declared and North embraces South.

To add to Bogart's disappointment, Flynn and Scott had free rein to indulge their outsize personalities, and each went on to bigger and better westerns. Flynn retained the single evocative placename title in several (*Dodge City* , *San Antonio* , *Silver River* , *Montana*) and Scott, in a fertile career that endured until he was on the verge of sixty, epitomizing the hard durable plainsman. The movie, however, is fast and exciting and the pace never lets up, the dialogue is crisp and flavorful, and there is only one female, Miriam Hopkins, a love interest for Flynn.

'A rousing and cheerful story lavishly produced' noted Monthly Film Bulletin. 'It is on the long side, but there is no lack of colourful incident, thrills and fight to keep it going. The period settings are effective and the atmosphere of the time convincingly suggested. Errol Flynn makes a dashing Kerry. His appearance is much

"John Murrell" – [*Virginia City*] *(1940)*

more impressive than his acting.'

Kine Weekly said: 'Fast action, sacrificial romance, crisp comedy and thrilling spectacle are the compelling keynotes of exhilarating and refreshing entertainment.'

'A skillfully conjected essay in colorful movement,' noted The Cinema, 'has been produced on a super-spectacular scale, and if its narrative interest is exclusively American, the appeal of its eventful incident is none the less assured.'

His talent continued to be unstretched in Raoul Walsh's *They Drive By Night*, as Paul Fabrini, the dour, volatile junior partner in a road haulage firm he owns with hard-boiled, ambitious brother Joe (George Raft). At a road stop frequented by other truckers, Joe meets Cassie (Ann Sheridan) a slick, assured waitress, and later along the road encounters her as a hitchhiker. Paul is married, resents the long hours away from home while Joe, a footloose bachelor, loves the freedom of the open road. Over fatigued one night, Paul dozes in front of the wheel, the truck smashes and he loses an arm. With their business literally wrecked, to make ends meet Joe joins a big trucking fleet run by Carlsen (Alan Hale) whose amorous young wife Lana (Ida Lupino) soon has him in her determined sights. Convinced that Carlsen stands in her way, Lana garages the car after a party, leaving her drunken husband asleep in it with the engine running – Carlsen's excessive drinking habits are not entirely unknown – and the police are satisfied that his death is accidental until Lana, in a towering rage when she discovers that Joe loves Cassie, accuses him of engineering her husband's murder. The cops follow up and the circumstantial evidence looks damaging for Joe, particularly since he had become Lana's business partner shortly after Carlsen's death. In the witness box under terse cross-examination, however, Lana's paranoia is chillingly evident, and Joe earns a deserved acquittal.

They Drive By Night is a brittle yarn, strong in atmosphere and filled with robust, bare-knuckle crosstalk but suffering from inner deficiencies in plot and motivation. Raft is in excellent form as the flinty, opportunist truck driver, and his demeanor, slightly smart-ass, vaguely knockabout, is perfect for the part. In the early scenes at the truckers' cafe, the mood is established quickly and expertly, and every line of the genial, raucous camaraderie of the long distance drivers rings true. Ann Sheridan's

wisecracking waitress ('Barney had twelve hands and I didn't like any of them') cool, honest, direct, the stereotype self-willed lady buoyant in rough male fraternity (echoed by the Bacall character in *To Have and Have Not*) contrasts well with Ida Lupino's devil woman.

Bogart, as the more subdued Paul, is carried along by the story rather than doing much of the carrying, but he gets a few salty lines. Retrieving Bogart's truck for non-payment of dues a collection agent is threatened with a monkey wrench. The man warns him: 'If you touch me I'll call a cop.' Bogart replies: 'If I touch you, you'll call an ambulance.' The accident which costs him his arm also costs him his place in the picture.

After the murder of Carlsen, with Joe grimly on the make, commercially speaking, while keeping the treacherous widow at bay, with Paul – who was never exactly a ball of fire – reduced to sour introspection about his injuries and with Cassie, the one bright element early on, relegated to an off-screen love interest, the splendidly raunchy, carefree atmosphere dissipates into a series of gloomy setpieces.

Raft's eclipse halfway through by Ida Lupino coincides with the film's loss of complexion. Early on, in the cafe and on the road, his scenes with Ann Sheridan are zestful and infectious and she gamely slugs it out with him, toe to toe, mellowing later in the apartment he rents for her just sufficiently for the softer feminine edges to intrude – but never obtrude – in what is basically a rip-roaring relationship. By contrast, his later scenes with Ida Lupino are frozen and inconclusive as, clearly on the defensive and not enjoying it, he parries her attacks like a fighter with broken knuckles. The main fault with *They Drive By Night* is its glossary of types rather than real people, but the enthusiasm of the players, lively dialogue, and Raoul Walsh's spirited handling of the mood and violent incident during the first 45 minutes give the movie the kind of momentum and buoyancy that sustain it through the heavier manufactured passages near the end.

Monthly Film Bulletin called it 'an absorbing document of the life of an American lorry-driver. Whether the picture is a true one or not, there is a realism about it, all which rings true, and which constitutes the real merit of the film. It is definitely one to see.'

'There are some humorous incidents but the picture as a whole fails to grip,' noted Picturegoer. 'There seems to be very little purpose to this meandering story of a truck driver who is chased by a married woman. George Raft has few chances but makes the most of those he has, as does Humphrey Bogart./.'

Motion Picture Herald said: 'A fascinating wrought piece of cinema merchandise which combines rough and ready action with a refined adventure into insanity. It is the story of the trucking industry./.'.told vigorously albeit bawdily in spots. Definitely adult classification.'

The Wagons Roll at Night , directed by Ray Enright was a revamping of the Warners' earlier Bogart-Edward G. Robinson success *Kid Galahad* which sacrificed the gangster theme in favor of a 'human relations' melodrama, and transposed the boxing backgrounds of the earlier film to that of a traveling circus. Bogart plays Nick Coster, hard baked boss of a mediocre roadshow whose convent-reared kid sister Mary (Joan Leslie, the crippled love interest of *High Sierra*) falls in love with Coster's lion-tamer, Matt Varney (Eddie Albert). Outrage at Mary's conduct veils Coster's own incestuous regard for her and when the lion-tamer resists his warnings to keep away from her, Coster devises a plan to murder him. Substituting a ferocious beast ordinarily kept caged for exhibition purposes for one of the performing lions, Coster inveigles the tamer to go into the cage with it. Varney is getting the worst of the tussle when the circus boss, appealed to on all sides to intervene, relents and dives in to save Varney at the cost of his own life.

Lacking the pace and punch of *Kid Galahad* , and with no Edward G. Robinson (whose central role in the earlier film he usurped) to draw out the worst in him, Bogart's circus boss is about as ferocious as the studio lions on temporary loan from M-G-M's 'Tarzan' backlot.

Eddie Albert, anticipating the dependable, but unexciting middle-of-the-road actor he was to become, is a vapid hero. Bogart is left to smoulder balefully at plastic images, which he is not convincingly good at, being an eyeball-to-eyeball actor and only capable of imaginative heights of menace and candor when there is a fellow-stalwart to bounce things off.

Monthly Film Bulletin noted: 'The restless,

"Paul Fabrini", Ann Sheridan and George Raft – [They Drive By Night] (1940)

colorful atmosphere of a traveling circus has been admirably caught in this tense though rather far-fetched drama, and the director has given each player full scope to develop his or her role in a plot which abounds in dramatic situations. Bogart as the hard, cynical Nick is an excellent contrast to Eddie Albert as the youthful and loyal Matt. Likewise against Sylvia Sidney's restrained and rather intense performance in the role of Flo is set the girlish freshness and charm of Joan Leslie as Mary.'

'A well-knit tale of triangular love,' said Today's Cinema. 'Humphrey Bogart's role is an admirable choice for the registration of smouldering arrogance which at times leaps into searing flame. The circus backgrounds are nothing if not vivid, complete with all the panorama of catch-penny turns, and the barker exercising his art on the sucker.'

The Wagons Roll at Night marked the effective end of Bogart's sourpuss period, covering some thirty films crammed into six years. Certainly, the quality was erratic, but bearing in mind the breathless rate of production (in 1937 he made seven films) and his lack of real choice in the parts or how he played them, there is a consistency of style, energy and professional technique, which in many of the films, was the only thing worth watching. He was to revert to his thirties type, the hard ingratiating single-dimension gangster, only one more time, in *The Big Shot* in 1942. But that after *The Maltese Falcon*, the turning point film which gave birth to the Bogart cult, and remains one of the three great cornerstones of our interest in him today.

PRODUCTION BOGART

DIRECTOR D. Mirunh.

CAMERAMAN M M n.

SCENE ECHOES OF RICK

TAKE 11

DATE M·1·80

While it was John Huston who sketched the outlines of the archetypal Bogart in *The Maltese Falcon* in 1941, it was Michael Curtiz who finished the canvas the following year by adding some subtle but classic shades of romanticism and personal commitment in *Casablanca*, considered by many to be the completest realization of the Bogart screen personality.

The character's weary resignation, his bleak detachment, aware of everything but participating in nothing, a guy who has turned off the tap because the hurt got too much and wallows in jaded resentment for the world at large – all these qualities fitted like a glove, Bogart's deepfrozen, battered face mirroring, we feel certain, an equally battered soul. Rick's penetration of our senses goes beyond an inspired script and craftsmanlike direction, his origins date back to the Bogart of *Bullets or Ballots* and *San Quentin*, where his cold impassive authority was forged under the tutelage of hard-driving directors like Curtiz, Lloyd Bacon and Lewis Seiler.

The Maltese Falcon, likewise, owes much of its strength to Bogart's gangster period, so that all Huston had to do to arrive at Spade's composite character was to overlay what existed with wit and cynicism – qualities abundant in Dashiell Hammett's original story.

The grand alliance of Hammett's hard-bitten words, Huston's interpretive visual sense and

Bogart's 'King Rat' heritage makes Spade the kind of flesh-and blood creation that could, and did, usher in an era and gave the world the most engaging of all private eye blueprints.

Like Spade, Rick functions from within, owing nothing to the world that lies beyond his personal horizon. It is a them-and-us world, where anybody who has not earned his personal allegiance can expect nothing. And woe betide those who blunder into his consciousness, or take for granted his patronage.

Applied to modern living, with the unsubtleties of the rat race, class and racial antipathy, our diminishing natural resources and the shift of political democratic power, Rick's I'm-All-Right-Jack mentality, that of the wary loner who sees the world stacking up the wrong way and wants no part of it, is very much a man of our times. We identify with this cynicism, and as the gloom deepens, so we embrace it more and more.

It is easy to see how Rick could be seen to a Europe locked in war to mirror America's political attitude, waiting and watching, avoiding a commitment of its youth and its resources until no alternative course exists.

Casablanca and its glum, world-weary hero was such a personal triumph for Bogart that for the next few years it overshadowed everything he attempted, as indeed, it tends to overshadow today everything else he did. At the end of *Casablanca* self-interest might induce Rick to hide out in Brazzaville for a while, as Renaud suggests, but with such a perfect formula and the cash customers baying for more, by 1943 it was no longer a question of when he would reappear, albeit under a new name, but how often. And the answer, if the outline story and vague political sentiments of *Casablanca* are to parameters, is in effect, three.

To Have and Have Not, the first and most important of them, began as a private wager between its author Ernest Hemingway and director Howard Hawks. The story goes that Hawks had been insisting he could make a good movie out of even the worst Hemingway novel. The author threw *To Have and Have Not* at Hawks and the challenge was eagerly grasped. For the screenplay job, Hawks brought together two distinguished scenarists whose work he knew well, having used each of them independently on several previous occasions.

William Faulkner was both novelist and screen writer, who had collaborated with Hawks

"Harry Morgan", Bacall and Marcel Dalio – [To Have and Have Not] (1945)

on *Today We Live* (1935), *The Road to Glory* (1935) and *Airforce* (1943). Jules Furthman had scripted for Hawks *Only Angels Have Wings* (1939) and *The Outlaw* (1940) the latter among the most publicized films of its day, introducing the 'mean, moody, magnificent' Jane Russell, and although billed as directed by Howard Hughes for Hughes' own production company, Hawks was the real creative brain behind it. Faulkner and Furthman would go on with Leigh Brackett to adapt Raymond Chandler's *The Big Sleep* for Hawks (and Bogart) two years later.

To convert the Hemingway piece to contemporary cinema, they moved the story base from Key West, Florida, to Martinique, the strategic French Possession in the West Indies and the villains of the original, Cuban revolutionaries and the idle American bourgeois

were transposed for the Vichyite French civil authorities. The central character, Harry Morgan was adapted along the lines of Rick in *Casablanca*, as were the settings, but with nine-tenths of the Hemingway novel abandoned in the transition, it is difficult to see how Hawks could go back and collect his bet.

Morgan (Bogart) plies his cabin cruiser for hire along the coastline of Martinique, mostly for private fishing trips. He lives at the Marquee Hotel, a shady bastion of international intrigue running under the surly nose of Vichyite police chief Captain Renard (Dan Seymour) in much the same way that Rick's Caf´e Am´ericain, operated by consent of Casablanca police chief Captain Renaud – even the names are practically the same.

The weasely hotelier Monsieur Gerard (Marcel Dalio), alias Frenchy, a staunch de Gaullist, pleads with Morgan to hire his boat to some French patriots converging on the hotel later, but the skipper is not interested ('I can't afford to get mixed up in your local politics').

In the hallway he gets the glad eye from Marie (Lauren Bacall), a footloose nightclub singer on her way home to the States from Trinidad, stranded in Martinique because she has run out of fare money. Later their paths cross when Marie lifts the wallet of an American fishing enthusiast who happens to be Morgan's current client, and Morgan lectures her ('You ought to pick on somebody to steal from that doesn't owe me money.')

The contents of the wallet reveal that his client was planning to abscond owing Morgan $800. Impervious to renewed pressure from the Free French ('I don't care who runs France'), he forces Marie to return the wallet, and blags the conman into signing travelers checks for the amount owed, but before the reluctant signatures are appended, a gun-happy police raid on the hotel, aimed at flushing out the de Gaullists, accidentally kills Morgan's client. 'He didn't write any faster than he could duck,' laments Morgan over the carcase.

Morgan and Marie are held for questioning by Renard and his dour monkeys, Lt Coyo (Sheldon Leonard) and a bodyguard (Aldo Nadi). Asked her business in Martinique, Marie informs them she came to buy a new hat, a piece of insolence that gets her a biff in the face from Coyo. Morgan thrusts forward, 'Go ahead, slap me,' he invites.

This, and much tossing to and fro of matchboxes, lighting cigarettes and languid patter establishes the main relationships. The cops confiscate all of Morgan's money pending further investigation of his affairs.

Marie, also penniless, hustles some booze, and more time-killing patter is leveled at us in the guise of a deepening relationship. The relationship is deepening, true, but off-screen, and much of the sleek squaring off that we see is the result of Bacall's part being hastily adjusted upward to take account of her new status after Bogart fell in love with her. Time, however, prevents her part being built up in other areas of the story, as in the action scenes outside the hotel, and the feeling generated by these rather tedious, self-indulgent scenes is one of impatience — firstly, because they slow down the bustling little yarn to a dead stop, and secondly, because Bacall's inexperience before the movie cameras is so obvious that, at times, she scarcely bears looking at.

Marie is determined to get back to the States, and Morgan, cleaned out by the police but with the Free French cash offer still valid, about-turns on his vow to Gerard. 'I need the money now, last night I didn't', he explains, putting his surprise decision in perspective. The mission involves the smuggling of two escaped patriots from a nearby island into Martinique from where a daring escape mission to Devil's Island to spring a top resistance fighter is to be mounted.

Morgan endeavors to ditch his alcoholic old partner Eddie (Walter Brennan) because of the dangers, but Eddie clambers back on board before the boat departs. One of his passengers turns out to be a woman, a discovery which irritates Morgan ('I don't understand what kind of war you guys are fighting, dragging your wives around. . .don't you get enough of them at home?'). Fired on by a Vichy patrol boat, Brussac (Walter Molnar) the husband, is seriously wounded, and has to be nursed in the hotel cellar. Marie, meanwhile has struck up a friendship with the hotel pianist Cricket (Hoagy Carmichael) and when Morgan returns, she flaunts her new job as a singer with the resident band.

Brussac's worsening condition and further entreaties by Frenchy persuade Morgan to try his hand at digging out the bullet and Brussac's wife Helene's (Dolores Moran) initial objection is smothered by one of the resistance group. 'She's not herself,' he explains. 'Who is she?' demands Morgan, flatly.

In the bar upstairs, the wily Renard plies Eddie with liquor to loosen his tongue unaware that booze has the opposite effect on him. When Morgan intervenes, Renard offers the return of his money, passport and an additional $500 blood money, but without success. Realizing that the cops are onto him, Morgan decides to vanish, news which genuinely grieves Frenchy, who had hoped to convert him gradually to the de Gaullist cause, and also Brussac, who openly covets his resilience ('I wish I could borrow your nature for a while, Captain. . .the word failure does not even exist for you.')

Their departure is forestalled by Eddie's arrest, and the police, alerted to the futility of getting him drunk, are instead withholding liquor in order to wring from him the information they need to put Morgan away. Trapped, but far from beaten, Morgan turns the tables on the gloating Renard, kills his bodyguard (spectacularly, with a gun concealed in his desk drawer which he fires up through the desk top) and urges him to make the move that will give Morgan an excuse to kill him, too. ('Go for it. Your boy needs company!') Renard is battered into signing harbor passes guaranteeing the Brussacs' safe conduct from Martinique, and into phoning through instructions for Eddie's release before being coldly abandoned by Morgan to a traitor's fate at hands of the freedom fighters.

Morgan throws in with the Brussacs whose mission in the area is to rescue a sub-Laszlo figure from Devil's Island ('a man that people who are persecuted and oppressed will believe and follow'), and his reasons, outlined to a delighted Frenchy are, simply, 'because I like you and I don't like them.'

Taken as a slice of popular entertainment, *To Have and Have Not* works superbly well because the elements making it up are nicely judged – too nicely judged, perhaps – and the plot moves purposefully towards the final settling up from the moment the gross Renard confiscates Morgan's cash and documents. The characters are sensibly balanced, and like many Hawksian sagas, the opposing teams exclude anyone totally good or irredeemably bad. The Vichyites act more like parochial bullies than real strong-arms, while Morgan's declared self-interest and money-motif (till the very end) makes him a scrappy hero by the standards of the period. In considering the loose political overtones – much looser than in *Casablanca* – Morgan's prickly lack of idealism for nine-tenths of the film is less acceptable than Rick's, coming three years later and with the war practically over. People who had been through hell and back found little to admire in a supposed tough guy 'minding his own business' in a safe, tropical backwater. Morgan demonstrates his shallow egocentricity on several occasions, dismissing the hostilities as a matter of 'local politics', refusing to acknowledge – as if acknowledgment would hasten commitment – that it is a global fight. 'You save France, I'll save my boat,' he tells Brussac, neatly summing up his priorities.

Because of the timing, his sideline attitude is incomprehensible. 'I don't care who runs France,' he declares but hasn't he read the papers? Not until the last ten minutes do we catch on to what Hawks and the rest of them are up to. By making Morgan fiercely neutral, oblivious to all appeals and patriotic sentiment, the anti-fascist statement contained is a personal one not a political one,

thus making the allegory between fascism and the surrender of individual liberty all the more devastatingly accurate, even though viewed as most of the movie is from Morgan's live-and-let-live viewpoint.

Integrity prompts the action against the evil abuses of power in both *Casablanca* and *To Have and Have Not*, but in the later film the outrage is a personal one, and Eddie is merely the tool to get at him. In *Casablanca*, Rick is not personally involved, his action is voluntary, out of affection for Ilsa and a genuine regard for what Laszlo represents. In *Casablanca* he could have done almost anything without compromising his personal integrity, whereas, in *To Have and Have Not*, because the seizure of Eddie is an act of calculated aggression against himself, the grim response (unlike the moral outrage which prompts it) is a spontaneous personal declaration of war.

Thus, in the final action, Bogart becomes the near perfect embodiment of all reasonable free-thinking souls when their freedom is encroached, striking back not out of sentiment or because he believes any of the crap put out by his own side, but simply because he refuses to tolerate erosion of his individual rights, and by that he includes those whose rights, like Eddie's, are more or less a matter for his judgment.

His demeanor in two earlier incidents clarify his thinking on what constitutes invasion of privacy. When Renard confiscates his cash during the interrogation, he accepts this matter-of-factly – it is an insult, but a man-to-man insult tolerable within the terms of their relationship. When Marie is slapped by Coyo, he reacts instinctively, taking her side, not out of bravado or even a feeling it was undeserved, but because the slap represents something outside his code of tolerable conduct, and that puts it into the context of an attack on himself, making the incident acutely personal.

In *To Have and Have Not*, Lauren Bacall made her debut and during the making of the picture Bogart fell in love with her, a fact that gives the film a pointedness it may not otherwise deserve. Ogling and circling each other like a pair of playful tigers, we are aware of being in at the birth of one of the century's great love affairs, and the knowledge colors our view of the movie.

Lauren Bacall was born Betty Joan Perske in the Bronx on September 16, 1924. The Bacall came from her mother's maiden name, Bacal (with one 'l') and the Lauren – which she despises – was studio manufactured. A former usherette and model, she was originally noticed on the cover of Harpers Bazaar by Howard Hawk's wife 'Slim' (the nickname Bogart affectionately calls her in *To Have and Have Not*) and brought to Hollywood by Hawks who lost no time in getting her before the cameras with Bogart. A Life magazine article shortly after the release of her debut film attributed her success to 'making the most of an insinuating look, a sultry voice, and an immense determination to succeed.' Her entrance is certainly auspicious, even audacious. Loitering in the Marquee hallway, she brassily demands a light for her cigarette from Bogart, who happens to be passing.

He pauses, grins, and tosses a box of matches at her. In that moment their future relationship is summarized. Later his synicism prompts her to ask: 'Who was the girl who left you with such a high opinion of women?' and he invites her to parade round him to satisy her mind that there are no strings attached. After a kiss, comes her rebuke, 'It's even better when you help,' and of course, the saucy, double-meaninged 'You know how to whistle, don't you, Steve. Just put your lips together and blow.'

If one can tear one's thoughts away from the Great Love Affair, the film works better when Bacall is not around. Her scenes with Bogart are stagey and loaded with bits of business but the main argument is, surely that they relate poorly to the central theme. Even after the build-up her part remains slight when its impact on the course of events is considered, and this is a cruel fact that no amount of padding or camera worship – and there is plenty of that – can obscure.

True, it is her lack of fare-money which prompts his involvement with the Free French initially, but one ought not to forget that after the surrender of his money to Renard he, too, is broke, and being the kind of man he is, the opportunity to earn some much-needed cash and at the same time score a point off the gross Renard would be difficult to resist. Bacall legitimises his actions in his own eyes, but despite his cautious, middle-of-the-path morality not for a moment can we believe he intends to keep off the grass forever.

"Harry Morgan" with Walter Brennan – [*To Have and Have Not*] *(1945)*

'Hooey but fun,' decided Time and Tide. 'I can assure you with authority that Lauren is torrid, sultry, slinky, exotic and wolverine. And you can have her. You can have, too, Humphrey Bogart, so he-man and monosyllabic that to heap adjectives would be offensive.'

News Chronicle called the film 'remarkable at least for the ingenuity and industry by which the original story and the individual rites of Faulkner and Hemingway have been rendered down into Hollywood basic. This indeed is just another of those resistance films from which it is about time we were liberated. Of all such pictures *Casablanca*, though no less false, alone has any buoyancy or self-relief.'

'Live steam too hot for kiddies,' thought Motion Picture Herald. 'The script, by Jules Furthman and William Faulkner, furnishes dialogue lines and business which vary from warmish to sizzling, Mr Bogart being on the receiving end of the lady's attentions and displaying considerably less of his accustomed reserve than usual. Some of this stuff verges on the mushy, by inadvertence and over-pretension.'

Sight and Sound noted: 'The whole to-do about this film seems to have centered around the debut of Lauren Bacall, a dour-faced vixen whom the critical boys have confused with Dietrich, the Empress Poppaea and certain of their more esoteric dreams. A more embarrassing portrayal of a *femme fatale* I have never seen. Like *Casablanca*, which it sets out to duplicate to the last desperate display of manliness, it will no doubt, earn a fortune.'

Kine Weekly agreed: 'Make no mistake, it will do a *Casablanca*. . .intrigue, dark dealings and romance have the Devil's own fling. It's life in the raw all right – the dialogue is as tough as the characterization and acting – but its many spectacular and arresting highlights are cunningly amplified and mellowed by masterly detail.'

Monthly Film Bulletin concludes: 'neither the plot nor the setting is convincing, and Humphrey Bogart has an over-familiar task as the toughly sentimental Harry. Lauren Bacall shows such real talent and personality as to maintain interest in a not very interesting film.'

'Sound, exciting war melodrama,' said the Daily Herald, 'with the magnetic Mr Bogart smuggling patriots away. At one point Lauren Bacall suddenly kisses him, "wondering if I'd like it" she blurts out. "What's the decision?" asks Humphrey. "I don't know yet." Regarding our Bacall, I don't know yet, either.'

The London Guardian wrote: 'Results are above average, especially for those who never saw *Casablanca*, a slightly better edition of the same kind of tale.'

News of The World called it: 'This rehashed version of an old Hemingway story. The story is the overtired *Casablanca* formula, in Martinique this time. How stale and remote is this fuss over Vichy police and virtuous loyalists, the inevitable pianist – charmingly played by Hoagy Carmichael – who sings nostalgic numbers while all France's fate is decided in a dirty bar!'

Today's Cinema noted: 'Newcomer Lauren Bacall certainly has an individual personality and invites one's interest in her future work, but it is Humphrey Bogart who dominates the portrayal and the artistes. Harry is another of those curiously intense characterizations in which he is so renowned a specialist. . .excellent melodramatic entertainment.'

One critic reflected: 'On these familiar paths, Bogart moves with his old nonchalant ease, and a pause now and then to take in Miss Bacall: still waters running deep as to be indistinguishable from stagnation, sulky fire running so hot as to be indistinguishable from a frost. I wouldn't say the film hasn't, in the absence of anything better, its enjoyable moments, but I could use something better.'

Tokyo Joe, the second of four films made by his own Santana production company and released through Columbia, is *Casablanca* with a distinctly oriental flavor. In this bizarrely cosmopolitan melodrama, Tokyo Joe of the title is Joe Barrett (Bogart), an expatriate American nightclub proprietor based in Tokyo prior to Pearl Harbor, married to the beautiful Trina (Florence Marly), a Russian. The nightclub is a great success, but after Pearl Harbor he ducks out on Trina, hands over the nightclub to his partner Ito (Teru Shimada) and volunteers for the American Air Corps, where coolness and sound judgment on numerous flying missions make him something of a celebrity.

After the war, he returns to his former haunts, hoping to pick up the threads of his life again. Trina, he discovers, is alive and well and living in Tokyo, married to Landis (Alexander Knox), a prosperous but shady lawyer. Joe's daughter Anya (Lora Lee Michel), whom he has not seen, lives with them.

Bitter at the way his personal fortunes have turned out, Joe attempts to win back Trina, but is betrayed into the hands of Kimura (Sessue Hayakawa), one-time head of the Japanese secret service and still boss of an active insurgents' organization, who threatens to make public Trina's wartime propaganda broadcasts, made under threat to their daughter's life, unless he obeys orders.

The orders entail securing an airline franchise, obtained with Landis's help, and the smuggling into Japan by air of three notorious Japanese war criminals. To protect Trina from exposure and arrest, Joe goes along with the scheme, but the kidnap of his daughter Anya, to tighten their grip on him, is the last straw.

He transports the fugitives, but engineers their arrest, and with Anya's life threatened, takes on the insurgents at their own nasty little game. Storming their hideout, Joe manages to rescue Anya, but is outnumbered and shot before help can arrive, dying with the mistaken idea that life with Trina and his daughter is about to resume. In fact, Trina has no intention of leaving Landis – a modest piece of truth, and certainly no secret, which to the bitter end Joe seems incapable of grasping.

For those who had blamed so many of Bogart's inferior roles on the slavish star system at Warners, where as a contract player he was often obliged to accept roles against his will, *Tokyo Joe* is a cruel slap in the face. Here is Bogart the Santana tycoon, boss of his own backyard, controller at long last of his own destiny, with the cream of Hollywood's diverse creative talents to choose from, in one of the most mawkish, sentiment-ridden and cliché-bound productions of the year. The film lacks practically all the incisiveness and most of the cleverly patchworked characters that makes *Casablanca* and to a lesser extent *To Have and Have Not* so interesting, and it seems all the more incredible that after twelve years on the inside at Warners, Bogart should discard so much of what he had learnt at the factory bench.

Tokyo Joe gives no relief whatever from Bogart's scowling, unshaven face as he lumbers around the Tokyo nightscape. There are endless ways in which the plot's early derailment could have been rectified, but instead it ploughs blindly along out of control, hoping at best for a soft belly landing. The talented international cast do what they can to help – notably Canadian Alexander Knox and Japanese Sessue Hayakawa (a one-time silent screen star most memorable in the 1957 war film *Bridge On the River Kwai* as

the unbowing prison camp commandant) but unfortunately the heavy task of redemption is beyond the lightweight support Bogart conscripts for this movie. Like the genteel, cold-eyed lawyer who moves in on the lovely Trina while Joe is off playing rough war games, Alexander Knox, who plays him, uses every moment available to him to good advantage, and makes Trina's loyalty to him despite Joe's gruff reappearance, the one startlingly commonsense feature of a movie loaded with trite, action-comic theatrics.

Motion Picture Herald wrote: 'Bogart again is the tough guy who can't deny his heart of gold in a standard melodrama set in Tokyo, where many of the background scenes were photographed. Performances are conventional, in the main. Knox with relatively little to do, delivers the best job.'

News of the World said: 'With anybody but Humphrey Bogart starring in this wildly fabulous drama of occupied Japan, it would have deserved and received an all-round thumbs down. It must be the tremendous sincerity and authority at his command that makes palatable such films as *Tokyo Joe*.'

'Escapism of a high order, and sure-fire stuff for Bogart fans,' announced the Sunday Pictorial. 'Joe dies surrounded by American officers with a bullet in his back and a look in his eyes which a doctor would recognize as oyster poisoning, but which his old fans know to be patriotism. Whatever his faults, the story packs a punch.'

The Herald noted: 'There are times, when I think Humphrey Bogart looks so tired I would like to offer him a chair to sit down on while acting. In this rather stupid, catch-as-catch-can drama he is so weary that Sessue Hayakawa, returning to the screen after thirty years rest, looks both boyish and spry by comparison. If you are one of those people who say "Oh I must go and see Bogart," then you must. If not, I think I should leave it alone.'

The Times found 'so many objections to this film it is difficult to know where to begin. It is throughout too childish to have any real political significance and had better be regarded as simply a tough fight by Mr Humphrey Bogart against (a) some wicked Japanese and (b) the bad relentless streak in Joe himself. Needless to say, Joe wins both battles. Sessue Hayakawa has little to say but his silence is even more eloquent than those clipped, monosyllabic wisecracks with which the screen Mr Bogart is apt to unburden his soul.'

'Lively action, strong suspense and sound

"Joe Barrett" – *[Tokyo Joe]* (1949)

acting,' cited Today's Cinema, 'are the basis of the film's considerable popular appeal. The title role does not provide Humphrey Bogart with many opportunities, yet the artist provides a competent and frequently incisive portrayal.'

The Star viewed the whole thing as 'pretty preposterous. . . "See you again soon Joe," says Miss Marly through her tears as Mr Bogart is carried out on a stretcher. Let's hope it will be in a rather better story next time.'

'Mr Bogart always looks as if he needs a shave and it suits him,' said London's Daily Express. 'I don't know any other film player who so easily suggests the possession of muscle, temper and dogged determination. He isn't a subtle man, but you could never call Mr Bogart a lah-di-dah.'

Sirocco, directed by Curtis Bernhardt (who made *Conflict*), and based on Joseph Kessel's novel *Coup de Grace*, follows the adventures of Harry Smith (Bogart), an American gunrunner in French-occupied Damascus in 1925. Smith supplies the Syrian Emir Hassan (Onslow Stevens) and his terrorists with arms and ammunition, at a tidy profit. Fighting guerilla

tactics on one hand and low morale among their troops on the other, General La Salle (Everett Sloane) leans on the slippery Syrians ('My soldiers didn't survive Verdun to have their throats cut in this stinking hole,') but despite the threat that 'for every Frenchman murdered five Syrians will be executed' terrorism flourishes, fanned by the black market supply of arms. French intelligence chief Colonel Feroud (Lee J. Cobb) is assigned the task of nobbling the gunrunners.

Smith is interrogated ('I believe in being co-operative, Colonel') and his checkered past – newspaperman, World War One volunteer, casino proprietor – rolled out for scrutiny. Noting his lack of political conviction, and indeed morality ('I've had them, they're left behind in America with my first wife') and a surly dislike of the French, who closed down his Damascus casino, Feroud decides that Smith is a man to keep an eye on.

The Syrians suspect him of fraternizing with the French and close the arms deal. Foolhardedly, Smith takes up Feroud's slinky Egyptian mistress Violette (Marta Toren), who is tired of Damascus low-life and bored, but afraid, of her influential lover.

120

Violette wants to kick the traces and sees Smith as a meal-ticket back to Cairo, but the gunrunner is in deep trouble, a fall guy between the opposing factions and eventually sold out by a flabby Armenian (Zero Mostel).

With two deadly scores to settle – the gunrunning and his affair with Violette – Feroud can hardly wait to blot him out ('I know I'm going to get shot, but not for running guns,' Smith tells him. 'I'm something special. I made a monkey out of you, I'm the guy who took your girl') but political expediency demands that Smith's value as a go-between is utilized. In return for an exit visa to Cairo, Smith is induced to set up a hush-hush meeting between Feroud and the Emir to see if a way can be found to stop the bloodshed.

The meeting is arranged, and Smith is packed ready to leave for Cairo when news filters through to the French headquarters that Feroud is a prisoner of the Syrians who are demanding a ransom of ten thousand dollars. Accompanied by Major Leon (Gerald Mohr), Smith attempts to get Feroud off the hook by again acting as go-between, but though the Syrians agree to release Feroud once they have the ransom delivered, they are by now convinced that Smith is a dangerous double agent and kill him with a hand-grenade before he can get away.

Harry Smith comes closer to Rick's persona than either the earlier Harry (Morgan) or Joe Barrett. Rick is the supreme opportunist, playing several ends against the middle, the superheel with the golden touch. Morgan is paler meat, his personal horizons do not extend beyond elementary physical comforts and the freedom to make up his mind, or not make it up, as the case may be.

Smith inherits much of Rick's past – battle-scarred war veteran, casino boss etc. – his taste for grimy, big-profit enterprises (and the nerve to go with it), and his ability to turn a fast buck. However, he has none of Rick's wry charm and sports his vocation a shade too openly, as well as being tactically naive when it comes to scoring minor points, alienating officialdom when Rick would have charmed it and bent it to suit his needs.

In *Casablanca*, when Rick thwarts one of Renaud's romantic conquests by fixing the roulette wheel so that the lady in question's husband makes a quick win, enough to get them both out of Casablanca, he is not tampering with something which matters very much to the French official. It is all part of the elaborate, raffish game between them. And besides, there will be another pretty girl along presently. By contrast, Feroud is violently jealous of Violette, and Smith's philandering seems to senselessly invite, in his own colorful words, 'a slug in the head and a hole in the ground'.

The hole in the ground is provided, at the end, by the Syrians, but having outlived his usefulness to either side it seems to matter little which one takes him out.

The movie is a tightly reined, but strictly mechanical excursion over old ground, and there are no commanding new sights or intriguing new signposts to divert one's attention as we pound over a bleak, familiar landscape. Grey interiors, dimly-lit streets after dark and a pageant of sombre characters flinging limp dialogue to and fro with little apparent enthusiasm (and who can blame them!) make us gasp for some light relief.

But, again, there is no relief from Bogey's weary, impassive features – attaining a composed lifelessness here not often encountered outside a funeral parlor – and when one considers the thrust and vitality of some of the earlier movies, and the acting heights yet to be exhibited (*The African Queen* , *Caine Mutiny* , *Sirocco*) is all the more disappointing coming from an actor who fought long and hard for the right to choose his material.

Kinematograph Weekly called it 'unblushing hokum. . .but impressive performances by Bogart as the tough hero, and Lee J. Cobb as a high-minded French officer invest it with some validity. The film contains slightly more talk than action but when it does flare up it very nearly sets the screen alight. The love interest intrigues, while the most is made of the hero's mighty sacrifice. Hardly vintage Bogart but nevertheless a powerful and popular brew.'

Variety noted: 'Curtis Bernhardt's direction pulls generally satisfactory performances from the cast, and had the story line been projected with more tension and clarity, the results would have rated more attention. The visual presentation interestingly depicts the locale, and it is given excellent low-key lensing in keeping with the yarn, but the story deals with sordid characters, with little redeeming uplift even in the climactic stretch.'

' *Sirocco* never completely realizes the drama and excitement inherent in its story,' wrote Motion Picture Herald. 'The picture is a slow starter, and when it finally does begin to

*"Harry Smith" with Marta Toren in a studio pose
for [Sirocco] (1951)*

move, the action is sporadic, never achieving the
suspense the situations seem to promise. Even so,
it is a satisfactory adventure-romance,
distinguished by the fine performances of Bogart,
Cobb and Miss Toren.'

Today's Cinema called Bogart's performance
'another of his specialist studies of tortured
intensity with only a rare smile breaking up his
accustomed expression of unremitting agony,' and
the movie 'an admirable thriller, especially
distinctive in its atmosphere of espionage and
intrigue.'

'The story follows a pattern familiar since
Casablanca,' said Monthly Film Bulletin. 'The
plot development is slow and lacks conviction, as
does the Damascus atmosphere. Bogart himself,
walking about the catacombs in a raincoat, gives
a performance so emotionless and expressionless
as to suggest a parody of his own acting
technique.'

Hollywood had shown interest in the war well before America's active involvement, and even in 1940, was casting glutinous eyes towards a blitzed Europe, in films like *Escape* and *Foreign Correspondent*. The propaganda machine was not slow to rumble out its biased commentary on what was going on, and separated from Europe by thousands of miles, it could only speculate, not always with pinpoint accuracy. But propaganda was the name of the game, and if all Nazi officers seemed cultured twits and lower ranks merely minor ghouls and idiots, it seems now an excusable piece of tail-pulling within the context of a wartime production code.

It is interesting to see how, as the war progressed, the character of the enemy, as depicted by moviemakers, changed from stupidity and greed to downright nastiness, taking in rape and sadism as a way of life. Common language, before America joined in the actual fighting, made its propaganda movies go down well in Britain; the Nazis were people who spoke in a ludicrous, jibbering way, and when America leapt – or was pushed according to one's point of view – into the war it was only right that its enemies were also people the propagandists and the caricaturists could really go to town on.

While the American cinema was prepared to invest the Nazi with a thin layer of civilized intelligence, Japanese soldiers were not even vaguely human. Squat, disgusting little sadists peering through horn rims, jabbering and

grunting like demented monkeys, this is how they were portrayed in endless war movies right up to the mid-fifties, and such is the unfortunate power of propaganda that quite a few of the older generation still manage to see them in this peculiar light.

War produces action and action creates heroes, thus in cinematograph terms the war years are important in understanding the nature of the modern screen hero. The pre-war hero, or matinee idol as he was sometimes called, was essentially clean-cut, with huge reserves of personal charm. John Barrymore, Warner Baxter, Warren William and Britain's Leslie Howard were paraded in tame, bespoke dramas, one after the other, like well-groomed, manicured poodles at a dog-show.

But when war started, audiences needed heroes who looked like they could stand up to rough treatment, guys who understood guns and killing, who could dish out anything that came their way and more. Who better, in fact, than our old friends, the gangsters.

In 1942, although it scarcely knew it at the time, Warner Brothers created the near-perfect symbol of cool, canny resistance, Rick of Casablanca, alias Humphrey Bogart.

Bogart's first encounter with fascists was in *All Through the Night*, the film he made before *Casablanca*, which also featured the latter's Major Strasser, Conrad Veidt, and which he reminds Veidt of momentarily in *Casablanca* when he says, 'There are certain sections of New York, Major, that I wouldn't advise you to try and invade!'

Bogart plays Gloves' Donahue, a Broadway gambler whose patch is infiltrated by enemy agents. A likable rogue, Donohue looks after people, like the friendly old baker whose cheesecake finds its way to all neighborhood caf'es, thanks to the gambler's persuasiveness. Stung by the baker's brutal murder, Donahue tracks Leda (Kaaren Verne) a mysterious lady seen leaving the baker shop, whom he suspects of involvement, to the caf'e of his former rackets rival Marty Callaghan (Barton MacLane), where he discovers she is a singer. The trail leads him into the twilight world of a gang of Nazi saboteurs led by Ebbing (Conrad Veidt), whose plan it is to detonate a ship in New York harbor.

Donohue infiltrates the infiltrators and, aided by a colorful retinue of Runyonesque characters who include William Demarest, Frank McHugh, Phil Silvers and Jackie Gleason, thwarts their little game, clinching a rather busy afternoon by sending the brains of the operation, Ebbing, to a watery grave in the very harbor they planned to destroy.

A good idea at the time, *All Through the Night* was unfortunately overtaken by events (Pearl Harbor) before its release, and understandably, the Jap attack dented the ability of an American audience to see the joke about an enemy, even a moderately comic enemy, planning to destroy a harbor. Nevertheless, the movie strides along at a canter, a better than average comedy-thriller which serves as both a witty send-up of the gangster genre, and a mild warning. Partisanship within the gangster world makes it easy to accept a story where they close ranks against shifty outsiders. Bogart and MacLane, lusty rednecks in four earlier movies, now wary bedfellows in an alliance to save New York, amuse because of what they have done before and what we know they will do again.

The Times noted: 'The film opens with a mingling of good comedy and a sense of menace and hints at exciting developments to come. It seems, in these early moments, that their pattern will not be too transparently clear, that imagination will play its part in them, and that a film as outstanding in its class as *The Maltese Falcon* may be in the making, but all too soon these expectations vanish and *All Through the Night* settles down to the familiar task of exposing Nazi agents.'

Another critic called it 'a thriller almost as exciting as the old *haute monde* of the gangster. The pace, the tension, the sardonic wise-cracking are all there. Except for some flagging moments halfway, the film tears along like its cars in the midnight streets; the thrills and the jokes have both been sharpened to a pinpoint.'

'Calculated to thrill the most blasé observer,' said The Cinema. 'Warner Bros have always been noted for their action pictures, but in *All Through the Night* they excel previous efforts for pace and vigor in a story that goes at a breathless speed from its amusing opening to its violent and spectacular finish. Bogart is splendidly suited to the role of the racketeer Gloves Donahue, entering into the spirit of the characterization with zest and enthusiasm. A cleverly treated and expertly directed melodrama.'

Daily Film Renter: 'There is little real plot, but tons of excitement of a familiar pattern. Bogart is, naturally, superior to his material. The rest of the cast enters into the rollicking, nerve-tingling proceedings with zest. If we have met them before, the adventures are thrilling and breathless.'

Monthly Film Bulletin decided that 'Bogart is as good as usual' in a 'reasonably well produced and directed melodrama. . .but there is nothing outstanding in the film.'

Across the Pacific was a spit-and-polish try by director John Huston to capture the verve and luster of *The Maltese Falcon* in a wartime setting. There were plans to reunite the four stars of the earlier movie in a straight sequel, taking up the pursuit of the priceless statuette from virtually where it had left off, but problems caused its abandonment – no doubt one of them being how to reintroduce Mary Astor after presumably 'taking the fall' for Archer's murder.

With the exception of Peter Lorre, the director and stars of *The Maltese Falcon* came up with *Across the Pacific*, a commendable but heavy-handled thriller if comparisons with *Falcon* are allowed (and how can they be avoided?). The story opens with the dishonorable discharge of US Army captain Rick Leland (Bogart) for misappropriating military funds. Disillusioned, he attempts to enlist in Canada but is rejected, and acting on impulse – or so we are snugly led to believe – books a passage on a Japanese freighter, the *Genoa Maru*, bound for Yokohama via New York, Panama and Honolulu. His fellow passengers include Alberta Marlow (Mary Astor) an enigmatic young lady from Medicine Head, Dr Lorenz (Sydney Greenstreet), a cultured Jap-lover ('to really know them is to feel the deepest affection for them') and his mysterious valet Tee Oko (Kam Tong).

Lorenz is impressed with Leland's detailed knowledge of armaments ('a 1918 flush-decker four 4-inch fifty caliber guns, one 3-inch twenty-three caliber anti-aircraft gun – not very formidable!' he observes slyly as a US warship overhauls them), but Alberta is casing him for other qualities, like chivalry, which do not materialize. 'Are you always blue?' he inquires as she sunbathes in the cold wind. Later, after a brief romantic interlude on deck during a storm she becomes seasick.

'Everything was going so beautifully,' he sighs. 'Why did you have to eat the bread pudding?'

Stopping off at New York, Leland meets Colonel Hart (Paul Stanton), an army intelligence chief, revealing what we suspected all along, that Leland is in military intelligence sniffing out a traitor. Back on board he feigns hatred of the uniform ('the brass-hats tied me up in pink ribbon and threw me to the wolves') and Lorenz nibbles the bait with a cash offer for information about defense installations in the canal zone. From a Panama-based contact, Leland learns that Alberta has made numerous mysterious trips abroad, which she is on the point of explaining to him later over a drink when, called to the telephone, she fails to return.

Although caught momentarily off-guard, beaten unconscious and left for dead by Lorenz when the true nature of his assignment is suspected, Leland manages to trace the subversives to a secluded plantation owned by Alberta's seedy, alcoholic father (whom she was innocently visiting all along). The rogues' intention, outlined by a startled Lorenz after Leland has caught up with the party, is to destroy the canal locks with torpedos dropped from a plane piloted by the strange Tee Oko from a nearby jungle clearing.

With a sudden onrush of the Errol Flynns, Leland disposes of the yellow peril, bringing down the evil midget Oko with a short burst of machinegun fire to the exposed torpedoes. Finding the defeated Lorenz attempting, but lacking the nerve to commit ceremonial Japanese suicide, Leland points to a squadron of US planes overhead and tells him, 'If any of your friends in Tokyo have trouble committing hara-kari, those boys will be glad to help them out.'

Huston keeps the actions, and the interplay of characters, very much in the *Falcon* spirit, even to similar snatches of dialogue.

As once again Mary Astor protests her innocence, Bogart mocks, 'You're good, Angel, you're very good.' Confronted with a robust-looking Bogart after leaving him for dead, Greenstreet concedes 'You are always furnishing surprises' – a line paraphrased from Gutman. The early scenes while the main protagonists are flippantly sizing each other up are quick and brash, and Bogart's pseudo-courtship of Miss Astor recalls their racy banter during the first half of *The Maltese Falcon*. It is a compliment to her holding power in *Falcon* that we are immediately suspicious of her from her first

"Rick Leland", Sydney Greenstreet and Mary Astor – [Across the Pacific] (1942)

encounter with Leland politely declining his offer to buy her a drink.

When she disappears and Leland is beaten senseless by Lorenz in her apartment, we assume that she has penetrated his cover and betrayed him, not because of anything she does, but because we expect no better of her. Her established innocence at the end is a genuine disappointment, like the anticlimactic revelation half-way through that Leland is a secret agent. So, too, is the unsatisfactory climax which turns Leland into a blend of Captain Marvel and John Wayne, thereby cheapening and distorting all that has happened before.

Allegedly, Huston wrote Bogart into that tight spot before departing impishly into the services, leaving replacement director Vincent Donahue and a gaggle of writers to sort out the muddle. The likelier story is that, with his enlistment imminent and feeling bored with his Humpty-Dumpty project, he simply pushed it off the wall, comforted by the knowledge that the heap of fragments could never be glued together in the time and limited budget available.

Bogart seems to share Huston's diminishing commitment to *Across the Pacific* with his earlier capricious tone congealing into glazed determination, and ending in acute horror, rather like someone driving leisurely along a quiet country lane who rounds a corner to find it terminated abruptly in a briar patch.

The Times stated: 'Here is a film which avoids the mistake that too often disfigures our screens, the mistake of making our enemies stupid and stereotyped. *Across the Pacific* strives successfully to tell a stock story in a fresh and imaginative idiom. Mr Bogart as the secret service agent, and Miss Mary Astor, who at one time appears to be working for Mr Greenstreet, have the advantage of good lines and intelligent direction.'

According to Motion Picture Herald: 'The picture is packed with interest, sticks to plausibility and delivers a punch. The story moves swiftly through surprises, captures, escapes, battles and thrills to an ending agreeable to everybody but Hirohito.'

Today's Cinema noted: 'This rather florid story of treachery in kid gloves has given John Huston every opportunity to exercise his talent. He is the master of those subtle touches that outline a character with economy of effort. Colorful backgrounds and snappy wisecracks contribute to the general entertainment, but an intrusive intermittent musical accompaniment does not encourage conviction.'

'A slow starter but its unhurried technique, neatly cloaked by a piquant love interest, more than justifies itself in the end,' wrote Kine Weekly. 'By punching with both hands and using its head and equally important, exercising a sense of humor between rounds, it represents thick-ear espionage fare of infallibly high-and-low-brow appeal. Humphrey Bogart contributes a cool and convincing portrayal as Rick.'

Monthly Film Bulletin complimented its 'many excellent and thrilling situations, some good lines and extremely able acting,' adding that Sydney Greenstreet's performance 'outclasses those of the other two.'

Daily Film Renter described *Across the Pacific* as 'a class picture which grips the imagination by its powerfully melodramatic story, its superb acting and its ultra-intelligent dialogue. As an example of directorial skill at its most intelligent it is a picture which could not be bettered. Amongst the melodrama are deliciously played, teasingly provocative love scenes, penetrating character sidelights, original and refreshing subsidiary parts, while all through it runs a vein of gently barbed-dialogue which is as lifelike as makes no matter.   .a treat for those who look below the surface.'

The Sunday Times called it 'a conventional spy story whose firm pictorial emphasis draws something new and stirring; a ship casting off, a man watching his shadower in a shop window – with such details John Huston turns a piece one might doze through into a piece alive and insistent of attention.'

Action in the North Atlantic, directed by Lloyd Bacon, casts Bogart as Joe Rossi, first mate aboard the liberty ship *Seawitch* under the command of skipper Steve Jarvis (Raymond Massey). Part of a task force in the north Atlantic bound for Murmansk, in the extreme north west of Russia, the *Seawitch* loses contact with the main convoy in heavy fog and, dogged by a persistent U-boat whose periscope the sharp-eyed Jarvis detects, the captain decides to change course in order to divert the enemy sub away from the main force.

The *Seawitch* cuts its engines to prevent sonar detection, and like two hungry sea monsters eager for the kill, the two vessels wait out the long night in eerie silence. By morning the U-boat has withdrawn, but merely as a prelude to a fierce aerial bombardment by the

Luftwaffe, during which Jarvis is wounded.

Rossi assumes command and quickly shows his mettle when the enemy submarine returns to gloatingly finish off what the air attack left undone. Deceiving the U-boat into believing that the *Seawitch* is mortally damaged – he even lights a fire on deck for effect – Rossi waits for the sub to surface to take a closer look.

When she eventually does, the *Seawitch* is waiting to ram her to the bottom of the sea, and quickly rejoin the convoy, now under Russian aerial protection, as it steams on towards Murmansk.

Action in the North Atlantic is a greater triumph for Warners' special effects department, supervised by Jack Cosgrove and Edwin B. DuPar, than for either star, with Massey, a superbly restrained and thoughtful actor, plainly more at sea than Bogart, whose portrayal of the impulsive first mate has some telling touches, like when he clobbers a loudmouth who is barracking the songstress at a seedy bar, never thinking she is going to lassoe him into marriage shortly afterwards.

Bogart and Massey make an excellent team, with Rossi's glib wiseguy masking an inner self-depreciation, and Jarvis, ponderous but goodnatured, ever ready to retrieve his maverick first officer from the debris, putting his life in order, his capabilities in perspective. Aside from the action scenes, which are vividly and realistically staged – at one point it seems as if the entire backlot must be ablaze – the 'inner story' of how an everyday guy is transformed by responsibility is feelingly and imaginatively sketched, as is its depiction of the hazards and loneliness of merchant ships in war.

The grim battle of wits between the *Seawitch* and the enemy sub (a similar showdown takes place between Robert Mitchum and Curt Jurgens in the 1957 sea drama *The Enemy Below*) is given a fine cutting edge by Lloyd Bacon's surehanded direction, which shrewdly avoids either synthetic bathtub heroics or maudlin sentiment. The test of the movie's heart comes during a burial-at-sea, when it would have been all too easy to relax the grip and slip from good taste to pious waffle, however the mood of restrained dignity is nicely kept going.

Even though, for obvious propaganda reasons, the Americans are shown as lusty men-of-action and the enemy, in the main, as a bunch of unsavory goons, the movie refrains from going overboard on the blood-and-guts. At times it manages to convey the mood of men in combat more skillfully than we have come to expect from movies of the period, as for instance, at the end, with one leg of the mission completed, Bogart remains slightly aloof from the movie's congratulatory mood, ruminating soberly on the dangers still to be faced.

One critic called it 'a story of the war as it should be presented, with human feeling, spectacle and strength of purpose. I cannot think I have ever seen more realistic battles, or lived so intimately with the characters who comprise the crew. Humphrey Bogart is at his best as the second-in-command, and Raymond Massey is excellent as the ship's captain.'

'Mr Bogart gives his usual superbly and minutely expressive performance,' noted the Sunday Times. 'This film, though overlong, is commonly above the general standard of American war films; it has many exciting passages. . .there is much that is convincing in the piece and not a little that is moving.'

'The bare title of this film cannot convey the unabated excitement that has been packed into more than two hours running time,' said Motion Picture Herald. 'It is a title which may profit by prominent display of the name Humphrey Bogart as the film does from his excellent performance in an unaccustomed role in an admirable and thrilling account of the men who carry weapons to our fighting allies.'

Today's Cinema noted: 'Warners say here just about all there is to say on the contribution to victory made by the Allied merchant seamen – and they say it superbly. They offer no study in facile heroics. . .but instead a realistic depiction of the hazards – vested with the screen's dramatic potentialities, of course – which are part and parcel of the Allied seaman's life in wartime, whatever his nationality. Bogart and Massey are first rate, but of course it is the action which takes precedence over all, and vividly spectacular action it is.'

Kine Weekly wrote: 'The heroic tale obviously inspired by fact opens and ends with some of the most exciting and realistic scenes ever presented on the screen of a lone ship's duels with U-boats. For the most part its profound, taut and breathtaking human drama springs from the brilliant way in which it cross-sections life above and below deck. Humphrey Bogart is excellent as Joe.'

Monthly Film Bulletin praised its 'exciting, quick moving action in which we feel we almost have a part. . .with a story which makes the most of almost every possible aspect of a sailor's life in wartime, Lloyd Bacon's direction has linked an energetic use of camera. A thoroughly good yarn.'

Sahara, directed by Zoltan Korda, is a visually stark desert rat drama, part tribute and part rally-round-the-flag, which examines the relationship of nations by throwing together representative individuals and stepping back to see if the ragbag comes to anything. Taking its inspiration from an incident in the 1937 Soviet film *Trinadstat* (English title *The Thirteen*), *Sahara* follows a group of stragglers stranded in the desert by the retreating Allied armies following the fall of Tobruk.

Star of the drama is the *Lulubelle* , a 28-ton US Army tank commanded by Sgt Joe Gunn (Bogart) who rather than allow her to be pressed into service by the all-conquering Panzers, heads her off into the desert vaguely on the heels of the retreating Eighth Army. Soon the *Lulubelle* has attracted a diverse collection of escapees and runaways – excluding one Italian prisoner – whom Gunn endeavors to bind into a small, viable fighting unit, but national barriers, clashes of temperament and a pervading sense of doom inhibits progress in this direction.

Inexorably overhauled by the advancing Germans, and weakened by sandstorms and diminishing water reserves, the exhausted oddball platoon stumble into Bir Acroma, a derelict caravan station, where fresh water exists but in limited quantities.

Soon a couple of unwilling extras have joined

them: a German pilot shot down while attacking them and a scout for a motorized German battalion, who reveals that an enemy battalion is just over the ridge and is desperately short of water.

Figuring that the advancing battalion is part of a massive clean-up operation heading for El Alamein, the last Allied stronghold, Gunn exhorts the diffident group to delay the Germans as long as possible at the waterhole, engaging them in a shoot-out – albeit a rather one-sided one – if necessary.

Realizing that the German contingent are unaware that the waterhole is dried up, and knowing also that it is only the promise of water which is detaining them, Gunn decides to fool them into thinking there is water aplenty, which he promises to share with them if they will only surrender, driving his point home by pretending to take a shower, making lots of gurgling noises and splashing about in fresh air.

The inescapable pitched battle occurs, but despite heavy losses, Gunn's dirty half-dozen hold them off.

With only one other survivor, the symbolic Britisher, Gunn braces himself for what is shaping up to be a final thrust, but instead of attacking, the thirsty Krauts are intent on surrender, in order to qualify for drinks all round. Ironically, one of their mortars has scored a direct hit on the waterhole opening up a fresh supply, so they are not disappointed. Later Gunn learns that the British have held El Alamein and

"Sgt Joe Gunn" and Bruce Bennett – [*Sahara*] *(1943)*

the tide of the war has turned back in the Allies favor, so the lives lost at Bir Acroma have not been in vain.

Sahara contains some of the more convincing desert fighting sequences to come out of Hollywood's war factory, and the hot, relentless desert, choking and blinding the dogged little troupe as they blunder on in search of water and shade, is most realistically caught in the harsh, impersonal camerawork of Rudolph Mat'e. Essentially a group effort, the movie suffers by making the individuals mere cyphers for whatever nationality they represent and being, again, blatantly propagandist in aim as well as presentation, the characters perform rigidly to expectation, for instance the dapper, bulldog British officer, likable Tommies, rugged, warloving Yanks, a spineless Italian, arrogant Germans and so on.

The story is merely an excuse to clip together representatives of the various nationalities, toss them into the North African melting-pot with the Yanks doing most of the stirring – although the Brits fare reasonably well – and deliver a tart little sermon on the need for men of good spirit to unite against the common foe. Unfortunately, the message is drilled home with a reckless lack of insight and the goodish adventure yarn, under the yoke of being politically meaningful, jettisons rather more of its logic than it can afford.

The business at the waterhole where a mere handful of stalwarts hold off hundreds of the enemy and dupe them into surrender on the slenderest of motives, simply cannot be taken seriously, and is an unforgivable lapse in a movie that constantly pins back the ears and eyes. Bogart's bullish tank commander suggests that Rick has wandered east from Casablanca to see what the fuss is all about, and in his lusty portrayal of a straight, non-conciliatory sort of guy who feels entitled to his square of desert because he found it first, smouldering with quiet determination that no way is he going to be moved on, Hollywood comes as close at it will ever get to depicting America's authentic fighting man.

Time Magazine noted: 'This story is told so expertly, detail by detail, that the whole unlikely affair seems believable. More than that – it often approximates hard and honest facts about war and about people. *Sahara* rings dozens of changes on old formulas, and in their simple way, they make more hard sense pictorially than most documentaries. Humphrey Bogart is the only well-known actor in the picture. To say that he is as good as the rest of the cast is high praise.'

'A straightforward narrative of excitement, heroism and devotion heightened by the solid performance of its star,' said Motion Picture Herald. 'Scenes of vast trackless wasteland and small but indomitable men are effectively caught in the camerawork of Rudolph Mat'e. These and the complete lack of unnecessary ornament add realism enough to the slight story to compensate for its heroic finale.'

Monthly Film Bulletin noted: 'Bogart struggles manfully with selfconsciously propagandist declarations on "why we fight". The acting is good but there are story weaknesses – notably having Germans attack the well from only one side when there are 500 Germans and equal or better cover for them from nearly every other direction.'

'The tale has the epic quality of adventure against tremendous odds,' wrote Today's Cinema. 'The hazards of heat and thirst in the Libyan desert are most realistically conveyed, while on the emotional side we have the domestic confidences of men who perhaps sense their approaching doom. But it is the sheer action and suspense and spectacle of heroic achievement that make the film most memorable. Humphrey Bogart enjoys another of his characteristically tough roles in the part of the enterprising tank sergeant.'

Bogart is the star of *Passage to Marseille*, directed by Michael Curtiz, but the center stage is not exclusively his, for he has for company three other *Casablanca* stalwarts, Claude Rains, Sydney Greenstreet and Peter Lorre. Freycinet (Claude Rains), liaison officer of a striker air base in rural England, is host to an influential journalist (John Loder) who vaguely recognizes Matrac (Bogart) a Bomber Command gunner at the start of a major sortie on Berlin. ('I've never seen a stronger face or a stranger one').

Freycinet volunteers Matrac's strange story, but not, as they say, for publication. At the outbreak of war, Freycinet and some other French army officers including Captain Duval (Sydney Greenstreet) return from the Orient to Marseille, via the Panama Canal, in a ship loaded with six thousand tons of nickel ore for the Allies. Duval, a Nazi sympathizer, barely conceals his resentment of his country's alliance with Britain ('The British will fight to the very last drop of French blood') and favors unconditional appeasement, an attitude that Freycinet and others, including the ship's captain, find wholly abhorrent.

Safely through Panama, they encounter a small boat adrift in the ocean with five semiconcious men aboard.

Their leader Matrac (Bogart) explains they have been without food for twenty days and without water for five, and later to Freycinet, whom he trusts, he admits they are escaped convicts from Devil's Island. The others are keen to get back to France to join the war, but Matrac, a former crusading journalist whose outspoken anti-fascist editorials have landed him on Devil's Island on a trumped-up murder charge, is sour and disillusioned and wants only to rejoin his wife Paula (Michele Morgan).

After the relayed news that France has fallen to the Nazis, the captain surreptitiously plots a course for England, but Duval cottons on and briefly commandeers the vessel. The convicts seize control, but not until the appeasers have radioed their location, which draws a German air attack onto them, Matrac's hatred for the

Germans surfaces after tracer bullets have killed the cabin boy, to the extent that he turns the ship's gun on the shot-down enemy air crew floundering in the water.

Ashore in Britain, Matrac enlists with Bomber Command, and his surviving compatriots eagerly join up too. On the night of the reporter's visit, as the story is brought up to date, Matrac's plane fails to rendezvous in time, because the gunner has been killed over Germany in an air duel with three Messerschmidts. At his funeral service, Freycinet reads aloud Matrac's final letter to his son, which was never delivered, urging the boy in later life to treasure and safeguard the freedoms he will inherit through the vigilance and sacrifice of others.

Today's Cinema opined: 'The crackling action and the patriotic motif will appeal powerfully to the generality of cinemagoers, who will also react to the dynamic all-round portrayals. Humphrey Bogart, for instance, plays the role of Matrac with a species of tortured concentration which does reveal something of the character's thwarted idealism.'
'Excellent characterization and skilled and

"Matrac" – [Passage to Marseilles] (1944)

imaginative direction,' wrote Kinematograph Weekly. 'Bogart gives a commanding performance as Matrac. . .a tough, exciting and moving tribute to the fighting French.'

Monthly Film Bulletin said: 'The film is meant as a tribute to France, but it does not altogether succeed. It is too dispersed in interest to grip the attention and its length is greater than its drama. The ending is given sentiment when it needed only simple dignity. Humphrey Bogart is sombrely monotonous as Matrac, but Michele Morgan gives depth to the very slight part of Paula, his wife.'

Chain Lightning, directed by Stuart Heisler, casts Bogart as Matt Brennan, a footloose ex-wartime flying ace who through a wartime buddy meets Leland Willis (Raymond Massey) an unscrupulous planemaker who hopes to make a quick sale of his YL-3 supersonic jet to the US Air Force. Willis sees that Brennan is just the man to help push the deal ahead, even though the machine is not yet perfected to the satisfaction of its fretful designer Troxell (Richard Whorf), also a one-time flying buddy of Brennan's.

Troxell implores Brennan not to report the plane ready for flight until the escape mechanism is put right, but the inducement of thirty thousand dollars to test fly from Alaska to Washington in a publicity bid to bring the lucrative deal forward, makes Brennan conveniently forgetful about the plane's lack of airworthiness. The flight is a success but Troxell, forced to rush his experimental work as a result of Brennan's vainglorious actions, is killed testing the faulty ejector equipment.

Brennan blames himself for the accident, a view shared by Troxell's girlfriend Jo (Eleanor Parker), formerly Brennan's lover in wartime Europe and now Willis's private secretary. Everything rests on a flying display for Air Force chiefs which Willis has arranged, and the routine stunts present no problems – which was all Willis intended to demonstrate – but as a post-script and a final vindication of Troxell's theories, Brennan ejects. The apparatus holds, and Brennan redeems himself in Jo's eyes.

The patent shock of seeing Bogart strapped inside a jet plane, giddily plummeting through the stratosphere, eyes owlishly peering out from under a space helmet, takes a while to adjust to, and as the reviews show, some of us never could. Judged on its flying sequences and technical merit, *Chain Lightning* is a topical, visual treat,

and the elation of space, speed and sudden danger is graphically conveyed. Out of the skies, the drama loses its touch, and much wrangling occurs to little purpose.

Eleanor Parker is a rather pretty, but negligible love interest, and Raymond Massey compares poorly with Ralph Richardson in a similar role in *The Sound Barrier*, as does Richard Whorf with Denholm Elliot's sacrificial lamb of the British film. But it is with Bogart that the real source of the trouble lies. He is plainly too old for the part, which probably explains why he looks so jaded and indifferent at times, forcing us to wonder more than once if he will manage to stay awake long enough to bring the plane down in one piece.

New Yorker noted: 'Humphrey Bogart, having by now exhausted almost all forms of ground-level strong-arm stuff, takes to the stratosphere in *Chain Lightning*! As long as he is aloft, flying everything from a B17 during the war to a jet plane afterwards. There is plenty of zip in the film. It gets pretty sad when it comes down to earth though.'

' *Chain Lightning* is one of those technically perfect pictures that Hollywood turns out almost automatically,' wrote the London Observer. 'You like this sort of thing or you don't. There is a love story that amounts to little and Raymond Massey who amounts to less. It seems a pity to waste actors like Humphrey Bogart and Raymond Massey on stuff like this where acting is the last thing that is required.'

Another reviewer said: 'In a variety of costumes, combining the less aesthetic aspects of a frogman's uniform and a rubber tyre, our Humphrey zooms through the stratosphere with smoke shooting out of his tail. I had hoped that when Humphrey started flying faster than the speed of sound, he might leave some of that hackneyed dialogue behind. But, unfortunately, those corny lines were right up with him all the time.'

Sunday Graphic thought much the same: 'Humphrey Bogart flies on a long-nosed jet plane (rather like a bad-tempered sword fish) at 1400 miles an hour. I can't think why unless he was trying to get away from the dialogue.'

Today's Cinema wrote: 'One would not say that Humphrey Bogart is ideally cast as the death-or-glory aviator. . .but the star again gives his celebrated study in tight-lipped taciturnity, and again his fans may well be pleased with the display.'

"Maj Jed Webbe" and June Allyson – [Battle Circus] (1953)

Time Magazine called it 'a great rush of supersonic hot air. With Humphrey Bogart as the devil-may-care test pilot, its heroics are built to scale. Tough guy Bogart still conveys emotion by baring his teeth in a grimace that gentlefolks reserve for the moment after biting into a wormy apple. And the girl for whom he carries a torch, Eleanor Parker, conveys no emotion at all.'

Monthly Film Bulletin said: 'In the intervals of a boorishly conducted romance, a demobilized, aging flying fortress pilot tests a fabulous new jet fighter. Without conviction or genuine technical interest, the film may have some superficial attraction for the scientifically curious.'

The Star added: 'Mr Bogart flies forward, backward, sideways and upside-down in a praiseworthy effort to sweep us off our feet with excitement, but I found it easy enough to keep mine on the ground.'

Battle Circus, written and directed by Richard Brooks, is an unmemorable pairing of Bogart and June Allyson of the husky voice, in a war hospital drama where love triumphs over the mud and bullets. Bogart is Major Jed Webbe, a weathered, disillusioned MASH surgeon, divorced, downbeat and rather grudgingly inclined towards women, who begins by bawling out rookie nurse Ruth McCara (June Allyson) for cutting corners, but softens when her effervescent do-good attitude begins to get through to him.

A fierce rainstorm, which demolishes the tent they are in, literally throws them together, but Ruth equates his reluctance to talk about himself as a sure indication that he is married, and they quarrel. Jed is of the view that both he and the human race are failures and that three wars and one marriage is enough for one lifetime ('Maybe whisky's as much a part of our life as war,' he muses, cracking open another bottle).

Threatened with a transfer by his commanding officer (Robert Keith) if the drinking continues, his attention is diverted by Ruth's courageous snatching of a grenade from a nutty Korean. Eventually hero and heroine jeep off into the sunset having patched up everything in sight, including their differences and Jed's drinking problem, and regaled us, till our teeth rattle, about the Futility of War.

As with *Chain Lightning*, the semi-documentary treatment and briskly topical story lend *Battle Circus* a tremendous visual momentum to which, alas, the fictional ingredients are never equal. Scenes of the frontline mobile hospital disassembling and repatching are both tense and actional, and one particular sequence showing a helicopter pick-up of front line casualties, executed under heavy enemy fire, is brilliantly done. The camera's fly-on-the-wall technique logs the field staff's battles against the lousy climate, primitive operating conditions, the patients themselves and their own resentments and frustrations in a vivid, impersonal sort of way which heightens and pinpoints its drama.

Director Richard Brooks canvasses the effects of war in a harsh focus and at times the newsreel sense raises the movie to the level of

William Wellman's *Story Of G. I. Joe* and Lewis Seiler's *Guadacanal Diary*, leaving one with a tangible taste of what it must be like at the mopping up end of the war game. Slipshod handling of the love scenes, however, which have neither wit nor truth, rob the movie of much of its merit, and one begins to wish, less than halfway through, that we could enjoy Brooks' Korea without having to watch Bogart – here hollowed out like a Hallowe'en turnip – or listen to June Allyson's reedy voice.

'Had there been a loftier central theme this might have been a pretty good film. Unfortunately Richard Brooks, who wrote the script and directed, seems to have been in much the same position as the hero of his own interesting novel, *The Producer*. He had to sacrifice truth to showmanship.'

The Spectator called it 'an extremely good Korean war picture. . .delightful and humorous at times, harsh at others, the picture is beautifully balanced. Mr Brooks takes no sentimental view of either love or war. Not a soldier of his dies leaving a message for Mum, no mention is made of his country or cause, not a flag is waved, not an axe is ground. The dialogue is both adult and charming.'

'Very novelettish warfare,' said Kine Weekly. 'The picture is presumably meant both as a pat on the back for army nurses and universal entertainment, but so much lassitude is allowed hero and heroine, portrayed somewhat self-consciously by Humphrey Bogart and June Allyson, that neither object is satisfactorily achieved. There is, however, no denying Bogart's popularity, and he may possibly pull the phoney opus through.'

One pointed critic wrote: 'Korea is a peculiar background for a flirtatious farce with June Allyson as a timid nurse and Humphrey Bogart as a doctor who won't take her "No" for an answer. Once this cheap flippancy has been discarded, the film shows war at its most spectacular and horrific.'

'The invasion of Korea by MGM, Humphrey Bogart and June Allyson in *Battle Circus* is one of the most unsavory of all the battles fought on celluloid,' commented News Chronicle. 'It contemptuously treats the sufferings of the soldier as mere props to the wooing of Lieut June Allyson by Major Humphrey Bogart.'

Today's Cinema called it 'a vivid impression of what must really be happening in Korea. The central love story, though slight and rather obviously contrived in some of its effects, benefits from fluent, natural dialogue and the polished personality of the stars. Humphrey Bogart gives a convincingly tough and intelligent performance.'

'What's wrong?' asked The Star. 'Chiefly, I think, the emphasis. A war in which men are fighting and dying becomes a mere backdrop for a boy-meets-girl story of the most trivial kind. . .'

Motion Picture Herald applauded its 'good box-office ingredients. . .engrossing incidents and well-timed flare-ups of excitement. However, the picture lacks an on-the-scene quality necessary to give it authenticity and complete credulity. . .Bogart hammers out his customary vigorous performance *in* a story as timely as a morning newspaper.'

Film Daily liked the way 'the current combat action in Korea is brought into vivid, exacting and even bloody focus. It is also a touching, happy love story that reaches that estate after considerable trial, perhaps even error, but with telling understanding.'

Variety said: 'Richard Brooks scripted and directed with varying and rather stock results. Bogart and Miss Allyson make a good, if incongruous, romantic team.'

The Times declared: 'The truth is that the formula of mixing war and romance, of using the battlefield and the casualty station as background for the amorous manoeuvres of conventional hero and heroine, here in the guise of surgeon and nurse, is distasteful. In one or two semi-documentary scenes the film achieves interest and dignity but such scenes are all too few.'

Others also took a tough line: '*Battle Circus* ruins an effective and sincere semi-documentary tribute to the US Medical Service in Korea by casting a galaxy of showgirls as nurses and cooking up a glutinous box-office love affair between Bogart and June Allyson. And if war must be made into a circus, then we must expect circus girls, however thinly disguised they may be as Army nurses.'

The Left Hand of God opens on a wildly intriguing note, with Bogart astride a wretched-looking mule clad in priestly black with just the suggestion of a revolver beneath the ill-fitting cassock. This, we discover, is outback China in 1947 and Bogart, as Jim Carmody, is a captured World War II flyer who dons the priest's disguise to evade the despotic Chinese warlord Mieh Yang (Lee J. Cobb) and the role of 'military adviser' to Yang's thuggish private army which he has been forced to fulfil since capture three years before.

An incident which results in the death of a Catholic priest en route to a remote mission colony gives Carmody his chance of escape, and masquerading as the replacement priest, he presents himself to Dr David Sigman (E. G. Marshall) the mission doctor, and his wife Beryl (Agnes Moorehead), at St Mary's Mission. His unpriestly demeanor does not pass unnoticed ('Work sure piles up,' he growls on hearing the confession line-up has started), nevertheless with the help of the mission library and some thundering good luck he gets by, and even manages to recharge the badly neglected community spirit with his unorthodox, and some might think refreshingly different, attitude towards saving souls.

Not everyone approves but mission nurse Ann Scott (Gene Tierney) does, from a safe distance.

Carmody finds himself strongly attracted to her, but unable to express his feelings for fear of blowing his cover, retreats grimly under the sign of the cross. Eventually tiring of the masquerade, he confesses his true identity in a letter to the Bishop, but communications being what they are in remote China, before the Bishop can get his representative along to sort out the mess, the vengeful Yang catches up with Carmody, surrounding the village and threatening to burn the place down.

Knowing Yang to be a compulsive gambler, Carmody challenges the bandit chief to a friendly game of dice, gambling five more years of uncomplaining service against freedom for himself and the village. Naturally, Carmody wins, and Yang, who cannot escape the parallel between losing two throws out of two and his own wickedness, withdraws his robbers from the village, a Somewhat Better Person. The phoney priest is the toast of the village until the Bishop's representative (Carl Benton Reid) arrives to ceremoniously unfrock him, but this late in the day, it scarcely matters. His display of true grit has made him a hero to the entire village, and an immediate compensation for losing the cloth materializes in the shape of Miss Scott, who can scarcely believe her good luck.

Bogart astride a sad looking mule (actually, their expressions are quite similar) is not a pretty sight. Neither is an unrecognizably almond-eyed Lee J. Cobb, sporting a Telly Savalas tonsure.

The movie aspires to be several things which it plainly is not, but that does not mean it is totally dispossessed of entertainment value. Viewed as a quaint variation on the standard western theme, it works relatively well. The hardfaced, guntoting stranger rides into town and endears himself to the local populace before the evil land-baron muscles in to hold the town for ransom. In a showdown the stranger wrests the township from the badman's clutches, later to reveal that he is a wanted man, but the grateful townsfolk rally to square things with the impassive lawman who arrives with a warrant.

At this simple level, *The Left Hand of God* is good clean fun and moderately inoffensive, with novel and realistic backgrounds to hold it up where it occasionally sags. Alas, the film seems to have convinced itself it is on the verge of being something deeper, and pokes around at messy theological questions which it has not a hope of doing anything with, even if it did manage to roll them over. Then having stirred them slightly, it takes fright and pulls back, leaving several rather sombre men in black stranded like stragglers from a vicarage outing who have missed the coach home. Bogart's playing is cleverly modulated, and he copes with the build-up of complications that result from his masquerade with just the right mixture of breezy confidence and dry candor. The romance they dare not show is mandatorily a tepid affair, a play-off of coy looks and seductive silences, with Gene Tierney over-anxious to show herself as not one of those profane priest-groupies and Bogart hinting broadly that he is fair game without actually putting himself in the window.

At the end, he labors to be nice, presumably indicating that the cloth affects for the good all who come into proximity with it. It is just possible he is trying to tell us that man's inner good equips him for things that look daunting at a distance, but are easy when the secret of one's inner resources are revealed. Then again, he might simply be saying 'don't believe a word of this mindless crap, for I certainly don't'. *The Left Hand of God* is that kind of picture, you pays your money and takes your choice. As we leave Bogart and his moist, bloodhound eyes contemplating the future, which presumably includes a steady job and marriage to the characterless Miss Scott, we come to the inescapable conclusion that he would have been much better off with Lee J. Cobb any day.

The London Daily Mail wrote: ' *In The Left*

Hand of God, Bogart has to start with three enemies – China, temptation, and most of the clich'es ever used in films about missionaries on foreign soil. Halfway through he tears off his collar revealing himself for what he truly is, a man without a collar. On the final fadeout, Mr Bogart is seen riding off to apologize to the local bishop for profaning the cloth. Since he was in the mood for apology I can't see why he should have stopped there.'

'Not by any means a great film, nor is it particularly profound, but it does try to be honest according to its lights and Mr Edward Dmytryk directs it with a straightforward simplicity,' noted The Times. 'Mr Bogart is no mean actor, and he does by a rigid economy of means succeed in suggesting that some sort of change of heart is taking place beneath the rugged exterior.'

One reviewer thought it was 'unintentionally the year's best comedy. Mr Bogart looks and acts about as priestly as 'Legs' Diamond.'

Tribune asked its readers: 'Have you ever in your wildest dreams expected to see Humphrey Bogart in the vestments of a Catholic priest delivering a sermon in impeccable Chinese? You can see this and much more in *The Left Hand of God*, a collector's piece for connoisseurs of the outrageous.'

'A smoothly, unthinking sort of cinemascope entertainment that might be expected with Bogey on the prowl,' said another. 'It seems unpleasing of a film to risk blasphemy at the outset and then to shirk the issue by fobbing us off with triviality.'

Variety thought: 'There are a number of scenes and incidents that strain the imagination. While at first glance, it's difficult to picture Bogart as a priest, his smooth portrayal of a spurious man of cloth is a compliment to his acting.'

Hollywood Reporter noted: 'My personal feeling is that this is one of Bogart's finest performances. He manages to be inspirational without being preachy, a thing rare in religious pictures.'

'A completely absorbing and thoroughly adult film,' was Film Daily's view. 'Although a first impression, after seeing Bogart in the robes of a priest, might be to imagine a routine religious picture, the plot involves more deception than devotion, more chance than conscience, more force than faith. Alfred Hayes' screenplay has brought forth these qualities straightforwardly.'

'Powerful, moving and thoroughly thought-provoking entertainment,' decided Today's Cinema. 'Little action, but the off-beat character of the story holds compelling and sustained interest. Bogart plays with great sincerity but with less authority than he can usually command.'

Monthly Film Bulletin listed its main drawbacks as 'obscure character motivation and an unpleasant mock religiosity in the worst Hollywood tradition. One suspects that the original novel may have provided more detailed and logical characterization than is apparent in the film's script – Carmody's allegiance to the Chinese War Lord is never satisfactorily explained – and Bogart's tired and uneasy playing fails to suggest the character's dilemma. Edward Dmytryk's handling of this theme displays little style or distinction.'

Two British newspapers had the final say. The Guardian summed it up as 'mawkish, silly and offensive,' while the Daily Herald noted: 'Not bad, but not very Bogart.'

PRODUCTION **BOGART**
DIRECTOR *D. Maranah.*
CAMERAMAN *Mm n.*
SCENE
TAKE

THEATRE CAREER

DATE *6·1·30*

2 January 1922. **DRIFTING**
Melodrama in six scenes by John Colton and D. H. Andrews. Presented at the Playhouse Theatre, New York. Producer, William A. Brady. Director, John Cromwell. 63 performances.
    Alice Brady (Cassie Cook), Humphrey D. Bogart (Ernie Crockett), H. Mortimer White (Deacon Cook), Robert Warwick (Badlands McKinney), Lumsden Hare, etc.

16 October 1922. **SWIFTY**
Comedy in three acts by John Peter Toohey and W. C. Percival. Presented at the Playhouse Theatre, New York. Producer, William A. Brady. Director, John Cromwell.
    Hale Hamilton (Swifty Morgan), Frances Howard (Miriam Proctor), Humphrey Bogart (Tom Proctor), William Holden (Jefferson Proctor), Robert Ayrton (Milton), Margaret Mosier (Alice), Grace Goodhall (Mrs Kimball), Elmer Nicholls (Chauffeur).

26 November 1923. **MEET THE WIFE**
Comedy in three acts by Lynn Starling. Presented at the Klaw Theatre, New York. Produced by Rosalie Stewart and French. 232 performances.
    Mary Boland (Gertrude Lennox), Clifton Webb (Victor Staunton), Ernest Lawford (Philip Lord), Charles Dalton (Harvey Lennox), Eleanor Griffith (Doris Bellamy), Humphrey Bogart (Gregory Brown), Patricia Calvert (Alice), Charles Bloomer (William).

1 September 1924. **NERVES**
War drama by John Farrar and Stephen Vincent Benet. Presented at the Comedy Theatre, New York. Producer, William A. Brady. Director, William A. Brady Jr. 16 performances.
    Winifred Lenihan (Peggy Thatch), Kenneth MacKenna (Jack Coates), Paul Kelly (Ted Hill), Humphrey Bogart (Bob Thatch), Mary Phillips (Jane), Walter Baldwin (Rook).

26 January 1926. **HELL'S BELLS**
Comedy by Barry Connors. Presented at Wallacks Theatre, New York. Producer, Herman Gantvoort. Director, John Hayden. 120 performances.
    Tom H. Walsh ('Jap' Stillson), Eddie Garvey (D. O'Donnell), Shirley Booth (Nan Winchester), Olive May (Mrs Buck), Humphrey Bogart (Jimmy Todhunter), Camilla Crume (Mrs Amos Todhunter), Virginia Howell (Abigail Stellson), Violet Dunn (Gladys Todhunter).

7 September 1925. **CRADLE SNATCHERS**
Comedy in Three Acts by Russel Medcraft and Norma Mitchell. Presented at the Music Box Theatre, New York. Producer, Sam H. Harris. Director, Sam Forrest. 332 performances.
    Mary Boland (Susan Martin), Edna May Oliver (Ethel Drake), Margaret Dale (Kitty Ladd), Humphrey Bogart (Jose Vallejo), William Barton (Roy Ladd), Cecil Owen (George Ladd), Stanley Jessup (Howard Drake).

9 June 1927. **BABY MINE**
Comedy in Three Acts by Margaret Mayo. Presented at the 46th Street Theatre, New York. Produced by John Tuerk. 12 performances.
    Roscoe 'Fatty' Arbuckle (Jimmy Jenks), Lee Patrick (Zoe Hardy), Humphrey Bogart (Alfred Hardy), W. J. Paul (Hardy's secretary), W. J. Brady (Michael O'Flaherty), etc.

9 April 1928. **SATURDAY'S CHILDREN**
Comedy in Three Acts by Maxwell Anderson. Presented at the Actors Theatre, New York.* Directed by Guthrie McClintic. 310 performances.
    Ruth Gordon (Bobby), Humphrey Bogart (Rims O'Neil), Ruth Hammond

(Florrie Sands), Richard Barbee (Willie Sands), Grace Roth Henderson (Mrs Halevy), Fredrick Perry (Mr Halevy), Anne Tonetti (Mrs Gorlick).

11 January 1928. **SKYROCKET**
Comedy in Three Acts by Mark Reed. Presented at the Lyceum Theatre, New York. Producers, Gilbert Miller and Guthrie McClintic. Director, Guthrie McClintic.
    Humphrey Bogart (Vic Ewing), Mary Phillips (Del Ewing), J. C. Nugent (Mr Ewing), Howard Freeman (Homer Bemis), Ian Wolfe (Frank Greer), Dorothy Bigelow (Kitty Marsh).

6 August 1929. **IT'S A WISE CHILD**
Comedy in Three Acts by Laurence E. Johnson. Presented at the Belasco Theatre, New York. Producer and director, David Belasco. 378 performances.
    Mildred McCoy (Joyce Stanton), Humphrey Bogart (Roger Baldwin), Harlan Briggs (G. A. Appleby), Minor Watson (James Stevens), Helen Lowell (Mrs Stanton), Sidney Toler (Cool Kelly), Porter Hall (Otho Peabody).

3 December 1931. **AFTER ALL**
Comedy in Three Acts by John Van Druten. Presented at the Booth Theatre, New York. Producer, Dwight Deere Wiman. Director, Auriol Lee. 20 performances.
    Edmund George (Ralph Thomas), Margaret Perry (Phyllis Thomas), Helen Haye (Mrs Thomas), Walter Kingsford (Mr Thomas), Humphrey Bogart (Duff Wilson), etc.

11 October 1932. **I LOVED YOU WEDNESDAY**
Romantic comedy in one prologue and Three Acts by Molly Ricardel and William Du Bois. Presented at the Harris Theatre, New York. Producer, Crosby Gaige. Director, Worthington Milner. 63 performances.
    Frances Fuller (Victoria Meredith), Humphrey Bogart (Randall Williams), Rose Hobart (Cynthia Williams), Jane Seymour (Dr. Mary Hansen), Henry O'Neill (Philip Fletcher), Henry Fonda (Eustace), Henry Bergman (Eddie).

15 November 1932. **CHRYSALIS**
A Melodrama in Ten Scenes by Rose Albert Porter. Presented at the Martin Beck Theatre, New York. Producers, Martin Beck, Lawrence Langner and Theresa Helburn. Director, Theresa Helburn. 23 performances.
    Margaret Sullivan (Lyda Cose), Osgood Perkins (Michael Averill), Humphrey Bogart (Don Ellis), Elisha Cook Jr. (Honey Rogers), June Walker (Eve Haron), Lily Cahill (Elizabeth Cose), Elia Kazan (Louis), Mary Orr (Ray).

2 March 1933. **OUR WIFE**
Comedy in Three Acts by Lynn Mearson and Lilian Day. Presented at the Booth Theatre, New York. Producers, Thomas J. R. Brotherton and Abe H. Halle. 20 performances.
    Rose Hobart (Margot Drake), Humphrey Bogart (Jerry Marvin), June Walker (Barbara Marvin), Edward Raquello (Antonio Di Mariano).

8 May 1933. **LA MASCHERA E IL VOLTE (THE MASK AND THE FACE)**
Comedy by Luigi Chiarelli, translation by W. Somerset Maugham. Presented at the Guild Theatre, New York. Producers, the Theatre Guild. Director, Philip Moeller. 40 performances.
    Stanley Ridges (Count Paulo Grazia), Shirley Booth (Elisa Zanotti), Humphrey Bogart (Luciano Spina), Judith Anderson (Savina Grazia), Leo G. Carroll (Cirillo Zanotti), Ernest Cossart, etc.

17 May 1934. **INVITATION TO A MURDER**
Murder mystery in Three Acts by Rufus King. Presented at the Masque Theatre, New York. Producer, Ben Stein. Director, A. H. Van Buren. 37 performances.
    Gale Sondergaard (Lorinda Channing), Walter Abel (Dr. Linton), Humphrey Bogart (Horatio Channing), Jane Seymour (Jeanette Thorn), etc.

7 January 1935. **THE PETRIFIED FOREST**
Drama in Two Acts by Robert E. Sherwood. Presented at the Broadhurst Theatre, New York. Producers, Gilbert Miller, Arthur Hopkins and Leslie Howard. Director, Arthur Hopkins. 181 performances.
    Leslie Howard (Alan Squier), Peggy Conklin (Gabrielle Maple), Charles Dow Clarke (Grandpa Maple), Frank Milan (Boze Hertzlinger), Blanche Sweet (Mrs Chisholm), Humphrey Bogart (Duke Mantee), Walter Vonnegut (Jason Maple), Tom Fadden (Ruby), Ross Hertz (Jackie), Robert Hudson (Mr Chisholm), John Alewander (Joseph), etc.

1930. **BROADWAY'S LIKE THAT** (Vitaphone Varieties No. 960)
Ruth Etting, Humphrey Bogart, Joan Blondell.
Produced by Vitaphone Corporation. Distributed by Warner Brothers.
Director-in-chief, Murray Roth. Story and dialogue by Stanley Rauh. Musical director, Harold Levey. Release Date, March 1930. Running time, 10 minutes.

1930. **A DEVIL WITH WOMEN** (Fox)
Victor McLaglen (Jerry Maxton), Mona Maris (Rosita Fernandez), Humphrey Bogart (Tom Standish), Luana Alcaniz (Dolores), Michael Vavitch (Morloff), Soledad Jiminez (Jiminez), Mona Rico (Alicia), John St. Polis (Don Diego), Robert Edeson (General Garcia).
Directed by Irving Cummings. Associate producer, George Middleton. Screenplay by Dudley Nichols and Henry M. Johnson. Based on the novel *Dust and Sun* by Clement Ripley. Director of photography, Arthur Todd. Music by Peter Brunelli. Film editor, Jack Murray. Art director, William Darling. Sound recorders, E. Clayton Ward and Harry M. Leonard. Song, 'Amor Mio' by James Monaco and Cliff Friend. Release Date, November 1930. Running time, 76 minutes.

1930. **UP THE RIVER** (Fox)
Spencer Tracy (St. Louis), Claire Luce (Judy), Warren Hymer (Dannemora Dan), Humphrey Bogart (Steve), William Collier, Sr. (Pop), Joan Marie Lawes (Jean), George MacFarlane (Jessup), Gaylord Pendleton (Morris), Sharon Lynn (Edith LaVerne), Noel Francis (Sophie), Goodee Montgomery (Kit), Robert Burns (Slim), John Swor (Clem), Robert E. O'Connor (The Warden), Louise MacIntosh (Mrs Massey), Richard Keene (Dick), Johnnie Walker (Happy), Pat Somerset (Beauchamp), Morgan Wallace (Frosby), Edythe Chapman (Mrs Jordan), Althea Henly (Cynthia), Keating Sisters (May and June), Joe Brown (Deputy Warden,) Wilbur Mack (Whiteley), Harvey Clarke (Nash), Carol Wines (Daisy Elmore), Adele Windsor (Minnie), Mildred Vincent (Annie).
Directed by John Ford. Original screenplay by Maurine Watkins. Director of photography, Joseph August. Staged by William Collier, Sr. Film editor Frank Hull. Sound recorder, W. W. Lindsay, Jr. Release Date, October 1930. Running time, 92 minutes.

1931. **BODY AND SOUL** (Fox)
Charles Farrell (Mal Andrews), Elissa Landi (Carla), Humphrey Bogart (Jim Watson), Myrna Loy (Alice Lester), Donald Dillaway (Tap Johnson), Craufurd Kent (Major Burke), Pat Somerset (Major Knowls), Ian MacLaren (General Trafford-Jones), Dennis D'Auburn (Lieutenant Meggs), Douglas Dray (Zane), Harold Kinney (Young), Bruce Warren (Sam Douglas).
Directed by Alfred Santell. Screenplay by Jules Furthman. From the play *Squadrons* by A. E. Thomas, based on the story "Big Eyes and Little Mouth" by Elliott White Springs. Director of photography, Glen MacWilliams. Music by Peter Brunelli. Film editor, Paul Weatherwax. Art director, Anton Grot. Special effects by Ralph Hammeras. Sound recorder, Donald Flick. Technical Adviser, Bogart Rogers. Release Date, February 1931. Running time, 83 minutes.

1931. **BAD SISTER** (Universal)
Conrad Nagel (Dick Lindley), Sidney Fox (Marianne Madison), Bette Davis (Laura Madison), ZaSu Pitts (Minnie), Slim Summerville (Sam), Charles Winninger (Mr. Madison), Emma Dunn (Mrs Madison), Humphrey Bogart (Valentine Corliss), Bert Roach (Wade Trumbull), David Durand (Hedrick Madison).
Directed by Hobart Henley. Produced by Carl Laemmle, Jr. Scenario by Raymond L. Schrock and Tom Reed. Dialogue by Edwin H. Knopf. Based on the story "The Flirt" by Booth Tarkington. Director of photography, Karl Freund. Film editor, Ted Kent. Sound recorder, C. Roy Hunter. Release Date, March 1931. Running time, 71 minutes.

1931. **WOMEN OF ALL NATIONS** (Fox)
Victor McLaglen (Sergeant Flagg), Edmund Lowe (Sergeant Quirt), Greta Nissen (Elsa), El Brendel (Olsen), Fifi Dorsay (Fifi), Marjorie White (Pee Wee), T. Roy Barnes (Captain of Marines), Bela Lugosi (Prince Hassan), Humphrey Bogart (Stone), Joyce Compton (Kiki), Jesse DeVorska (Izzie), Charles Judels (Leon), Marion Lessing (Gretchen), Ruth Warren (Ruth).
Directed by Raoul Walsh. Original screenplay by Barry Connors. Based on the characters created by Laurence Stallings and Maxwell Anderson. Director of photography, Lucien Andriot. Music by Reginald H. Bassett. Film editor, Jack Dennis. Art director, David Hall. Sound recorder, George H. Leverett. Musical director, Carli D. Elinor. Production manager, Archibald Buchanan. Release Date, May 1931. Running time, 72 minutes.

1931. **A HOLY TERROR** (Fox)
George O'Brien (Tony Bard), Sally Eilers (Jerry Foster), Rita LaRoy (Kitty Carroll), Humphrey Bogart (Steve Nash), James Kirkwood (William Drew), Stanley Fields (Butch Morgan), Robert Warwick (Thomas Woodbury), Richard Tucker (Tom Hedges), Earl Pingree (Jim Lawler).
Directed by Irving Cummings. Associate producer, Edmund Grainger. Scenario by Ralph Block. Dialogue by Alfred A. Cohn and Myron Fagan. Based on the novel *Trailin'* by Max Brand. Director of photography, George Schneiderman. Film editor, Ralph Dixon. Sound recorder, Donald Flick. Release Date, July 1931. Running time, 53 minutes.

1932. **LOVE AFFAIR** (Columbia)
Dorothy MacKaill (Carol Owen), Humphrey Bogart (Jim Leonard), Jack Kennedy (Gilligan), Barbara Leonard (Felice), Astrid Allwyn (Linda Lee), Bradley Page (Georgie), Halliwell Hobbes (Kibbee), Hale Hamilton (Bruce Hardy), Harold Minjir (Antone).
Directed by Thornton Freeland. Adaptation and dialogue by Jo Swerling. Continuity by Dorothy Howell. Based on the College Humor story by Ursula Parrott. Director of photography, Ted Tetzlaff. Film editor, Jack Dennis. Sound recorder, Charles Noyes. Release Date, March 1932, Running time, 68 minutes.

1932. **BIG CITY BLUES** (Warner Bros.)
Joan Blondell (Vida), Eric Linden (Bud), Inez Courtney (Faun), Evalyn Knapp (Jo-Jo), Guy Kibbee (Hummel), Lyle Talbot (Sully), Gloria Shea (Agnes), Walter Catlett (Gibbony), Jobyna Howland (Serena), Humphrey Bogart (Adkins), Josephine Dunn (Jackie), Grant Mitchell (Station Agent), Thomas Jackson (Quelkin), Ned Sparks (Stackhouse), Sheila Terry (Lorna), Tom Dugan (Red), Betty Gillette (Mabel), Edward McWade (Baggage Master).
Directed by Mervyn LeRoy. Screenplay by Ward Morehouse and Lillian Hayward. Based on the play *New York Town* by Ward Morehouse. Director of photography, James Van Trees. Film editor, Ray Curtis. Music and arrangements by Ray Heindorf and Bernhard Kaun. Musical director, Leo. F. Forbstein. Release Date, September 1932. Running time, 65 minutes.

1932. **THREE ON A MATCH** (First National for Warner Bros.)
Joan Blondell (Mary Keaton), Warren William (Henry Kirkwood), Ann Dvorak (Vivian Revere), Bette Davis (Ruth Westcott), Lyle Talbot (Mike Loftus), Humphrey Bogart (The Mug), Patricia Ellis (Linda), Sheila Terry (Naomi), Grant Mitchell (Principal of School), Glenda Farrell (Vivian's Chum), Frankie Darro (Bobby), Clara Blandick (Mrs Keaton), Hale Hamilton (Defence Attorney), Dick Brandon (Horace), Junior Johnson (Max), Anne Shirley (Vivian as a child), Virginia Davis (Mary as a child), Betty Carrs (Ruth as a child), Buster Phelps (Junior).
Directed by Mervyn LeRoy. Scenario by Lucien Hubbard. Dialogue by Kubec Glasmon and John Bright. Based on a story by Kubec Glasmon and John Bright. Director of photography, Sol Polito. Film editor, Ray Curtis. Art director, Robert Haas. Orchestral arrangements by Ray Heindorf. Musical director, Leo F. Forbstein. Release Date, October 1932. Running time 64 minutes.

1934. **MIDNIGHT** (Released by Universal)
Sidney Fox (Stella Weldon), O. P. Heggie (Edward Weldon), Henry Hull (Nolan), Margaret Wycherly (Mrs Weldon), Lynne Overman (Joe Biggers), Katherine Wilson (Ada Biggers), Richard Whorf (Arthur Weldon), Humphrey Bogart (Garboni), Granville Bates (Henry McGrath), Cora Witherspoon (Elizabeth McGrath), Moffat Johnston (District Attorney Plunkett), Henry O'Neill (Ingersoll), Helen Flint (Ethel Saxon).
Produced and directed by Chester Erskine. Screenplay by Chester Erskine. Based on the play by Paul and Claire Sifton. Release Date, January 1934. Running time, 80 minutes.

1936. **THE PETRIFIED FOREST** (Warner Bros.)
Leslie Howard (Alan Squier), Bette Davis (Gabrielle Maple), Genevieve Tobin (Mrs Chisholm), Dick Foran (Boze Hertzlinger), Humphrey Bogart (Duke Mantee), Joseph Sawyer (Jackie), Porter Hall (Jason Maple), Charles Grapewin (Gramp Maple), Paul Harvey (Mr Chisholm), Eddie Acuff (Lineman), Adrian Morris (Ruby), Nina Campana (Paula), Slim Thompson (Slim), John Alexander (Joseph).
Directed by Archie Mayo. Associate producer, Henry Blanke. Screenplay by Charles Kenyon and Delmer Davis. Based on the play by Robert E. Sherwood. Director of photography, Sol Polito. Music by Bernhard Kaun. Film editor, Owen Marks. Assistant director, Dick Mayberry. Art director, John Hughes. Gowns by Orry-Kelly. Special effects by Warren E. Lynch, Fred Jackman and Willard Van Enger. Sound recorder, Charles Lang. Release Date, February 1936. Running time, 83 minutes.

1936. **BULLETS OR BALLOTS** (A First National Picture for Warner Bros.)
Edward G. Robinson (Johnny Blake), Joan Blondell (Lee Morgan), Barton MacLane (Al Kruger), Humphrey Bogart (Nick "Bugs" Fenner), Frank McHugh (Herman), Joseph King (Captain Dan McLaren), Richard Purcell (Driscoll), George E. Stone (Wires), Joseph Crehan (Grand Jury Spokesman), Henry O'Neill (Bryant), Henry Kolker (Hollister), Gilbert Emery (Thorndyke), Herbert Rawlinson (Caldwell), Louise Beavers (Nellie), Norman Willis (Vinci), William Pawley (Crail), Ralph Remley (Kelly), Frank Faylen (Gatley).
Directed by William Keighley. Associate producer, Louis F. Edelman. Screenplay by Seton I. Miller. Based on an original story by Martin Mooney and Seton I. Miller. Director of photography, Hal Mohr. Music by Heinz Roemheld.

Film editor, Jack Killifer. Assistant director, Chuck Hansen. Art director, Carl Jules Weyl. Special effects by Fred Jackman, Fred Jackman, Jr., and Warren E. Lynch. Sound recorder, Oliver S. Garretson. Release Date, June 1936. Running time, 81 minutes.

1936 **TWO AGAINST THE WORLD** (A First National Picture for Warner Bros.)
Humphrey Bogart (Sherry Scott), Beverly Roberts (Alma Ross), Helen MacKellar (Martha Carstairs), Henry O'Neill (Jim Carstairs), Linda Perry (Edith Carstairs), Carlyle Moore, Jr. (Billy Sims), Virginia Brissac (Mrs Marion Sims), Robert Middlemass (Bertram C. Reynolds), Clay Clement (Mr Banning), Harry Hayden (Martin Leavenworth), Claire Dodd (Cora Latimer), Hobart Cavanaugh (Tippy Mantus), Douglas Wood (Malcolm Sims), Bobby Gordon (Herman O'Reilly), Paula Stone (Miss Symonds), Frank Orth (Tommy), Howard Hickman (Dr. McGuire), Ferdinand Schumann-Heink (Sound Mixer).
Directed by William McGann. Associate producer, Bryan Foy. Screenplay by Michel Jacoby. Based on the play *Five Star Final* by Louis Weitzenkorn. Director of photography, Sid Hickox. Music by Heinz Roemheld. Film editor, Frank Magee. Dialogue director, Irving Rapper. Assistant director, Carrol Sax. Art director, Esdras Hartley. Special effects by Fred Jackman, Jr., and Rex Wimpy. Sound recorder, C. A. Riggs. Release Date, July 1936. Running time, 64 minutes.

1936 **CHINA CLIPPER** (A First National Picture for Warner Bros.)
Pat O'Brien (Dave Logan), Beverly Roberts (Jean Logan), Ross Alexander (Tom Collins), Humphrey Bogart (Hap Stuart), Marie Wilson (Sunny Avery), Henry B. Walthall (Dad Brunn), Joseph Crehan (Jim Horn), Joseph King (Mr Pierson), Addison Richards (B. C. Hill), Ruth Robinson (Mother Brunn), Carlyle Moore, Jr. (Radio Operator), Lyle Moraine (Co-Pilot), Dennis Moore (Co-Pilot), Wayne Morris (Navigator), Alexander Cross (Bill Andrews), William Wright (Pilot), Kenneth Harlan (Commerce Inspector), Anne Nagel (Secretary), Marjorie Weaver (Secretary), Milburn Stone (Radio Operator), Owen King (Radio Operator).
Directed by Ray Enright. Associate producer, Louis F. Edelman. Original screenplay by Frank Wead. Director of photography, Arthur Edeson. Music by Bernhard Kaun and W. Franke Harling. Film editor, Owen Marks. Dialogue director, Gene Lewis. Assistant director, Lee Katz. Art director, Max Parker. Gowns by Orry-Kelly. Aerial photography by Elmer G. Dyer and H. F. Koenekamp. Special effects by Fred Jackman, Willard Van Enger, and H. F. Koenekamp. Sound recorder, Everett A. Brown. Technical adviser, William I. Van Dusen, Pan-American Airways. Release Date, August 1936. Running time, 85 minutes.

1936. **ISLE OF FURY** (Warner Bros.)
Humphrey Bogart (Val Stevens), Margaret Lindsay (Lucille Gordon), Donald Woods (Eric Blake), Paul Graetz (Captain Deever), Gordon Hart (Anderson), E. E. Clive (Dr. Hardy), George Regas (Otar), Sidney Bracy (Sam), Tetsu Komai (Kim Lee), Miki Morita (Oh Kay), Houseley Stevenson, Sr. (The Rector), Frank Lackteen (Old Native).
Directed by Frank McDonald. Associate producer, Bryan Foy. Screenplay by Robert Andrews and William Jacobs. Based on the novel *The Narrow Corner* by W. Somerset Maugham. Director of photography, Frank Good. Music by Howard Jackson. Film editor, Warren Low. Assistant director, Frank Heath. Art director, Esdras Hartley. Gowns by Orry-Kelly. Special effects by Fred Jackman, Willard Van Enger, and H. F. Koenekamp. Sound recorder, Charles Lang. Release Date, October 1936. Running time, 60 minutes.

1937. **BLACK LEGION** (Warner Bros.)
Humphrey Bogart (Frank Taylor), Dick Foran (Ed Jackson), Erin O'Brien-Moore (Ruth Taylor), Ann Sheridan (Betty Grogan), Robert Barrat (Brown), Helen Flint (Pearl Davis), Joseph Sawyer (Cliff Moore), Addison Richards (Prosecuting Attorney), Eddie Acuff (Metcalf), Clifford Soubier (Mike Grogan), Paul Harvey (Billings), Samuel S. Hinds (Judge), John Litel (Tommy Smith), Alonzo Price (Alexander Hargrave), Dickie Jones (Buddy Taylor), Dorothy Vaughan (Mrs Grogan), Henry Brandon (Joe Dombrowski), Charles Halton (Osgood), Pat C. Flick (Nick Strumpas), Francis Sayles (Charlie), Paul Stanton (Dr. Barham), Harry Hayden (Jones), Egon Brecher (Old Man Dombrowski).
Directed by Archie Mayo. Associate producer, Robert Lord. Screenplay by Abem Finkel and William Wister Haines. Based on an original story by Robert Lord. Director of photography, George Barnes, Music by Bernhard Kaun. Film editor, Owen Marks. Assistant director, Jack Sullivan. Art director, Robert Haas. Gowns by Milo Anderson. Special effects by Fred Jackman, Jr. and H. F. Koenekamp. Sound recorder, C. A. Riggs. Release Date, January 1937. Running time, 83 minutes.

1937. **THE GREAT O'MALLEY** (Warner Bros.)
Pat O'Brien (James Aloysius O'Malley), Sybil Jason (Barbara Phillips), Humphrey Bogart (John Phillips), Ann Sheridan (Judy Nolan), Frieda Inescort (Mrs Phillips), Donald Crisp (Captain Cromwell), Henry O'Neill (Defence Attorney), Craig Reynolds (Motorist), Hobart Cavanaugh (Pinky Holden), Gordon Hart (Doctor), Mary Gordon (Mrs O'Malley), Mabel Colcord (Mrs Flaherty), Frank Sheridan (Father Patrick), Lillian Harmer (Miss Taylor), Delmar Watson (Tubby), Frank Reicher (Dr. Larson).
Directed by William Dieterle. Associate producer, Harry Joe Brown. Screenplay by Milton Krims and Tom Reed. Based on the story *The Making of O'Malley* by Gerald Beaumont. Director of photography, Ernest Haller. Music by Heinz Roemheld. Film editor, Warren Low. Dialogue director, Irving Rapper. Assistant director, Frank Shaw. Art director, Hugh Reticker. Gowns by Milo Anderson. Special effects by James Gibbons, Fred Jackman, Jr., and H. F. Koenekamp. Sound recorder, Francis J. Scheid. Orchestrations by Hugo Friedhofer. Release Date, February 1937. Running time, 71 minutes.

1937 **MARKED WOMEN** A First National Picture for Warner Bros.
Bette Davis (Mary Dwight), Humphrey Bogart (David Graham), Lola Lane (Gabby Marvin), Isabel Jewell (Emmy Lou Egan), Eduardo Cianelli (Johnny Vanning), Rosalind Marquis (Florrie Liggett), Mayo Methot (Estelle Porter), Jane Bryan (Betty), Allen Jenkins (Louie), John Litel (Gordon), Ben Welden (Charlie), Damian O'Flynn (Ralph Krawford), Henry O'Neill (Arthur Sheldon), Raymond Hatton (Lawyer at Jail), Carlos San Martin (Headwaiter), William B Davidson (Bob Crandall), Kenneth Harlan (Eddie), Robert Strange (George Beler), James Robbins (Bell Captain), Arthur Aylesworth (John Truble), John Sheehan (Vincent), San Wren (Mac), Edwin Stanley (Detective Casey), Alan Davis (Henchman), Allen Mathews (Henchman), Guy Usher (Detective Ferguson), Gordon Hart (Judge at first Trial), Pierre Watkin (Judge at Second Trial), Herman Marks (Joe).
Directed by Lloyd Bacon. Associate producer, Louis F. Edelman. Original screenplay by Robert Rossen and Abem Finkel. Director of photography, George Barnes. Music by Bernhard Kaun and Heinz Roemheld. Film editor, Jack Killifer. Assistant director, Dick Mayberry. Art director, Max Parker. Gowns by Orry-Kelly. Special effects by James Gibbons and Robert Burks. Sound recorder, Everett A. Brown. Songs: "My Silver Dollar Man" by Harry Warren and Al Dubin; "Mr and Mrs Doaks" by M. K. Jerome and Jack Scholl. Release Date, April 1937. Running time, 96 minutes.

1937. **KID GALAHAD** (Warner Bros.)
Edward G. Robinson (Nick Donati), Bette Davis (Fluff), Humphrey Bogart (Turkey Morgan), Wayne Morris (Ward Guisenberry), Jane Bryan (Marie Donati), Harry Carey (Silver Jackson), William Haade (Chuck McGraw), Soledad Jiminez (Mrs Donati), Joe Cunningham (Joe Taylor), Ben Welden (Buzz Barett), Joseph Crehan (Brady), Veda Ann Borg (The Redhead), Frank Faylen (Barney), Harland Tucker (Gunman), Bob Evans (Sam), Hank Hankinson (Burke), Bob Nestell (O'Brien), Jack Kranz (Denbaugh), George Blake (Referee).
Directed by Michael Curtiz. Associate producer, Samuel Bischoff. Screenplay by Seton I. Miller. Based on the novel by Francis Wallace. Director of photography, Tony Gaudio. Music by Heinz Roemheld and Max Steiner. Film editor, George Amy. Dialogue director, Irving Rapper. Assistant director, Jack Sullivan. Art director, Carl Jules Weyl. Gowns by Orry-Kelly. Special effects by James Gibbons and Edwin B. DuPar. Sound recorder, Charles Lang. Orchestrations by Hugo Friedhofer. Song, "The Moon Is In Tears Tonight", by M. K. Jerome and Jack Scholl. Release Date, May 1937. Running time, 101 minutes.

1937 **SAN QUENTIN** (A First National Picture for Warner Bros.)
Pat O'Brien (Capt. Stephen Jameson), Humphrey Bogart (Joe "Red" Kennedy), Ann Sheridan (May Kennedy), Barton MacLane (Lieut. Druggin), Joseph Sawyer (Sailer Boy Hansen), Veda Ann Borg (Helen), James Robbins (Mickey Callahan), Joseph King (Warden Taylor), Gordon Oliver (Captain), Garry Owen (Dopey), Marc Lawrence (Venetti), Emmett Vogan (Leiutenant), William Pawley (Convict), Al Hill (Convict), Max Wagner (Prison Runner), George Lloyd (Convict), Ernie Adams (Fink).
Directed by Lloyd Bacon. Associate producer, Samuel Bischoff. Screenplay by Peter Milne and Humphrey Cobb. Based on an original story by Robert Tasker and John Bright. Director of photography, Sid Hickox. Music by Heinz Roemheld, Charles Maxwell and David Raksin. Film editor, William Holmes. Assistant director, Dick Mayberry. Art director, Esdras Hartley. Gowns by Howard Shoup. Special effects by James Gibbons and H. F. Koenekamp. Sound recorder, Everett A. Brown. Orchestrations by Joseph Nussbaum and Ray Heindorf.. Song, "How Could You?" by Harry Warren and Al Dubin. Release Date, August 1937. Running time, 70 minutes.

1937. **DEAD END** (Released through United Artists)
Sylvia Sidney (Drina), Joel McCrea (Dave Connell), Humphrey Bogart (Baby Face Martin), Wendy Barrie (Kay Burton), Claire Trevor (Francey), Allen Jenkins (Hunk), Marjorie Main (Mrs Martin), Billy Halop (Tommy), Huntz Hall (Dippy), Bobby Jordan (Angel), Leo Gorcey (Spit), Gabriel Dell (T. B.), Bernard Punsley (Milty), Charles Peck (Philip Griswold), Minor Watson (Mr Griswold), James Burke (Officer Mulligan), Ward Bond (Doorman), Elisabeth Risdon (Mrs Connell), Esther Dale (Mrs Fenner), George Humbert (Mr Pascagli), Marcelle Corday (Governess), Charles Halton (Whitey).
A Samuel Goldwyn Production. Directed by William Wyler. Produced by Samuel Goldwyn. Associate producer, Merritt Hulburd. Screenplay by Lillian Hellman. Based on the play by Sidney Kingsley. Director of photography, Gregg Toland. Film editor, Daniel Mandell. Dialogue director, Edward P. Goodnow. Assistant director, Eddie Bernoudy. Art director, Richard Day. Set decorations by Julia Heron. Costumes by Omar Kiam. Special effects by James Basevi. Sound recorder, Frank Maher. Musical director, Alfred Newman. Release Date, August 1937. Running time, 93 minutes.

1937. **STAND-IN** (Released through United Artists)
Leslie Howard (Atterbury Dodd), Joan Blondell (Lester Plum), Humphrey Bogart (Douglas Quintain), Alan Mowbray (Koslofski), Marla Shelton (Thelma Cheri), C. Henry Gordon (Ivor Nassau), Jack Carson (Potts), Tully Marshall (Pennypacker, Sr.), J. C. Nugent (Pennypacker, Jr.), William V. Mong (Pennypacker).
Directed by Tay Garnett. Produced by Walter Wanger. Screenplay by Gene Towne and Graham Baker. Based on the Saturday Evening Post serial by Clarence Budington Kelland. Director of photography, Charles Clarke. Music by Heinz Roemheld. Film editors, Otho Lovering and Dorothy Spencer. Assistant director, Charles Kerr. Art Director, Alexander Toluboff; associate, Wade Rubottom. Costumes by Helen Taylor. Sound recorder, Paul Neal. Musical director, Rox Rommel. Release Date, October 1937. Running time, 90 minutes.

1938. **SWING YOUR LADY** (Warner Bros.)
Humphrey Bogart (Ed Hatch), Frank McHugh (Popeye Bronson), Louise Fazenda (Sadie Horn), Nat Pendleton (Joe Skopapoulos), Penny Singleton (Cookie Shannon), Allen Jenkins (Shiner Ward), Leon Weaver (Waldo Davis), Frank Weaver (Ollie Davis), Elviry Weaver (Mrs Davis), Ronald Reagan (Jack Miller), Daniel Boone Savage (Noah Webster), Hugh O'Connell (Smith), Tommy Bupp (Rufe Horn), Sonny Bupp (Len Horn), Joan Howard (Mattie Horn), Sue Moore (Mabel), Olin Howland (Hotel Proprietor), Sammy White (Speciality Number).
Directed by Ray Enright. Associate producer, Samuel Bischoff. Screenplay by Joseph Schrank and Maurice Leo. Based on the play by Kenyon Nicholson and Charles Robinson. Director of photography, Arthur Edeson. Music by Adolph Deutsch. Film editor, Jack Killifer. Dialogue director, Jo Graham. Assistant director, Jesse Hibbs. Art director, Esdras Hartley. Gowns by Howard Shoup. Sound recorder, Charles Lang. Orchestrations by Hugo Friedhofer. Musical numbers created and directed by Bobby Connolly. Songs: "Mountain Swingaroo", "Hillbilly from Tenth Avenue", "The Old Apple Tree", "Swing Your

Lady", and "Dig Me a Grave in Missouri" by M. K. Jerome and Jack Scholl. Release Date, January 1938. Running time, 79 minutes.

1938. **CRIME SCHOOL** (First National Picture for Warner Bros.)
Humphrey Bogart (Mark Braden), Gale Page (Sue Warren), Billy Halop (Frankie Warren), Bobby Jordan (Squirt), Huntz Hall (Goofy), Leo Gorcey (Spike Hawkins), Bernard Punsley (Fats Papadopolo), Gabriel Dell (Bugs Burke), George Offerman, Jr. (Red), Weldon Heyburn (Cooper), Cy Kendall (Morgan), Charles Trowbridge (Judge Clinton), Spencer Charters (Old Doctor), Donald Briggs (New Doctor), Frank Jaquet (Commissioner), Helen MacKellar (Mrs Burke), Al Bridge (Mr Burke), Sibyl Harris (Mrs Hawkins), Paul Porcasi (Nick Papadopolo), Frank Otto (Junkie), Ed Gargan (Officer Hogan), James B. Carson (Schwartz).
Directed by Lewis Seiler. Associate producer, Bryan Foy. Screenplay by Crane Wilbur and Vincent Sherman. Based on an original story by Crane Wilbur. Director of photography, Arthur Todd. Music by Max Steiner. Film editor, Terry Morse. Dialogue director, Vincent Sherman. Assistant director, Fred Tyler. Art director, Charles Novi. Gowns by N'Was McKenzie. Sound recorder, Francis J. Scheid. Orchestrations by Hugo Friedhofer and George Parrish. Release Date, May 1938. Running time, 86 minutes.

1938. **MEN ARE SUCH FOOLS** (Warner Bros.)
Wayne Morris (Jimmy Hall), Priscilla Lane (Linda Lawrence), Humphrey Bogart (Harry Galleon), Hugh Herbert (Harvey Bates), Penny Singleton (Nancy), Johnnie Davis (Tad), Mona Barrie (Beatrice Harris), Marcia Ralston (Wanda Townsend), Gene Lockhart (Bill Dalton), Kathleen Lockhart (Mrs Dalton), Donald Briggs (George Onslow), Renie Riano (Mrs Pinkel), Claude Allister (Rudolf), Nedda Harrigan (Mrs Nelson), Eric Stanley (Mr Nelson), James Nolan (Bill Collyer), Carole Landis (June Cooper).
Directed by Busby Berkeley. Associate producer, David Lewis. Screenplay by Norman Reilly Raine and Horace Jackson. Based on the novel by Faith Baldwin. Director of photography, Sid Hickox. Music by Heinz Roemheld. Film editor, Jack Killifer. Dialogue director, Jo Graham. Assistant director, Chuck Hansen. Art director, Max Parker. Gowns by Howard Shoup. Sound recorder, Stanley Jones. Orchestrations by Ray Heindorf. Release Date, July 1938. Running time, 70 minutes.

1938. **THE AMAZING DR. CLITTERHOUSE** (A First National Picture for Warner Bros.)
Edward G. Robinson (Dr. Clitterhouse), Claire Trevor (Jo Keller), Humphrey Bogart (Rocks Valentine), Allen Jenkins (Okay), Donald Crisp (Inspector Lane), Gale Page (Nurse Randolph), Henry O'Neill (Judge), John Litel (Prosecuting Attorney), Thurston Hall (Grant), Maxie Rosenbloom (Butch), Bert Hanlon (Pal), Curt Bois (Rabbit), Ward Bond (Tug), Vladimir Sokoloff (Popus), Billy Wayne (Candy), Robert Homans (Lieutenant Johnson), Irving Bacon (Foreman of the Jury).
Directed by Anatole Litvak. Associate producer, Robert Lord. Screenplay by John Wexley and John Huston. Based on the play by Barré Lyndon. Director of photography, Tony Gaudio. Music by Max Steiner. Film editor, Warren Low. Dialogue director, Jo Graham. Assistant director, Jack Sullivan. Art director, Carl Jules Weyl. Wardrobe by Milo Anderson. Sound recorder, C. A. Riggs. Orchestrations by George Parrish. Technical adviser, Dr. Leo Schulman. Release Date, July 1938. Running time, 87 minutes.

1938. **RACKET BUSTERS** (Warner Bros.)
Humphrey Bogart (Pete Martin), George Brent (Denny Jordan), Gloria Dickson (Nora Jordan), Allen Jenkins (Horse Wilson), Walter Abel (Thomas Allison), Henry O'Neill (Governor), Penny Singleton (Gladys), Anthony Averill (Crane), Oscar O'Shea (Pop Wilson), Elliott Sullivan (Charlie Smith), Fay Helm (Mrs Smith), Joseph Downing (Joe), Norman Willis (Gus), Don Rowan (Kimball).
A Cosmopolitan Production. Directed by Lloyd Bacon. Associate producer, Samuel Bischoff. Original screenplay by Robert Rossen and Leonardo Bercovici. Director of photography, Arthur Edeson. Music by Adolph Deutsch. Film editor, James Gibbon. Assistant director, Dick Mayberry. Art director, Esdras Hartley. Gowns by Howard Shoup. Sound recorder, Robert B. Lee. Orchestrations by Hugo Friedhofer. Release Date, August 1938. Running time, 71 minutes.

1938 **ANGELS WITH DIRTY FACES** (A First National Picture for Warner Bros.)
James Cagney (Rocky Sullivan), Pat O'Brien (Jerry Connolly), Humphrey Bogart (James Frazier), Ann Sheridan (Laury Ferguson), George Bancroft (Mac Keefer), Billy Halop (Soapy), Bobby Jordan (Swing), Leo Gorcey (Bim), Gabriel Dell (Pasty), Huntz Hall (Crab), Bernard Punsley (Hunky), Joseph Downing (Steve), Edward Pawley (Edwards), Adrian Morris (Blackie), Frankie Burke (Rocky as a boy), William Tracy (Jerry as a boy), Marilyn Knowlden (Laury as a child), St. Brendan's Church Choir.
Directed by Michael Curtiz. Associate producer, Samuel Bischoff. Screenplay by John Wexley and Warren Duff. Based on an original story by Rowland Brown. Director of photography, Sol Polito. Music by Max Steiner. Film editor, Owen Marks. Dialogue director, Jo Graham. Assistant director, Sherry Shourds. Art director, Robert Haas. Gowns by Orry-Kelly. Sound recorder, Everett A. Brown. Orchestrations, Hugo Friedhofer. Technical adviser, Father J. J. Devlin. Release Date, November 1938. Running time, 97 minutes.

1939. **KING OF THE UNDERWORLD** (Warner Bros.)
Humphrey Bogart (Joe Gurney), Kay Francis (Carol Nelson), James Stephenson (Bill Forrest), John Eldredge (Niles Nelson), Jessie Busley (Aunt Margaret), Arthur Aylesworth (Dr. Sanders), Raymond Brown (Sheriff), Harland Tucker (Mr Aimes), Ralph Remley (Mr Robert), Charley Foy (Eddie), Murray Alper (Butch), Joe Devlin (Porky), Elliott Sullivan (Mugsy), Alan Davis (Slick), John Harmon (Slats), John Ridgely (Jerry), Richard Bond (Interne), Pierre Watkin (District Attorney), Charles Trowbridge (Dr. Ryan), Edwin Stanley (Dr. Jacobs).
Directed by Lewis Seiler. Associate producer, Bryan Foy. Screenplay by George Bricker and Vincent Sherman. Based on the Liberty Magazine serial *Dr. Socrates* by W. R. Burnett. Director of photography, Sid Hickox. Music by Heinz Roemheld. Film editor, Frank Dewar. Dialogue director, Vincent Sherman. Assistant director, Frank Heath. Art director, Charles Novi. Gowns by Orry-Kelly. Sound recorder, Everett A. Brown. Technical adviser, Dr. Leo Schulman. Release Date, January 1939. Running time, 69 minutes.

1939. **THE OKLAHOMA KID** (Warner Bros.)
James Cagney (Jim Kincaid), Humphrey Bogart (Whip McCord), Rosemary Lane (Jane Hardwick), Donald Crisp (Judge Hardwick), Harvey Stephens (Ned Kincaid), Hugh Sothern (John Kincaid), Charles Middleton (Alex Martin), Edward Pawley (Doolin), Ward Bond (Wes Handley), Lew Harvey (Curly), Trevor Bardette (Indian Jack Pasco), John Miljan (Ringo), Arthur Aylesworth (Judge Morgan), Irving Bacon (Hotel Clerk), Joe Devlin (Keely), Wade Boteler (Sheriff Abe Collins).
Directed by Lloyd Bacon. Associate producer, Samuel Bischoff. Screenplay by Warren Duff, Robert Buckner and Edward E. Paramore. Based on an original story by Edward E. Paramore and Wally Klein. Director of photography, James Wong Howe. Music by Max Steiner. Film editor, Owen Marks. Assistant director, Dick Mayberry. Art director, Esdras Hartley. Gowns by Orry-Kelly. Sound recorder, Stanley Jones. Orchestrations by Hugo Friedhofer, Adolph Deutsch, George Parrish, and Murray Cutter. Technical adviser, Al Jennings. Release Date, March 1939. Running time, 80 minutes.

1939 **DARK VICTORY** (A First National Picture for Warner Bros.)
Bette Davis (Judith Traherne), George Brent (Dr. Frederick Steele), Humphrey Bogart (Michael O'Leary), Geraldine Fitzgerald (Ann King), Ronald Reagan (Alec Hamm), Henry Travers (Dr. Parsons), Cora Witherspoon (Carrie Spottswood), Dorothy Peterson (Miss Wainwright), Virginia Brissac (Martha), Charles Richman (Colonel Mantle), Herbert Rawlinson (Dr. Carter), Leonard Mudie (Dr. Driscoll), Fay Helm (Miss Dodd), Lottie Williams (Lucy).
Directed by Edmund Goulding. Associate producer, David Lewis. Screenplay by Casey Robinson. Based on the play by George Emerson Brewer, Jr., and Bertram Bloch. Director of photography, Ernest Haller. Music by Max Steiner. Film editor, William Holmes. Assistant director, Frank Heath. Art director, Robert Haas. Gowns by Orry-Kelly. Sound recorder, Robert B. Lee. Orchestrations by Hugo Friedhofer. Song, "Oh, Give Me Time for Tenderness", by Elsie Janis and Edmund Goulding. Technical adviser, Dr. Leo Schulman. Release Date, April 1939. Running time, 106 minutes.

1939. **YOU CAN'T GET AWAY WITH MURDER** (A First National Picture for Warner Bros.)
Humphrey Bogart (Frank Wilson), Billy Halop (Johnnie Stone), Gale Page (Madge Stone), John Litel (Attorney Carey), Henry Travers (Pop), Harvey Stephens (Fred Burke), Harold Huber (Scappa), Joseph Sawyer (Red), Joseph Downing (Smitty), George E. Stone (Toad), Joseph King (Principal Keeper), Joseph Crehan (Warden), John Ridgely (Gas Station Attendant), Herbert Rawlinson (District Attorney).
Directed by Lewis Seiler. Associate producer, Samuel Bischoff. Screenplay by Robert Buckner, Don Ryan and Kenneth Gamet. Based on the play *Chalked Out* by Warden Lewis E. Lawes and Jonathan Finn. Director of photography, Sol Polito. Music by Heinz Roemheld. Film editor, James Gibbon. Dialogue director, Jo Graham. Assistant director, William Kissel. Art director, Hugh Reticker. Gowns by Milo Anderson. Sound recorder, Francis J. Scheid. Orchestrations by Hugo Friedhofer, Arthur Kay and Rudolph Kopp. Release Date, May 1939. Running time, 78 minutes.

1939. **THE ROARING TWENTIES** (A Warner Bros.-First National Picture)
James Cagney (Eddie Bartlett), Priscilla Lane (Jean Sherman), Humphrey Bogart (George Hally), Gladys George (Panama Smith), Jeffrey Lynn (Lloyd Hart), Frank McHugh (Danny Green), Paul Kelly (Nick Brown), Elizabeth Risdon (Mrs Sherman), Edward Keane (Pete Henderson), Joseph Sawyer (Sergeant Pete Jones), Joseph Crehan (Mr Fletcher), George Meeker (Masters), John Hamilton (Judge), Robert Elliott (First Detective), Eddie Chandler (Second Detective), Abner Biberman (Lefty), Vera Lewis (Mrs Gray), Elliott Sullivan (Eddie's Cellmate), Bert Hanlon (Piano Accompanist), Murray Alper (First Mechanic), Dick Wessel (Second Mechanic), George Humbert (Restaurant Proprietor), Ben Welden (Tavern Proprietor).
Directed by Raoul Walsh. Executive producer, Hal B. Wallis. Associate producer Samuel Bischoff. Screenplay by Jerry Wald, Richard Macaulay and Robert Rossen. Based on an original story by Mark Hellinger. Director of photography, Ernest Haller. Music by Heinz Roemheld and Ray Heindorf. Film editor, Jack Killifer. Dialogue director, Hugh Cummings. Assistant director, Dick Mayberry. Art director, Max Parker. Wardrobe by Milo Anderson. Makeup artist, Perc Westmore. Special effects by Byron Haskin and Edwin B. DuPar. Sound recorder, Everett A. Brown. Songs: "My Melancholy Baby" by Ernie Burnett and George A. Norton; "I'm Just Wild About Harry" by Eubie Blake and Noble Sissle: "It Had to be You" by Isham Jones and Gus Kahn; "In a Shanty in Old Shanty Town" by Jack Little, Joseph Young and John Siras. Orchestral arrangements by Ray Heindorf. Narrated by John Deering. Release Date, October 1939. Running time, 106 minutes.

1939 **THE RETURN OF DOCTOR X** (A First National Picture for Warner Bros.)
Wayne Morris (Walter Barnett), Rosemary Lane (Joan Vance), Humphrey Bogart (Marshall Quesne), Dennis Morgan (Michael Rhodes), John Litel (Dr. Francis Flegg), Lya Lys (Angela Merrova), Huntz Hall (Pink), Charles Wilson (Detective Ray Kincaid), Vera Lewis (Miss Sweetman), Howard Hickman (Chairman), Olin Howland (Undertaker), Arthur Aylesworth (Guide), Jack Mower (Detective Sgt. Moran), Creighton Hale (Hotel Manager), John Ridgely (Rodgers), Joseph Crehan (Editor), Glenn Langan (Interne), William Hopper (Interne).
Directed by Vincent Sherman. Associate producer, Bryan Foy. Screenplay by Lee Katz. Based on the story *The Doctor's Secret* by William J. Makin. Director of photography, Sid Hickox. Music by Bernhard Kaun. Film editor, Thomas Pratt. Dialogue director, John Langan. Assistant director, Dick Mayberry. Art director, Esdras Hartley. Gowns by Milo Anderson. Makeup artist, Perc Westmore. Sound recorder, Charles Lang. Technical adviser, Dr. Leo Schulman. Release Date, December 1939. Running time, 62 minutes.

1939. **INVISIBLE STRIPES** (A Warner Bros.-First National Picture)
George Raft (Cliff Taylor), Jane Bryan (Peggy), William Holden (Tim Taylor), Humphrey Bogart (Chuck Martin), Flora Robson (Mrs Taylor),

Paul Kelly (Ed Kruger), Lee Patrick (Molly), Henry O'Neill (Parole Officer Masters), Frankie Thomas (Tommy), Moroni Olsen (Warden), Margot Stevenson (Sue), Marc Lawrence (Lefty), Joseph Downing (Johnny), Leo Gorcey (Jimmy), William Haade (Shrank), Tully Marshall (Old Peter).
Directed by Lloyd Bacon. Executive producer, Hal B. Wallis. Associate producer, Louis F. Edelman. Screenplay by Warren Duff. From an original story by Jonathan Finn, based on the book by Warden Lewis E. Lawes. Director of photography, Ernest Haller. Music by Heinz Roemheld. Film editor, James Gibbon. Dialogue director, Irving Rapper. Assistant director, Elmer Decker. Art director, Max Parker. Gowns by Milo Anderson. Makeup artist, Perc Westmore. Special effects by Byron Haskin. Sound recorder, Dolph Thomas. Orchestrations by Ray Heindorf. Release Date, December 1939. Running time, 82 minutes.

1940. **VIRGINIA CITY** (A Warner Bros.-First National Picture)
Errol Flynn (Kerry Bradford), Miriam Hopkins (Julia Hayne), Randolph Scott (Vance Irby), Humphrey Bogart (John Murrell), Frank McHugh (Mr Upjohn), Alan Hale (Olaf Swenson), Guinn "Big Boy" Williams (Marblehead), John Litel (Marshall), Douglass Dumbrille (Major Drewery), Moroni Olsen (Dr. Cameron), Russell Hicks (Armistead), Dickie Jones (Cobby), Frank Wilcox (Union Soldier), Russell Simpson (Gaylord), Victor Kilian (Abraham Lincoln), Charles Middleton (Jefferson Davis).
Directed by Michael Curtiz. Executive producer, Hal B. Wallis. Associate producer, Robert Fellows. Original screenplay by Robert Buckner. Director of photography, Sol Polito. Music by Max Steiner. Film editor, George Amy. Dialogue director, Jo Graham. Assistant director, Sherry Shourds. Art director, Ted Smith. Makeup artist, Perc Westmore. Special effects by Byron Haskin and H. F. Koenekamp. Sound recorders, Oliver S. Garretson and Francis J. Scheid. Orchestrations by Hugo Friedhofer. Release Date, March 1940. Running time, 121 minutes.

1940. **IT ALL CAME TRUE** (A Warner Bros.-First National Picture)
Ann Sheridan (Sarah Jane Ryan), Jeffrey Lynn (Tommy Taylor), Humphrey Bogart (Grasselli and Chips Maguire), ZaSu Pitts (Miss Flint), Una O'Connor (Maggie Ryan), Jessie Busley (Norah Taylor), John Litel (Mr Roberts), Grant Mitchell (Mr Salmon), Felix Bressart (Mr Boldini), Charles Judels (Leantopopulos), Brandon Tynan (Mr Van Diver), Howard Hickman (Mr Prendergast), Herbert Vigran (Monks).
Directed by Lewis Seiler. Executive producer, Hal B. Wallis. Associate producer Mark Hellinger. Screenplay by Michael Fessier and Lawrence Kimble. Based on the story *Better Than Life* by Louis Bromfield. Director of photography, Ernest Haller. Music by Heinz Roemheld. Film editor, Thomas Richards. Dialogue director, Robert Foulk. Assistant director, Russ Saunders. Art director, Max Parker. Gowns by Howard Shoup. Makeup artist, Perc Westmore. Special effects by Byron Haskin and Edwin B. DuPar. Sound recorder, Dolph Thomas. Dance director, Dave Gould. Songs: "Angel in Disguise" by Kim Gannon, Stephen Weiss, and Paul Mann; "The Gaucho Serenade" by James Cavanaugh, John Redmond and Nat Simon. Orchestral arrangements by Ray Heindorf and Frank Perkins. Release Date, April 1940. Running time ,97 minutes.

1940. **BROTHER ORCHID** (A Warner Bros.-First National Picture)
Edward G. Robinson (Little John Sarto), Ann Sothern (Flo Addams), Humphrey Bogart (Jack Buck), Donald Crisp (Brother Superior), Ralph Bellamy (Clarence Fletcher), Allen Jenkins (Willie the Knife), Charles D. Brown (Brother Wren), Cecil Kellaway (Brother Goodwin), Morgan Conway Philadelphia Powell), Richard Lane (Mugsy O'Day), Paul Guilfoyle (Red Martin), John Ridgely (Texas Pearson), Joseph Crehan (Brother MacEwen), Wilfred Lucas (Brother MacDonald), Tom Tyler (Curly Matthews), Dick Wessel (Buffalo Burns), Granville Bates (Pattonsville Supt.), Paul Phillips (French Frank), Don Rowan (Al Muller), Nanette Vallon (Fifi), Tim Ryan (Turkey Malone), Joe Caites (Handsome Harry), Pat Gleason (Dopey Perkins), Tommy Baker (Joseph).
Directed by Lloyd Bacon. Executive producer, Hal B. Wallis. Associate producer, Mark Hellinger. Screenplay by Earl Baldwin. Based on the Collier's magazine story by Richard Connell. Director of photography, Tony Gaudio. Music by Heinz Roemheld. Film editor, William Holmes. Dialogue director, Hugh Cummings. Assistant director, Dick Mayberry. Art director, Max Parker. Gowns by Howard Shoup. Makeup artist, Perc Westmore. Special effects by Byron Haskin, Willard Van Enger, and Edwin B. DuPar. Montages by Don Siegel and Robert Burks. Sound recorder, C. A. Riggs. Orchestrations by Ray Heindorf. Release Date, June 1940. Running time, 91 minutes.

1940. **THEY DRIVE BY NIGHT** (Warner Bros.-First National Picture)
George Raft (Joe Fabrini), Ann Sheridan (Cassie Hartley), Ida Lupino (Lana Carlsen), Humphrey Bogart (Paul Fabrini), Gale Page (Pearl Fabrini), Alan Hale (Ed Carlsen), Roscoe Karns (Irish McGurn), John Litel (Harry McNamara), George Tobias (George Rondolos), Henry O'Neill (District Attorney), Charles Halton (Farnsworth), Paul Hurst (Pete Haig), John Ridgely (Hank Dawson), George Lloyd (Barney), Joyce Compton (Sue Carter), Charles Wilson (Mike Williams), Pedro Regas (McNamara's Helper), Norman Willis (Neves), Joe Devlin (Fatso), William Haade (Driver), Vera Lewis (Landlady), John Hamilton (Defence Attorney).
Directed by Raoul Walsh. Executive producer, Hal B. Wallis. Associate producer, Mark Hellinger. Screenplay by Jerry Wald and Richard Macaulay. Based on the novel *Long Haul* by A. I. Bezzerides. Director of photography, Arthur Edeson. Music by Adolph Deutsch. Film editor, Thomas Richards. Dialogue director, Hugh MacMullen. Assistant director, Elmer Decker. Art director, John Hughes. Gowns by Milo Anderson. Makeup artist, Perc Westmore. Special effects by Byron Haskin, H. F. Koenekamp, James Gibbons, John Holden and Edwin B. DuPar. Montages by Don Siegel and Robert Burks. Sound recorder, Oliver S. Garretson. Orchestrations by Arthur Lange. Release Date, August 1940. Running time, 93 minutes.

1941. **HIGH SIERRA** (A Warner Bros.-First National Picture)
Ida Lupino (Marie Garson), Humphrey Bogart (Roy Earle), Alan Curtis (Babe Kozak), Arthur Kennedy (Red Hattery), Joan Leslie (Velma), Henry Hull (Doc Banton), Henry Travers (Pa Goodhue), Jerome Cowan (Healy), Minna Gombell (Mrs Baughman), Barton MacLane (Jake Kranmer), Elizabeth Risdon (Ma Goodhue), Cornel Wilde (Louis Mendoza), Donald MacBride (Big Mac), Paul Harvey (Mr Baughman), Isabel Jewell (Blonde), Willie Best (Algernon), Spencer Charters (Ed), George Meeker (Pfiffer), Robert Strange (Art), John Eldredge (Lon Preiser), Sam Hayes (Announcer).
Directed by Raoul Walsh. Executive producer, Hal B. Wallis. Associate producer, Mark Hellinger. Screenplay by John Huston and W. R. Burnett. Based on the novel by W. R. Burnett. Director of photography, Tony Gaudio. Music by Adolph Deutsch. Film editor, Jack Killifer. Dialogue director, Irving Rapper. Art director, Ted Smith. Gowns by Milo Anderson. Makeup artist, Perc Westmore. Special effects by Byron Haskin and H. F. Koenekamp. Sound recorder, Dolph Thomas. Orchestrations by Arthur Lange. Release Date, January 1941. Running time, 100 minutes.

1941. **THE WAGONS ROLL AT NIGHT** (A W.B.-First National Picture)
Humphrey Bogart (Nick Coster), Sylvia Sidney (Flo Lorraine), Eddie Albert (Matt Varney), Joan Leslie (Mary Coster), Sig Rumann (Hoffman the Great), Cliff Clark (Doc), Charley Foy (Snapper), Frank Wilcox (Tex), John Ridgely (Arch), Clara Blandick (Mrs Williams), Aldrich Bowker (Mr Williams), Garry Owen (Gus), Jack Mower (Bundy), Frank Mayo (Wally),
Directed by Ray Enright. Associate producer, Harlan Thompson. Screenplay by Fred Niblo, Jr. and Barry Trivers. Based on the novel *Kid Galahad* by Francis Wallace. Director of photography, Sid Hickox. Music by Heinz Roemheld. Film editor, Frederick Richards. Assistant director, Jesse Hibbs. Art director, Hugh Reticker. Special effects by Byron Haskin and H. F. Koenekamp. Orchestrations by Ray Heindorf. Release Date, April 1941. Running time, 84 mins.

1941. **THE MALTESE FALCON** (A Warner Bros.-First National Picture)
Humphrey Bogart (Sam Spade), Mary Astor (Brigid O'Shaughnessy), Gladys George (Iva Archer), Peter Lorre (Joel Cairo), Barton MacLane (Lieutenant Dundy), Lee Patrick (Effie Perine), Sydney Greenstreet (Casper Gutman), Ward Bond (Detective Tom Polhaus), Jerome Cowan (Miles Archer), Elisha Cook, Jr. (Wilmer Cook), James Burke (Luke), Murray Alper (Frank), John Hamilton (District Attorney Bryan), Emory Parnall (Mate of the *La Paloma*), Walter Huston (Captain Jacobi).
Directed by John Huston. Executive producer, Hal B. Wallis. Associate producer, Henry Blanke. Screenplay by John Huston. Based on the novel by Dashiell Hammett. Director of photography, Arthur Edeson. Music by Adolph Deutsch. Film editor, Thomas Richards. Dialogue director, Robert Foulk. Assistant director, Claude Archer. Art director, Robert Haas. Gowns by Orry-Kelly. Makeup artist Perc Westmore. Sound recorder, Oliver S. Garretson. Orchestrations by Arthur Lange. Release Date, October 1941. Running time, 100 minutes.

1942. **ALL THROUGH THE NIGHT** (A Warner Bros.-First National Picture)
Humphrey Bogart (Gloves Donahue), Conrad Veidt (Hall Ebbing), Kaaren Verne (Leda Hamilton), Jane Darwell (Ma Donahue), Frank McHugh (Barney), Peter Lorre (Pepi), Judith Anderson (Madame), William Demarest (Sunshine), Jackie Gleason (Starchie), Phil Silvers (Waiter), Wallace Ford (Spats Hunter), Barton MacLane (Marty Callahan), Edward Brophy (Joe Denning), Martin Kosleck (Steindorff), Jean Ames (Annabelle), Ludwig Stossel (Mr Miller), Irene Seidner (Mrs Miller), James Burke (Forbes), Ben Welden (Smitty), Hans Schumm (Anton), Charles Cane (Spence), Frank Sully (Sage), Sam McDaniel (Deacon).
Directed by Vincent Sherman. Produced by Jerry Wald. Screenplay by Leonard Spigelgass and Edwin Gilbert. Based on an original story by Leonard Q. Ross (Leo Rosten) and Leonard Spigelgass. Director of photography, Sid Hickox. Music by Adolph Deutsch. Film editor, Rudi Fehr. Assistant director, William Kissel. Art director Max Parker. Special effects by Edwin B. DuPar. Sound recorder, Oliver S. Garretson. Orchestrations by Frank Perkins. Song, "All Through the Night", by Johnny Mercer and Arthur Schwartz. Release Date, January 1942. Running time, 107 minutes.

1942. **THE BIG SHOT** (A Warner Bros.-First National Picture)
Humphrey Bogart (Duke Berne), Irene Manning (Lorna Fleming), Richard Travis (George Anderson), Susan Peters (Ruth Carter), Stanley Ridges (Martin Fleming), Minor Watson (Warden Booth), Chick Chandler (Dancer), Joseph Downing (Frenchy), Howard da Silva (Sandor), Murray Alper (Quinto), Roland Drew (Faye), John Ridgely (Tim), Joseph King (Toohey), John Hamilton (Judge), Virginia Brissac (Mrs Booth), William Edmunds (Sarto), Virginia Sale (Mrs Miggs), Ken Christy (Kat), Wallace Scott (Rusty).
Directed by Lewis Seiler. Produced by Walter MacEwen. Original screenplay by Bertram Millhauser, Abem Finkel and Daniel Fuchs. Director of photography, Sid Hickox. Music by Adolph Deutsch. Film editor, Jack Killifer. Dialogue director, Harold Winston. Assistant director, Art Lueker. Art director, John Hughes. Gowns by Milo Anderson. Makeup artist, Perc Westmore. Sound recorder, Stanley Jones. Orchestrations by Jerome Moross. Release Date, June 1942. Running time, 82 minutes.

1942. **ACROSS THE PACIFIC** (A Warner Bros.-First National Picture)
Humphrey Bogart (Rick Leland), Mary Astor (Alberta Marlow), Sydney Greenstreet (Dr. Lorenz), Charles Halton (A. V. Smith), Victor Sen Yung (Joe Totsuiko), Roland Got (Sugi), Lee Tung Foo (Sam Wing On), Frank Wilcox (Captain Morrison), Paul Stanton (Colonel Hart), Lester Matthews (Canadian Major), John Hamilton (Court-martial President), Tom Stevenson (Tall Thin Man), Roland Drew (Captain Harkness), Monte Blue (Dan Morton), Chester Gan (Captain Higoto), Richard Loo (First Officer Miyuma), Keye Luke (Steamship Office Clerk), Kam Tong (T. Oki), Spencer Chan (Chief Engineer Mitsudo), Rudy Robles (Filipino Assassin).

Directed by John Huston. Produced by Jerry Wald and Jack Saper. Screenplay by Richard Macaulay. Based on the Saturday Evening Post serial *Aloha Means Goodbye* by Robert Carson. Director of photography, Arthur Edeson. Music by Adolph Deutsch. Film editor, Frank Magee. Dialogue director, Edward Blatt. Assistant director, Lee Katz. Art directors, Robert Haas and Hugh Reticker. Gowns by Milo Anderson. Makeup artist, Perc Westmore. Special effects by Byron Haskin and Willard Van Enger. Montages by Don Siegel. Sound recorder, Everett A. Brown. Orchestrations by Clifford Vaughan. Release Date, September 1942. Running time, 97 minutes.

1943. CASABLANCA (A Warner Bros.-First National Picture)
Humphrey Bogart (Rick), Ingrid Bergman (Ilsa), Paul Henreid (Victor Laszlo), Claude Rains (Captain Louis Renault), Conrad Veidt (Major Strasser), Sydney Greenstreet (Senor Ferrari), Peter Lorre (Ugarte), S. Z. Sakall (Carl), Madeleine LeBeau (Yvonne), Dooley Wilson (Sam), Joy Page (Annina Brandel), John Qualen (Berger), Leonid Kinsky (Sascha), Helmut Dantine (Jan Brandel), Curt Bois (Pickpocket), Marcel Dalio (Croupier), Corinna Mura (Singer), Ludwig Stossel (Mr Leuchtag), Ilka Gruning (Mrs Leuchtag), Charles La Torre (Italian Officer Tonelli), Frank Puglia (Arab Vendor), Dan Seymour (Abdul).
Directed by Michael Curtiz. Produced by Hal B. Wallis. Screenplay by Julius J. & Philip G. Epstein and Howard Koch. Based on the play *Everybody Comes to Rick's* by Murray Burnett and Joan Alison. Director of photography, Arthur Edeson. Music by Max Steiner. Film editor, Owen Marks. Dialogue director, Hugh MacMullen. Assistant director, Lee Katz. Art director, Carl Jules Weyl. Set decorations by George James Hopkins. Gowns by Orry-Kelly. Makeup artist Perc Westmore. Special effects by Lawrence Butler and Willard Van Enger. Montages by Don Seigel and James Leicester. Sound recorder, Francis J. Scheid. Orchestrations by Hugo Friedhofer. Songs: "As Time Goes By" by Herman Hupfeld; "Knock on Wood" by M. K. Jerome and Jack Scholl. Technical adviser, Robert Aisner. Narrated by Lou Marcelle. Release Date, January 1943. Running time, 102 minutes.

1943. ACTION IN THE NORTH ATLANTIC (A Warner Bros.-First National Picture)
Humphrey Bogart (Joe Rossi), Raymond Massey (Captain Steve Jarvis), Alan Hale (Boats O'Hara), Julie Bishop (Pearl), Ruth Gordon (Mrs Jarvis), Sam Levene (Chips Abrams), Dane Clark (Johnny Pulaski), Peter Whitney (Whitey Lara), Dick Hogan (Cadet Robert Parker), Minor Watson (Rear Admiral Hartridge), J. M. Kerrigan (Caviar Jinks), Kane Richmond (Ensign Wright), William von Brincken (German Sub Captain), Chick Chandler (Goldberg), George Offerman, Jr. (Cecil), Don Douglas (Lieutenant Commander), Art Foster (Pete Larson), Ray Montgomery (Aherne), Glenn Strange (Tex Mathews), Creighton Hale (Sparks), Elliott Sullivan (Hennessy), Alec Craig (McGonigle), Ludwig Stossel (Captain Ziemer), Dick Wessel (Cherub), Frank Puglia (Captain Carpolis), Iris Adrian (Jenny O'Hara), Irving Bacon (Bartender), James Flavin (Lieutenant Commander).
Directed by Lloyd Bacon. Produced by Jerry Wald. Screenplay by John Howard Lawson. Additional dialogue by A. I. Bezzerides and W. R. Burnett. Based on the novel by Guy Gilpatric. Director of photography, Ted McCord. Music by Adolph Deutsch. Film editors, Thomas Pratt and George Amy. Dialogue director, Harold Winston. Assistant director, Reggie Callow. Art director, Ted Smith. Set decorations by Clarence I. Steensen. Gowns by Milo Anderson. Makeup artist, Perc Westmore. Special effects by Jack Cosgrove and Edwin B. DuPar. Montages by Don Siegel and James Leicester. Sound recorder, C. A. Riggs. Orchestrations by Jerome Moross. Release Date, June 1943. Running time, 127 minutes.

1943. THANK YOUR LUCKY STARS (A W.B.-First National Picture)
Humphrey Bogart (Himself), Eddie Cantor (Himself and Joe Simpson), Bette Davis (Herself), Olivia De Havilland (Herself), Errol Flynn (Himself), John Garfield (Himself), Joan Leslie (Pat Dixon), Ida Lupino (Herself), Dennis Morgan (Tom Randolph), Ann Sheridan (Herself), Dinah Shore (Herself), Alexis Smith (Herself), Jack Carson (Himself), Alan Hale (Himself), George Tobias (Himself), Edward Everett Horton (Farnsworth), S. Z. Sakall (Dr. Schlenna), Hattie McDaniel (Gossip), Ruth Donnelly (Nurse Hamilton), Don Wilson (Announcer), Willie Best (Soldier), Henry Armetta (Angelo), Joyce Reynolds (Girl with a book), Spike Jones and His City Slickers.
Directed by David Butler. Produced by Mark Hellinger. Screenplay by Norman Panama, Melvin Frank and James V. Kern. Based on an original story by Everett Freeman and Arthur Schwartz. Director of photography, Arthur Edeson. Film editor, Irene Morra. Dialogue director, Herbert Farjean. Assistant director, Phil Quinn. Art directors, Anton Grot and Leo K. Kuter. Set decorations by Walter F. Tilford. Gowns by Milo Anderson. Makeup artist, Perc Westmore. Special effects by H. F. Koenekamp. Sound recorders, Francis J. Scheid and Charles David Forrest. Dance numbers created and staged by Leroy Prinz. Songs by Arthur Schwartz and Frank Loesser. Orchestral arrangements by Ray Heindorf. Vocal arrangements by Dudley Chambers. Musical adaptation by Heinz Roemheld. Orchestrations by Maurice de Packh. Release Date, September 1943. Running time, 127 minutes.

1943 SAHARA (Columbia)
Humphrey Bogart (Sergeant Joe Gunn), Bruce Bennett (Waco Hoyt), J. Carrol Naish (Guiseppe), Lloyd Bridges (Fred Clarkson), Rex Ingram (Tambul), Richard Nugent (Capt. Jason Halliday), Dan Duryea (Jimmy Doyle), Carl Harbord (Marty Williams), Patrick O'Moore (Ozzie Bates), Louis Mercier (Jean Leroux), Guy Kingsford (Peter Stegman), Kurt Krueger (Capt. Von Schletow), John Wengraf (Major Von Falken), Hans Schumm (Sergeant Krause).
Directed by Zoltan Korda. Produced by Harry Joe Brown. Screenplay by John Howard Lawson and Zoltan Korda. Adaptation by James O'Hanlon. From an original story by Philip MacDonald, based on an incident in the Soviet film *Trinadstat* (*The Thirteen*). Director of photography, Rudolph Maté. Music by Miklos Rozsa. Film editor, Charles Nelson. Assistant director, Abby Berlin. Art director, Lionel Banks; associate, Eugene Lourie. Set decorations by William Kiernan. Sound recorder, Lodge Cunningham. Musical director, Morris Stoloff. Release Date, October 1943. Running time, 97 minutes.

1944. PASSAGE TO MARSEILLE (A W.B.-First National Picture)
Humphrey Bogart (Matrac), Claude Rains (Capt. Freycinet), Michele Morgan (Paula), Philip Dorn (Renault), Sydney Greenstreet (Major Duval), Peter Lorre (Marius), George Tobias (Petit), Helmut Dantine (Garou), John Loder (Manning), Victor Francen (Capt. Malo), Vladimir Sokoloff (Grandpere), Eduardo Cianelli (Chief Engineer), Corinna Mura (Singer), Konstantin Shayne (First Mate), Stephen Richards (Lt. Hastings), Charles La Torre (Lt. Lenoir), Hans Conried (Jourdain), Monte Blue (Second Mate), Billy Roy (Mess Boy), Frederick Brunn (Bijou), Louis Mercier (Second Engineer).
Directed by Michael Curtiz. Produced by Hal B. Wallis. Screenplay by Casey Robinson and Jack Moffitt. Based on the novel *Men Without Country* by Charles Nordhoff and James Norman Hall. Director of photography, James Wong Howe. Music by Max Steiner. Film editor, Owen Marks. Dialogue director, Herschel Daugherty. Assistant director, Frank Heath. Art director, Carl Jules Weyl. Set decorations by George James Hopkins. Gowns by Leah Rhodes. Makeup artist, Perc Westmore. Special effects by Jack Cosgrove, Edwin B. DuPar, Byron Haskin, E. Roy Davidson and Rex Wimpy. Montages by James Leicester. Sound recorder, Everett A. Brown. Orchestrations by Leonid Raab. Song, "Someday I'll Meet You Again" by Max Steiner and Ned Washington. Technical adviser, Sylvain Robert. Release Date, March 1944. Running time, 109 minutes.

1944. REPORT FROM THE FRONT
Prepared by the Red Cross Drive Committee of the Motion Picture Industry. Distributed by National Screen Service. Running time, 3 minutes.

1945. TO HAVE AND HAVE NOT (A Warner Bros.-First National Picture)
Humphrey Bogart (Harry Morgan), Walter Brennan (Eddie), Lauren Bacall (Marie), Dolores Moran (Helene de Brussac), Hoagy Carmichael (Cricket), Walter Molnar (Paul de Brussac), Sheldon Leonard (Lieutenant Coyo), Marcel Dalio (Gerard), Walter Sande (Johnson), Dan Seymour (Captain Renard), Aldo Nadi (Renard's Bodyguard), Paul Marion (Beauclerc), Patricia Shay (Mrs Beauclerc), Emmett Smith (Bartender), Sir Lancelot (Horatio).
Produced and directed by Howard Hawks. Screenplay by Jules Furthman and William Faulkner. Based on the novel by Ernest Hemingway. Director of photography, Sid Hickox. Music by Franz Waxman. Film editor, Christian Nyby. Assistant director, Jack Sullivan. Art director, Charles Novi. Set decorations by Casey Roberts. Gowns by Milo Anderson. Makeup artist, Perc Westmore. Special effects by E. Roy Davidson and Rex Wimpy. Sound recorder, Oliver S. Garretson. Orchestrations by Leonid Raab. Songs: "How Little We Know" by Hoagy Carmichael and Johnny Mercer; "Hong Kong Blues" by Hoagy Carmichael and Stanley Adams; "Am I Blue?" by Harry Akst and Grant Clarke. Technical adviser, Louis Comien. Release Date, January 1945. Running time, 100 minutes.

1945. CONFLICT (A Warner Bros.-First National Picture)
Humprey Bogart (Richard Mason), Alexis Smith (Evelyn Turner), Sydney Greenstreet (Dr. Mark Hamilton), Rose Hobart (Kathryn Mason), Charles Drake (Prof. Norman Holdsworth), Grant Mitchell (Dr. Grant), Patrick O'Moore (Detective Lt. Egan), Ann Shoemaker (Nora Grant), Frank Wilcox (Robert Freston), Edwin Stanley (Phillips), James Flavin (Detective Lt. Workman), Mary Servoss (Mrs Allman).
Directed by Curtis Bernhardt. Produced by William Jacobs. Screenplay by Arthur T. Horman and Dwight Taylor. Based on an original story by Robert Siodmak and Alfred Neumann. Director of photography, Merritt Gerstad. Music by Frederick Hollander. Film editor, David Weisbart. Dialogue director, James Vincent. Assistant director, Elmer Decker. Art director Ted Smith. Set decorations by Clarence I. Steensen. Gowns by Milo Anderson. Makeup artist Perc Westmore. Sound recorder, Oliver S. Garretson. Orchestrations by Jerome Moross. Release Date, June 1945. Running time, 86 minutes.

1945 HOLLYWOOD VICTORY CARAVAN
Robert Benchley, Humphrey Bogart, Joe Carioca, Carmen Cavallero and his Orchestra, Bing Crosby, William Demarest, Dona Drake, Bob Hope, Betty Hutton, Alan Ladd, Diana Lynn, Noreen Nash, Franklin Pangborn, Olga San Juan, Barbara Stanwyck, Charles Victor, Marjorie Weaver, Virginia Welles, and the U.S. Maritime Service Training Station Choir.
Produced for the War Activities Committee and the Treasury Department by Paramount Pictures. War Activities Committee release No. 136. Directed by William Russell. Produced by Louis Harris. Supervisor, Bernard Luber. Script by Melville Shavelson. Song, "We've Got Another Bond to Buy", by Jimmy McHugh and Harold Adamson. Running time, 20 minutes.

1946. TWO GUYS FROM MILWAUKEE (A Warner Bros.-First National Picture)
Dennis Morgan (Prince Henry), Jack Carson (Buzz Williams), Joan Leslie (Connie Reed), Janis Paige (Polly), S. Z. Sakall (Count Oswald), Patti Brady (Peggy), Tom D'Andrea (Happy), Rosemary DeCamp (Nan), John Ridgely (Mike Collins), Pat McVey (Johnson), Franklin Pangborn (Theatre Manager), Francis Pierlot (Dr. Bauer), Lauren Bacall (Herself), Humphrey Bogart (Himself),
Directed by David Butler. Produced by Alex Gottlieb. Original screenplay by Charles Hoffman and I. A. L. Diamond. Director of photography, Arthur Edeson. Music by Frederick Hollander. Film editor, Irene Morra. Dialogue director, Felix Jacoves. Assistant director, Jesse Hibbs. Art director, Leo K. Kuter. Set decorations by Jack McConaghy. Gowns by Leah Rhodes. Makeup artist, Perc Westmore. Special effects by Harry Barndollar and Edwin B. DuPar. Montages by James Leicester. Sound recorder, Stanley Jones. Orchestrations by Leonid Raab. Song, "And Her Tears Flowed Like Wine" by Charles Lawrence, Joe Greene and Stan Kenton. Running time, 90 minutes.

1946. THE BIG SLEEP (A Warner Bros.-First National Picture)
Humphrey Bogart (Philip Marlowe), Lauren Bacall (Vivian Rutledge), John Ridgely (Eddie Mars), Martha Vickers (Carmen Sternwood), Dorothy Malone (Bookshop Proprietress), Peggy Knudsen (Mrs Eddie Mars), Regis Toomey (Bernie Ohls), Charles Waldron (General Sternwood), Charles D. Brown (Norris), Bob Steele (Canino), Elisha Cook, Jr. (Harry Jones), Louis Jean Heydt (Joe Brody), Sonia Darrin (Agnes), James Flavin (Captain Cronjager), Thomas Jackson (District Attorney Wilde), Dan Wallace (Carol Lundgren), Theodore Von Eltz (Arthur Gwynn Geiger), Joy Barlowe (Taxicab Driver), Tom Fadden (Sidney), Ben Welden (Pete), Trevor Bardette (Art Huck), Joseph Crehan (Medical Examiner).
Produced and directed by Howard Hawks. Screenplay by William Faulkner, Leigh Brackett and Jules Furthman. Based on the novel by Raymond Chandler. Director of photography, Sid Hickox. Music by Max Steiner. Film editor, Christian Nyby. Assistant director, Robert Vreeland. Art director, Carl Jules Weyl. Set decorations by Fred M. MacLean. Gowns by Leah Rhodes. Special effects by E. Roy Davidson, Warren E. Lynch, William McGann, Robert Burks and Willard Van Enger. Sound recorder, Robert B. Lee. Orchestrations by Simon Bucharoff. Release Date, August 1946. Running time, 114 minutes.

1947. DEAD RECKONING (Columbia)
Humphrey Bogart (Rip Murdock), Lizabeth Scott (Coral Chandler), Morris Carnovsky (Martinelli), Charles Cane (Lieutenant Kincaid), William Prince (Johnny Drake), Marvin Miller (Krause), Wallace Ford (McGee), James Bell

(Father Logan), George Chandler (Louis Ord), William Forrest (Lt. Col. Simpson), Ruby Dandridge (Hyacinth).
Directed by John Cromwell. Produced by Sidney Biddell. Screenplay by Oliver H. P. Garrett and Steve Fisher. Adaptation by Allen Rivkin. Based on an original story by Gerald Adams and Sidney Biddell. Director of photography, Leo Tover. Music by Marlin Skiles. Assistant director, Seymour Friedman. Art directors, Stephen Goosson and Rudolph Sternad. Set decorations by Louis Diage. Gowns by Jean Louis. Makeup artist, Clay Campbell. Hair styles by Helen Hunt. Sound recorder, Jack Goodrich. Song, "Either It's Love or It Isn't" by Allan Roberts and Doris Fisher. Musical director, Morris Stoloff. Release Date, February 1947. Running time, 100 minutes.

1947. **THE TWO MRS CARROLLS** (A W.B.-First National Picture)
Humphrey Bogart (Geoffrey Carroll), Barbara Stanwyck (Sally Carroll), Alexis Smith (Cecily Latham), Nigel Bruce (Dr. Tuttle), Isobel Elsom (Mrs Latham), Patrick O'Moore (Charles Pennington), Ann Carter (Beatrice Carroll), Anita Bolster (Christine), Barry Bernard (Mr Blagdon), Colin Campbell (MacGregor), Peter Godfrey (Race Track Tout).
Directed by Peter Godfrey. Produced by Mark Hellinger. Screenplay by Thomas Job. Based on the play by Martin Vale. Director of photography, Peverell Marley. Music by Franz Waxman. Film editor, Frederick Richards. Assistant director, Claude Archer. Art director Anton Grot. Set decorations by Budd Friend. Gowns by Edith Head and Milo Anderson. Makeup artist, Perc Westmore. Special effects by Robert Burks. Sound recorder, C. A. Riggs. Orchestrations by Leonid Raab. Release Date, May 1947. Running time, 99 minutes.

1947. **DARK PASSAGE** (A Warner Bros.-First National Picture)
Humphrey Bogart (Vincent Parry), Lauren Bacall (Irene Jansen), Bruce Bennett (Bob Rapf), Agnes Moorehead (Madge Rapf), Tom D'Andrea (Sam), Clifton Young (Baker), Douglas Kennedy (Detective), Rory Mallinson (George Fellsinger), Houseley Stevenson (Dr. Walter Coley).
Directed by Delmer Daves. Produced by Jerry Wald. Screenplay by Delmer Daves. Based on the novel by David Goodis. Director of photography, Sid Hickox. Music by Franz Waxman. Film editor, David Weisbart. Assistant director, Dick Mayberry. Art director, Charles H. Clarke. Set decorations by William Kuehl. Wardrobe by Bernard Newman. Makeup artist, Perc Westmore. Special effects by H. F. Koenekamp. Sound recorder, Dolph Thomas. Orchestrations by Leonid Raab. Release Date, September 1947. Running time, 106 minutes.

1948. **ALWAYS TOGETHER** (A Warner Bros.-First National Picture)
Robert Hutton (Don Masters), Joyce Reynolds (Jane Barker), Cecil Kellaway (Jonathan Turner), Ernest Truex (Mr Bull), Don McGuire (McIntyre), Ransom Sherman (Judge), Douglas Kennedy (Doberman).
Directed by Frederick de Cordova. Produced by Alex Gottlieb. Original screenplay by Phoebe & Henry Ephron and I. A. L. Diamond. Director of photography, Carl Guthrie. Music by Werner Heymann. Film editor, Folmer Blangsted. Dialogue director, John Maxwell. Assistant director, James McMahon. Art director, Leo K. Kuter. Set decorations by Jack McConaghy. Wardrobe by Travilla. Makeup artist, Perc Westmore. Special effects by William McGann and Edwin B. DuPar. Montages by James Leicester. Sound recorder, C. A. Riggs. Orchestrations by Leonid Raab. Running time, 78 minutes.

1948. **THE TREASURE OF THE SIERRA MADRE**
(A Warner Bros.-First National Picture)
Humphrey Bogart (Dobbs) Walter Huston (Howard), Tim Holt (Curtin), Bruce Bennett (Cody), Barton MacLane (McCormick), Alfonso Bedoya (Gold Hat), A. Soto Rangel (Presidente), Manuel Donde (El Jefe), Jose Torvay (Pablo), Margarito Luna (Pancho), Jacqueline Dalya (Flashy Girl), Bobby Blake (Mexican Boy), John Huston (White Suit), Jack Holt (Flophouse Bum).
Directed by John Huston. Produced by Henry Blanke. Screenplay by John Huston. Based on the novel by B. Traven. Director of photography, Ted McCord. Music by Max Steiner. Film editor, Owen Marks. Assistant director, Dick Mayberry. Art director, John Hughes. Set decorations by Fred M. MacLean. Makeup artist, Perc Westmore. Special effects by William McGann and H. F. Koenekamp. Sound recorder, Robert B. Lee. Orchestrations by Murray Cutter. Release Date, January 1948. Running time, 126 minutes.

1948. **KEY LARGO** (A Warner Bros.-First National Picture)
Humphrey Bogart (Frank McCloud), Edward G. Robinson (Johnny Rocco), Lauren Bacall (Nora Temple), Lionel Barrymore (James Temple), Claire Trevor (Gaye Dawn), Thomas Gomez (Curly Hoff), Harry Lewis (Toots Bass), John Rodney (Deputy Clyde Sawyer), Marc Lawrence (Ziggy), Dan Seymour (Angel Garcia), Monte Blue (Sheriff Ben Wade), William Haade (Ralph Feeney), Jay Silverheels (Tom Osceola), Rodric Redwing (John Osceola).
Directed by John Huston. Produced by Jerry Wald. Screenplay by Richard Brooks and John Huston. Based on the play by Maxwell Anderson. Director of photography, Karl Freund. Music by Max Steiner. Film editor, Rudi Fehr. Assistant director, Art Lueker. Art director, Leo K. Kuter. Set decorations by Fred M. MacLean. Wardrobe by Leah Rhodes. Makeup artist, Perc Westmore. Special effects by William McGann and Robert Burks. Sound recorder, Dolph Thomas. Orchestrations by Murray Cutter. Song, "Moanin' Low". by Ralph Rainger and Howard Dietz. Release Date, July 1948. Running time, 101 minutes.

1949. **KNOCK ON ANY DOOR** (A Santana Production. Released by Columbia Pictures)
Humphrey Bogart (Andrew Morton), John Derek (Nick Romano), George Macready (Kerman), Allene Roberts (Emma), Susan Perry (Adele Morton), Mickey Knox (Vito), Barry Kelley (Judge Drake), Cara Williams (Nelly), Jimmy Conlin (Kid Fingers), Sumner Williams (Jimmy), Sid Melton (Squint), Pepe Hern (Juan), Dewey Martin (Butch), Robert A. Davis (Sunshine), Houseley Stevenson (Junior), Vince Barnett (Bartender), Thomas Sully (Officer Hawkins), Florence Auer (Aunt Lena), Pierre Watkin (Purcell), Gordon Nelson (Corey), Argentina Brunetti (Ma Romano), Dick Sinatra (Julian Romano), Carol Coombs (Ang Romano), Joan Baxter (Maria Romano).
Directed by Nicholas Ray. Produced by Robert Lord. Associate producer, Henry S. Kesler. Screenplay by Daniel Taradash and John Monks, Jr. Based on the novel by Willard Motley. Director of photography, Burnett Guffey. Music by George Antheil. Film editor, Viola Lawrence. Assistant director, Arthur S. Black. Art director, Robert Peterson. Set decorations by William Kiernan. Gowns by Jean Louis. Makeup artist, Clay Campbell. Hair styles by Helen Hunt. Sound recorder, Frank Goodwin. Orchestrations by Ernest Gold. Musical director, Morris Stoloff. Technical advisers, National Probation and Parole Association. Release Date, April 1949. Running time, 100 minutes.

1949. **TOKYO JOE** (A Santana Production. Released by Columbia Pictures)
Humphrey Bogart (Joe Barrett), Alexander Knox (Mark Landis), Florence Marly (Trina), Sessue Hayakawa (Baron Kimura), Jerome Courtland (Danny), Gordon Jones (Idaho), Teru Shimada (Ito), Hideo Mori (Kanda), Charles Meredith (General Ireton), Rhys Williams (Colonel Dahlgren), Lora Lee Michael (Anya), Kyoko Kamo (Nani-San), Gene Gondo (Kamikaze), Harold Goodwin (Major Loomis), James Cardwell (M.P. Captain), Frank Kumagai (Truck Driver), Tetsu Komai (Takenobu), Otto Han (Hara), Yosan Tsuruta (Goro).
Directed by Stuart Heisler. Produced by Robert Lord. Associate producer, Henry S. Kesler. Screenplay by Cyril Hume and Bertram Millhauser. Adaptation by Walter Doniger. Based on a story by Steve Fisher. Director of photography, Charles Lawton Jr. Music by George Antheil. Film editor, Viola Lawrence. Dialogue director, Jason Lindsey. Assistant director, Wilbur McGaugh. Art director, Robert Peterson. Set decorations by James Crowe. Gowns by Jean Louis. Makeup artist, Clay Campbell. Hair styles by Helen Hunt. Sound recorder, Russell Malmgren. Orchestrations by Ernest Gold. Musical director, Morris Stoloff. Release Date, November 1949. Running time, 88 minutes.

1950. **CHAIN LIGHTNING** (A Warner Bros.-First National Picture)
Humphrey Bogart (Matt Brennan), Eleanor Parker (Jo Holloway), Raymond Massey (Leland Willis), Richard Whorf (Carl Troxell), James Brown (Major Hinkle), Roy Roberts (General Hewitt), Morris Ankrum (Ed Bostwick), Fay Baker (Mrs Willis), Fred Sherman (Jeb Farley).
Directed by Stuart Heisler. Produced by Anthony Veiller. Screenplay by Liam O'Brien and Vincent Evans. Based on an original story by J. Redmond Prior. Director of photography, Ernest Haller. Music by David Buttolph. Film editor, Thomas Reilly. Assistant director, Don Page. Art director, Leo K. Kuter. Set decorations by William Wallace. Gowns by Leah Rhodes. Makeup artist, Perc Westmore. Special effects by William McGann, Harry Barndollar, H. F. Koenekamp and Edwin B. DuPar. Sound recorder, Francis J. Scheid. Orchestrations by Maurice de Packh. Song, "Bless 'Em All", by J. Hughes, Frank Lake and Al Stillman. Release Date, February 1950. Running time, 94 minutes.

1950. **IN A LONELY PLACE** (A Santana Production. Released by Columbia Pictures)
Humphrey Bogart (Dixon Steele), Gloria Grahame (Laurel Gray), Frank Lovejoy (Brub Nicolai), Carl Benton Reid (Captain Lochner), Art Smith (Mel Lippman), Jeff Donnell (Sylvia Nicolai), Martha Stewart (Mildred Atkinson), Robert Warwick (Charlie Waterman), Morris Ankrum (Lloyd Barnes), William Ching (Ted Barton), Steven Geray (Paul), Hadda Brooks (Singer), Alice Talton (Frances Randolph), Jack Reynolds (Henry Kesler), Ruth Warren (Effie), Ruth Gillette (Martha), Guy Beach (Swan), Lewis Howard (Junior).
Directed by Nicholas Ray. Produced by Robert Lord. Associate producer, Henry S. Kesler. Screenplay by Andrew Solt. Adaptation by Edmund H. North. Based on the novel by Dorothy B. Hughes. Director of photography, Burnett Guffey. Music by George Antheil. Film editor, Viola Lawrence. Assistant director, Earl Bellamy. Art director, Robert Peterson. Set decorations by William Kiernan. Gowns by Jean Louis. Makeup artist, Clay Campbell. Hair styles by Helen Hunt. Sound recorder, Howard Fogetti. Orchestrations by Ernest Gold. Musical director, Morris Stoloff. Technical adviser, Rodney Amateau. Release Date, August 1950. Running time, 94 minutes.

1951. **THE ENFORCER** (A United States Picture for Warner Bros.)
Humphrey Bogart (Martin Ferguson), Zero Mostel (Big Babe Lazich), Ted De Corsia (Joseph Rico), Everett Sloane (Albert Mendoza), Roy Roberts (Capt. Frank Nelson), Lawrence Tolan (Duke Malloy), King Donovan (Sgt. Whitlow), Bob Steele (Herman), Adelaide Klein (Olga Kirshen), Don Beddoe (Thomas O'Hara), Tito Vuolo (Tony Vetto), John Kellogg (Vince), Jack Lambert (Philadelphia Tom Zaca), Patricia Joiner (Angela Vetto), Susan Cabot (Nina Lombardo), Mario Siletti (Louis the Barber).
Directed by Bretaigne Windust. Produced by Milton Sperling. Original Screenplay by Martin Rackin. Director of photography, Robert Burks. Music by David Buttolph. Film editor, Fred Allen. Assistant director, Chuck Hansen. Art director, Charles H. Clarke. Set decorations by William Kuehl. Sound recorder, Dolph Thomas. Orchestrations by Maurice de Packh. Release Date, February 1951. Running time, 87 minutes.

1951. **SIROCCO** (A Santana Production. Released by Columbia Pictures)
Humphrey Bogart (Harry Smith), Marta Toren (Violette), Lee J. Cobb (Colonel Feroud), Everett Sloane (General LaSalle), Gerald Mohr (Major Leon), Zero Mostel (Balukjian), Nick Dennis (Nasir Aboud), Onslow Stevens (Emir Hassan), Ludwig Donath (Flophouse Proprietor), David Bond (Achmet), Vincent Renno (Arthur), Martin Wilkins (Omar), Peter Ortiz (Major Robbinet), Edward Colmans (Colonel Corville), Al Eben (Sergeant), Peter Brocco (Barber), Jay Novello (Hamal), Leonard Penn (Rifat), Harry Guardino (Lieutenant Collet).
Directed by Curtis Bernhardt. Produced by Robert Lord. Associate producer, Henry S. Kesler. Screenplay by A. I. Bezzerides and Hans Jacoby. Based on the novel *Coup de Grâce* by Joseph Kessel. Director of photography, Burnett Guffey. Music by George Antheil. Film editor, Viola Lawrence. Assistant director, Earl Bellamy. Art director, Robert Peterson. Set decorations by Robert Priestley. Makeup artist, Clay Campbell. Hair styles by Helen Hunt. Sound recorder, Lodge Cunningham. Orchestrations by Ernest Gold. Musical director, Morris Stoloff. Release Date, July 1951. Running time, 98 minutes.

1951. **THE AFRICAN QUEEN** (A Horizon-Romulus Production. Released through United Artists)

Humphrey Bogart (Charlie Allnut), Katharine Hepburn (Rose Sayer), Robert Morley (Rev. Samuel Sayer), Peter Bull (Captain of the Louisa), Theodore Bikel (First Officer (Louisa)), Walter Gotell (Second Officer (Louisa)), Gerald Onn (Petty Officer (Louisa)), Peter Swanwick (First Officer (Shona)), Richard Marner (Second Officer (Shona)).

Color by Technicolor. Directed by John Huston. Produced by S. P. Eagle (Sam Spiegel). Screenplay by James Agee and John Huston. Based on the novel by C. S. Forester. Director of photography, Jack Cardiff. Music by Alan Gray, played by the Royal Philharmonic Orchestra conducted by Norman Del Mar. Film editor, Ralph Kemplen. Assistant director, Guy Hamilton. Art director, Wilfred Shingleton; associate John Hoesli. Production Managers, Leigh Aman and T. S. Lyndon-Haynes. Miss Hepburn's costumes by Doris Langley Moore; other clothes by Connie De Pinna. Makeup artist, George Frost. Second unit photography by Ted Scaife. Special effects by Cliff Richardson. Sound recorder, John Mitchell. Sound editor, Eric Wood. Camera operator, Ted Moore. Hairdresser, Eileen Bates. Wardrobe mistress, Vi Murray. Continuity by Angela Allen. Release Date, March 1952. Running time, 105 minutes.

1952. **DEADLINE — U.S.A.** (A 20th Century-Fox Picture)

Humphrey Bogart (Ed Hutchinson), Ethel Barrymore (Mrs Garrison), Kim Hunter (Nora), Ed Begley (Frank Allen), Warren Stevens (George Burrows), Paul Stewart (Harry Thompson), Martin Gabel (Thomas Rienzi), Joe De Santis (Herman Schmidt), Joyce MacKenzie (Kitty Garrison Geary). Audrey Christie (Mrs Willebrandt), Fay Baker (Alice Garrison Courtney), Jim Backus (Jim Cleary), Carleton Young (Crane), Selmer Jackson (Williams), Fay Roope (Judge), Parley Baer (Headwaiter), John Douchette (Hal), Florence Shirley (Miss Barndollar), Kasia Orzazewski (Mrs Schmidt), Raymond Greenleaf (Lawrence White), Tom Powers (Wharton), Thomas Browne Henry (Fenway), Philip Terry (Lewis Schaefer), Joseph Sawyer (Whitey), Lawrence Dobkin (Larry Hansen), Alex Gerry (Prentiss), Clancy Cooper (Captain Finlay), Willis Bouchey (Henry), Joseph Crehan (White's City Editor).

Directed by Richard Brooks. Produced by Sol C. Siegel. Original Screenplay by Richard Brooks. Director of photography, Milton Krasner. Music by Cyril Mockridge and Sol Kaplan. Film editor, William B. Murphy. Assistant director, Dick Mayberry. Art directors, Lyle Wheeler and George Patrick. Set decorations by Thomas Little and Walter M. Scott. Wardrobe direction, Charles Le Maire. Costumes by Eloise Jenssen. Makeup artist, Ben Nye. Special effects by Ray Kellogg. Sound recorders, E. Clayton Ward and Harry M. Leonard. Orchestrations by Edward Powell and Bernard Mayers. Musical director, Lionel Newman. Release Date, May 1952. Running time, 87 minutes.

1952. **U.S. SAVINGS BONDS TRAILER**

Bogart presented the Series E. Savings Bonds in a special trailer made by Metro-Goldwyn-Mayer and attached to the July 25-26 newsreel releases.

1953. **BATTLE CIRCUS** (A Metro-Goldwyn-Mayer Picture)

Humphrey Bogart (Major Jed Webbe), June Allyson (Lt. Ruth McCara), Keenan Wynn (Sgt. Orvil Statt), Robert Keith (Lt. Col. Hillary Whalters), William Campbell (Capt. John Rustford), Perry Sheehan (Lt. Laurence), Patricia Tiernan (Lt. Rose Ashland), Jonathan Cott (Adjutant), Adele Longmire (Lt. Jane Franklin), Ann Morrison (Lt. Edith Edwards), Helen Winston (Lt. Graciano), Sarah Selby (Capt. Dobbs), Danny Chang (Danny), Philip Ahn (Korean Prisoner), Steve Forrest (Sergeant), Jeff Richards (Lieutenant), Dick Simmons (Capt. Norson).

Directed by Richard Brooks. Produced by Pandro S. Berman. Screenplay by Richard Brooks. Based on an original story by Allen Rivkin and Laura Kerr. Director of photography, John Alton. Music by Lennie Hayton. Film editor, George Boemler. Assistant director, Al Jennings. Art directors, Cedric Gibbons and James Basevi. Set decorations by Edwin B. Willis and Alfred E. Spencer. Makeup artist, William Tuttle. Special effects by A. Arnold Gillespie. Recording supervisor, Douglas Shearer. Orchestrations by Robert Franklyn. Technical advisers, Lt. Col. K. E. Van Buskirk and Lt. Mary Couch. Release Date, March 1953. Running time, 90 minutes.

1954. **BEAT THE DEVIL** (A Santana-Romulus Production. Released through United Artists)

Humphrey Bogart (Billy Danreuther), Jennifer Jones (Gwendolen Chelm), Gina Lollobrigida (Maria Danreuther), Robert Morley (Petersen), Peter Lorre (O'Hara), Edward Underdown (Harry Chelm), Ivor Barnard (Major Ross), Bernard Lee (C.I.D. Inspector), Marco Tulli (Ravello), Mario Perroni (Purser), Alex Pochet (Hotel Manager), Aldo Silvani (Charles), Guilio Donnini (Administrator), Saro Urzi (Captain), Juan de Landa (Hispano-Suiza Driver), Manuel Serano (Arab Officer), Mimo Poli (Barman).

Directed by John Huston. Associate producer, Jack Clayton. Screenplay by John Huston and Truman Capote. Based on the novel by James Helvick. Director of photography, Oswald Morris. Music by Franco Mannino. Film editor, Ralph Kemplen. Art director, Wilfred Shingleton. Sound recorders, George Stephenson and E. Law. Musical director, Lambert Williamson. Release Date, March 1954. Running time, 93 minutes.

1954. **THE CAINE MUTINY** (A Stanley Kramer Company Production. Released by Columbia Pictures)

Humphrey Bogart (Captain Queeg), Jose Ferrer (Lt. Barney Greenwald), Van Johnson (Lt. Steve Meryk), Fred MacMurray (Lt. Tom Keefer), Robert Francis (Ensign Willie Keith), May Wynn (May Wynn), Tom Tully (Captain DeVriess), E. G. Marshall (Lt. Comdr. Challee), Arthur Franz (Lt. Paynter), Lee Marvin (Meatball), Warner Anderson (Captain Blakely), Claude Akins (Horrible), Katharine Warren (Mrs Keith), Jerry Paris (Ensign Harding), Steve Brodie (Chief Budge), Todd Karns (Stilwell), Whit Bissell (Lt. Comdr. Dickson), James Best (Lt. Jorgensen), Joe Haworth (Ensign Carmody), Guy Anderson (Ensign Rabbit), James Edwards (Whittaker), Don Dubbins (Urban), David Alpert (Engstrand).

Color by Technicolor. Directed by Edward Dmytryk. Produced by Stanley Kramer. Screenplay by Stanley Roberts. Additional dialogue by Michael Blankfort. Based on the novel by Herman Wouk. Director of photography, Franz Planer. Music by Max Steiner. Production design by Rudolph Sternad. Film editors, William Lyon and Henry Batista. Assistant director, Carter De Haven, Jr. Art director, Cary Odell. Set decorations by Frank Tuttle. Gowns by Jean Louis. Makeup artist, Clay Campbell. Hair styles by Helen Hunt. Second unit photography by Ray Cory. Special effects by Lawrence Butler. Sound recorder, Lambert Day. Songs: "I Can't Believe That You're in Love With Me" by Jimmy McHugh and Clarence Gaskill; "Yellowstain Blues" by Fred Karger and Herman Wouk. Colour consultant, Francis Cugat. Technical adviser, Comdr. James C. Shaw, U.S.N. Release Date, September 1954. Running time, 125 minutes.

1954. **SABRINA** (Paramount)

Humphrey Bogart (Linus Larrabee), Audrey Hepburn (Sabrina Fairchild), William Holden (David Larrabee), Walter Hampden (Oliver Larrabee), John Williams (Thomas Fairchild), Martha Hyer (Elizabeth Tyson), Joan Vohs (Gretchen Van Horn), Marcel Dalio (Baron), Marcel Hillaire (The Professor), Nella Walker (Maude Larrabee), Francis X. Bushman (Mr Tyson), Ellen Corby (Miss McCardle).

Produced and directed by Billy Wilder. Screenplay by Billy Wilder, Samuel Taylor and Ernest Lehman. Based on the play *Sabrina Fair* by Samuel Taylor. Director of photography, Charles Lang, Jr. Music by Frederick Hollander. Film editor, Arthur Schmidt. Assistant director, C. C. Coleman, Jr. Art directors Hal Pereira and Walter Tyler. Set decorations by Sam Comer and Ray Moyer. Costumes by Edith Head. Makeup artist, Wally Westmore. Special effects by John P. Fulton and Farciot Edouart. Sound recorders, Harold Lewis and John Cope. Release Date, October 1954. Running time, 113 minutes.

1954. **THE BAREFOOT CONTESSA**

(A Figaro Incorporated Production. Released through United Artists)

Humphrey Bogart (Harry Dawes), Ava Gardner (Maria Vargas), Edmond O'Brien (Oscar Muldoon), Marius Goring (Alberto Bravano), Valentina Cortesa (Eleanora Torlato-Favrini), Rossano Brazzi (Vincenzo Torlato-Favrini), Elizabeth Sellars (Jerry), Warren Stevens (Kirk Edwards), Franco Interlenghi (Pedro), Mari Aldon (Myrna), Bessie Love (Mrs Eubanks), Diana Decker (Drunken Blonde), Bill Fraser (J. Montague Brown), Alberto Rabagliati (Night Club Proprietor), Enzo Staiola (Busboy), Haria Zanoli (Maria's Mother), Renato Chiantoni (Maria's Father), John Parrish (Mr Black), Jim Gerald (Mr Blue), Riccardo Rioli (Gypsy Dancer), Tonio Selwart (The Pretender), Margaret Anderson (The Pretender's Wife), Gertrude Flynn (Lulu McGee), John Horne (Hector Eubanks), Robert Christopher (Eddie Blake), Anna Maria Paduan (Chambermaid), Carlo Dale (Chauffeur).

Color by Technicolor. Directed by Joseph L. Mankiewicz. Original screenplay by Joseph L. Mankiewicz. Production supervisor, Forrest E. Johnston. Production associates, Franco Magli and Michael Waszynski. Director of photography, Jack Cardiff. Music by Mario Nascimbene. Film editor, William Hornbeck. Assistant director, Pietro Mussetta. Art director, Arrigo Equini. Gowns by Fontana. Sound recorder, Charles Knott. Release Date, October 1954. Running time, 128 minutes.

1955. **WE'RE NO ANGELS** (Paramount Picture. In VistaVison)

Humphrey Bogart (Joseph), Aldo Ray (Albert), Peter Ustinov (Jules), Joan Bennett (Amelia Ducotel), Basil Rathbone (Andre Trochard), Leo G. Carroll (Felix Ducotel), John Baer (Paul Trochard), Gloria Talbot (Isabelle Ducotel), Lea Penman (Madame Parole), John Smith (Arnaud).

Color by Technicolor. Directed by Michael Curtiz. Produced by Pat Duggan. Screenplay by Ranald MacDougall. Based on the play *La Cuisine des Anges* by Albert Husson. Director of photography, Loyal Griggs. Music by Frederick Hollander. Film editor, Arthur Schmidt. Assistant director, John Coonan. Dialogue assistant, Norman Stuart. Art directors, Hal Pereira and Roland Anderson. Set decorations by Sam Comer and Grace Gregory. Costumes by Mary Grant. Makeup artist, Wally Westmore. Special effects by John P. Fulton. Sound recorders, Hugo Grenzbach and John Cope. Songs: "Sentimental Moments" by Frederick Hollander and Ralph Freed; "Ma France Bien-Aimée" by G. Martini and Roger Wagner. Colour consultant, Richard Mueller. Release Date, July 1955. Running time,103 minutes.

1955. **THE LEFT HAND OF GOD** (A 20th Century-Fox Picture)

Humphrey Bogart (Jim Carmody), Gene Tierney (Anne Scott), Lee J. Cobb (Mieh Yang), Agnes Moorehead (Beryl Sigman), E. G. Marshall (Dr. David Sigman), Jean Porter (Mary Yin), Carl Benton Reid (Reverend Cornelius), Victor Sen Yung (John Wong), Philip Ahn (Jan Teng), Benson Fong (Chun Tien), Richard Cutting (Father O'Shea), Leon Lontoc (Pao Ching), Don Forbes (Father Keller), Noel Toy (Woman in Sarong), Peter Chong (Feng Tso Lin), Marie Tsien (Woman in Kimono), Stephen Wong (The Boy), Sophie Chin (Celeste), George Chan (Li Kwan), Walter Soo Hoo (Hospital Orderly), Henry S. Quan (Orderly), Doris Chung (Nurse), Moy Ming (Old Man), George Lee (Mi Lu), Beal Wong (Father), Stella Lynn (Pao Chu), Robert Burton (Reverend Marvin), Soo Young (Midwife).

CinemaScope. Color by DeLuxe. Directed by Edward Dmytryk. Produced by Buddy Adler. Screenplay by Alfred Hayes. Based on the novel by William E. Barrett. Director of photography, Franz Planer. Music by Victor Young. Film editor, Dorothy Spencer. Assistant director, Ben Kadish. Art directors, Lyle Wheeler and Maurice Ransford. Set decorations by Walter M. Scott and Frank Wade. Wardrobe director, Charles Le Maire. Costumes by Travilla. Makeup artist, Ben Nye. Hair styles by Helen Turpin. Special effects by Ray Kellogg. Sound recorders, Eugene Grossman and Harry M. Leonard. Orchestrations by Leo Shuken and Sidney Cutner. Colour consultant, Leonard Doss. Technical adviser, Frank Tang. Release Date, September 1955. Running time, 87 minutes.

1955. **THE DESPERATE HOURS** (A Paramount Picture. In VistaVison)

Humphrey Bogart (Glenn Griffin), Frederic March (Dan Hilliard), Arthur Kennedy (Jesse Bard), Martha Scott (Eleanor Hilliard), Dewey Martin (Hal Griffin), Gig Young (Chuck), Mary Murphy (Cindy Hilliard), Richard Eyer (Ralphie Hilliard), Robert Middleton (Sam Kobish), Alan Reed (Detective), Bert Freed (Winston), Ray Collins (Masters), Whit Bissell (Carson), Ray Teal (Fredericks), Michael Moore (Detective), Don Haggerty (Detective), Ric Roman (Sal), Pat Flaherty (Dutch), Beverly Garland (Miss Swift), Louis Lettieri (Bucky Walling), Ann Doran (Mrs Walling), Walter Baldwin (Patterson).

Produced and directed by William Wyler. Associate producer, Robert Wyler. Screenplay by Joseph Hayes, based on his novel and play. Director of photography, Lee Garmes. Music by Gail Kubik. Film editor, Robert Swink. Assistant director, C. C. Coleman, Jr. Art directors, Hal Pereira and Joseph MacMillan Johnston. Set decorations by Sam Comer and Grace Gregory. Costumes by Edith Head. Makeup artist, Wally Westmore. Special effects by John P. Fulton and Farciot Edouart. Sound recorders, Hugo Grenzbach and Winston Leverette. Release Date, November 1955. Running time, 112 minutes.

1956. **THE HARDER THEY FALL** (Columbia)
Humphrey Bogart (Eddie Willis), Rod Steiger (Nick Benko), Jan Sterling (Beth Willis), Mike Lane (Toro Moreno), Max Baer (Buddy Brannen), Jersey Joe Walcott (George), Edward Andrews (Jim Weyerhause), Harold J. Stone (Art Leavitt), Carlos Montalban (Luis Agrandi), Nehemiah Persoff (Leo), Felice Orlandi (Vince Fawcett), Herbi Faye (Max), Rusty Lane (Danny McKeogh), Jack Albertson (Pop), Val Avery (Frank), Tommy Herman (Tommy), Vinnie DeCarlo (Joey), Pat Comiskey (Gus Dundee), Matt Murphy (Sailor Rigazzo), Abel Fernandez (Chief Firebird), Marion Carr (Alice).
Directed by Mark Robson. Produced by Philip Yordan. Screenplay by Philip Yordan. Based on the novel by Budd Schulberg. Director of photography, Burnett Guffey. Music by Hugo Friedhofer. Film editor, Jerome Thoms. Assistant director, Milton Feldman. Art director, William Flannery. Set decorations by William Kiernan and Alfred E. Spencer. Makeup artist, Clay Campbell. Hair styles by Helen Hunt. Sound recorder, Lambert Day. Orchestrations by Arthur Morton. Musical director, Lionel Newman. Technical adviser, John Indrisano. Release Date, April 1956. Running time, 109 minutes.